INHERITING CHINA

A Memoir

INHERITING CHINA

A Memoir

Margaret Hollister

Eastern Branch Press – Washington
2010

Published by Eastern Branch Press

ISBN: 978-0-578-07069-8

Manufactured in the United States of America

First Edition

For Paul, Sarah, Rebecca, and Michael,
who also inherit

ACKNOWLEDGEMENTS

First and foremost, this book would never have appeared without David Minckler, editor, author, video-maker, perfect friend, and neighbor. He has watched over it many months and years, spurring me on through discouragement, diversions, and computer disasters, always resourceful, supportive, imaginative, keen-minded, and next door.

I thank Dr. Lewis Kurtz, a former colleague, for his insistence that the memoir be written in order to preserve the life stories of my minister grandfathers and for his support throughout.

I have depended on the encouragement, gentleness, editorial work, and advice of my son, Paul Hollister, without whom it seemed impossible to negotiate the hazards of recalling a long and complicated life.

I am also grateful to my editors: Elizabeth Macklin, who guided my initial efforts with poetic imagination, long magical discussions, and rigorous line-editing; and Jane Friedman, whose journalistic skills drove the narrative forward, and whose generosity I can never repay.

Members of the writers' group that succeeded an exciting course in memoir taught by Suzannah Lessard offered monthly appraisals and support: Cecelia Cassidy, Jane, Cathy Schoults, and Diane Zimmerman.

Dr. Stephen Quint, a friend and colleague, offered wisdom that helped clarify and stabilize the remembrance of a long life. Other friends have read sections and offered comments: Deborah Brown, Marianne Burke, Deborah Danielson, Billie Day, Louise Fenner, my brother John Hayes and his wife Jocelyn, my cousin Robert Johnson,

Suzanne Kulik, Lewis and Gwendolyn Kurtz, Lawrence and Roslyn Latton, John Marks, Alan Myers, and John Wennersten. Alexiss Kurtz cheerfully provided needed help in organizing materials and choosing pictures. To all of them I am grateful for their interest and support, and above all, their honesty.

I want to thank my Scottish cousins, who organized trips to Petercultur and Edinburgh for this book: Isobel Miller arranged a visit to Dr. Kelman's church and manse at Petercultur, and my cousin and "Scottish sister," Janet Craig arranged visits to family sites in Edinburgh, including my mother's school, St. George's Free Church, and to the River Dee, where Grandfather fished.

Dr. Chen Yang kindly reviewed the section on the Chinese language. Ms. Shu of the Freer Gallery generously provided the print characters for it, and Michael Smith of the Freer translated some Chinese into English. And thanks to Jim Reed for the wonderful title, "Inheriting China."

To all those who during the writing of this memoir have helped with comments, suggestions, and encouragement, and have thus enriched it and eased the writing, my gratitude and delight.

Finally, I am grateful to my grandchildren, Sarah, Rebecca, and Michael, *luminaria* of my life, for the pleasure their interest in the stories of this book has given me.

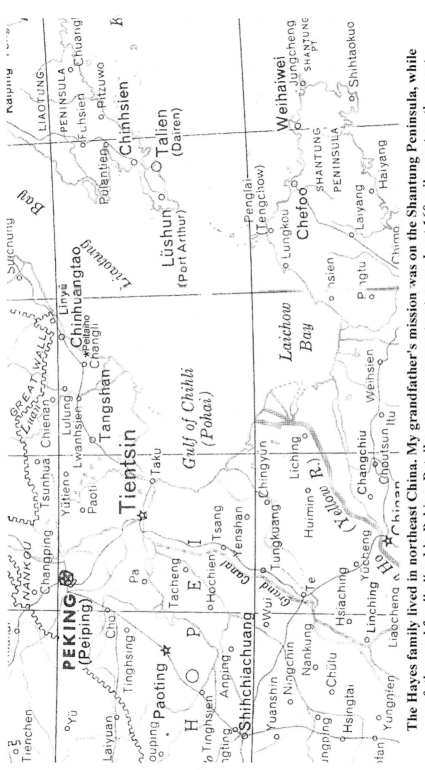

The Hayes family lived in northeast China. My grandfather's mission was on the Shantung Peninsula, while my father and family lived in Peking. Petaiho, our summer retreat, was about 160 miles east on the coast.

TABLE OF CONTENTS

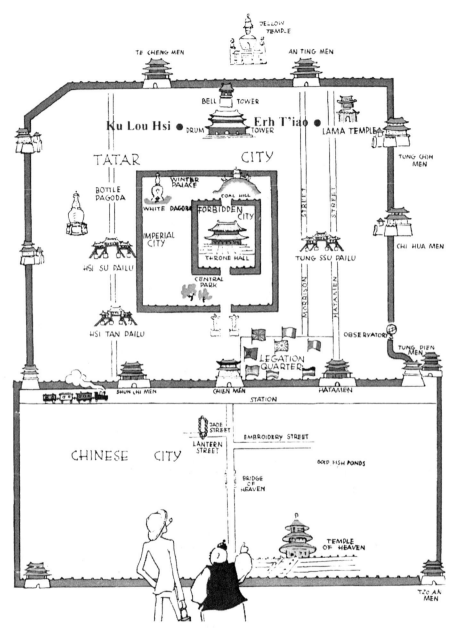

Map of Peking, circa 1930. The Presbyterian mission compounds were at Ku Lou Hsi and Erh T'iao *hutung*.

I

MY HOME TOWN

Outside view of south wall between Shun Chi Men and Ch'ien Men, circa 1920.

I was raised in a walled city. The walls of Peking were thick, about twelve feet wide at the top, of earth faced with brick, and with wooden, metal-bound gates. Guardian lions and gods scowled from temples nearby. The tops of the walls were paved roads from which we could look down on waves of gray-tiled roofs surging to the red walls of the Forbidden City. There were twelve gates to Peking. The southern gate was the central gate, so named, facing and leading to the great studded gate of the Forbidden City. When I was a child the gates were closed at night, and one felt somehow protected, cared about. Within the walls watchmen walked the narrow streets, tapping

1

wooden blocks together, as much, I used to wonder, to let us know that they were awake, as to assure us of our safety. Residents lived in one-story rooms, arranged around small courtyards, whose outer walls framed narrow unpaved lanes, called *hutungs*.

Peking! Now, that was a city. People had lived on its site for over five thousand years. The walls that surrounded it had protected its residents for over a thousand years. To live in it, to come from it, to intone its standard-setting language, was definition enough. Proudly I claimed it as my home town; to me the name chimed the air. World wide, the name Peking stood for the country. Tientsin was a busy, grimy seaport; Shanghai was all business and show; Canton was a culture all its own; Peking was the banner city of a quarter of the world's people. A world explorer once called the Forbidden City the perfect expression of power in space. In all the humility that I learned, both as a missionary's child and as a girl, and was expected to deliver, I had a secret pride. I was, in the Chinese term, *Beijing ren*, a Peking person.

Forbidden City, Peking, 1920s: gold tiles, red pillars, white marble.

Outside a western gate of Peking stood a little outdoor courtyard. From just north of the gate, a short wall extended to meet a longer wall on the west. To the south, a large opening admitted camel trains, carts, wagons, and people coming in from the countryside to enter the city. Such an arrangement was designed to protect Peking from evil spirits, which were believed to travel only in straight lines and to come from the north.

But the little space provided more than that; it served as an antechamber to the city. I could rest on the benches in front of a small temple on the northern wall and look out through the gate to the city, with its bustle and traffic, and also out the opening to the south, to the

Camel caravan passing through the outer gate at Hsi Pien Men, circa 1920.

low bridge over the city moat and the little village beyond it. Inside the courtyard, there might be chanting from the temple, or the sound of a drum, or of camels and donkeys lapping from water troughs. People and animals mingled as they rested from their journey and prepared to enter the gate. Merchants bargained while selling goods not subject to the city tax; travelers could sit on the benches in front of the temple, or squat before the food stalls drinking tea and eating steamed buns. Small pyramids of coal balls stood against the western side of the court to be brought through the gate on long, squeaking poles to the stores and houses inside.

I would halt in the passage from countryside to the city, to draw breath, to prepare for a change from the stillnesses of the country to the clangor of the city streets. It was as if the city was saying to me, "Not yet. Not yet. Prepare yourself to enter the Imperial city of China. Have a cup of tea. Welcome—but prepare." I would then get on my bicycle, ride through the deep shadow of the gate, emerge into the sunlight and the bustle and say to the city, "I am home."

From the time I was one until I was eighteen, Peking was my world. I listened to the sounds of families on the streets and watched people through the windows of our house. I was more comfortable with their language than with my own. I could see life being lived, and think of their culture as my own. But from the beginning there was no future in that. Early in our lives my sisters and brother and I knew that our future would be in another country, one we may not have seen, where we were to survive and succeed.

There were other walls. I was born into a closed universe: Presbyterians all around, two generations deep, a famous missionary in China on my father's side, an equally famous minister from Scotland on my mother's, both of them listed in the 1921 edition of *Who's Who in the World*, unassailable. The Presbyterian God was totally in charge. From that universe there was simply no exit. Those baptized into the

View of Peking from the Drum Tower, looking west towards our compound at Ku Lou Hsi, 1920s.

Presbyterian faith were predestined either for heaven or for hell, and according to doctrine there was nothing specific anyone could do to influence this fate. Only God's grace could alter it, and that was unreliable, because it could not be known. You might, however, try to become eligible, which meant being unwaveringly good, but it was never a sure thing. My father's brother, our beloved uncle Ernest, who married a USO hostess my father's mother dubbed a chorus girl, used to say that most missionary children would like to be bad; they just didn't know how.

In addition, my parents were not only Presbyterian, they were missionaries in China, a land famous for ancestor worship. Among the millions of people in that country at that time there were only a few hundred surnames. A person in those days was primarily a descendant, with the responsibility of honorably representing his or her ancestors. I knew that my father and mother were in China to represent God, so there was a double obligation at the very least for their children to be good, but it was much better if they were perfect. Since the Presbyterian doctrine of predestination made a risky business of experimenting with being naughty, I lived anxiously, ferreting out rules, and abiding by them, within expectations of behavior that felt like walls.

Finally I built a wall of my own, a few weeks before my second birthday, in 1919, just after my sister Elinor was born. My father, John Hayes, had been sent on a drought relief expedition to far northwest China, and my mother, newborn sister and I went to stay with fellow-missionaries in Chefoo, a coastal city about two hundred miles southeast of the capital. My sister's birth had been difficult, and she was fragile. In Chefoo I came down with scarlet fever, and was told to stay away from my mother and the baby in order not to endanger their lives. I do not remember who cared for me, but I do know that I was told that I could be fatal, and thus should keep my distance from people. This wall would last for decades.

*　　　*　　　*

My parents met at Oxford University in 1912, where my father was at Merton College and my mother was at Somerville. They were studying, separately, with the same tutor, and one evening when he invited his students to tea, they first saw each other. My mother,

Barbara Kelman, recalled that when she saw the handsome young American standing by the fireplace she said to herself, "That's the man I'm going to marry." Not "I want to," but "I'm going to."

My father was dashing, athletic and irrepressible. My mother, for the first time away from her somber home in gray Edinburgh, was ready for twinkles in the eye. She would later tell stories of unchaperoned day excursions on the river Cher, and equally unsupervised picnics in the countryside, all infused with American gaiety and ingenuity. My grandmother used to say that "John had a way with fences."

This soon changed. All through the summer of 1914 war had been building in Europe, and on August 4, 1914, the German army invaded Belgium, and Britain entered the war. The following week my father bicycled the 413 miles from London to Edinburgh. Although he and mother saw a great deal of each other, my mother's report was "nothing doing."

In the fall my mother's father, Dr. John Kelman, prepared to join the British army as a chaplain, but on the eve of his departure suffered a breakdown and left immediately for Australia, then considered a rehabilitative climate and society. My father entered New College seminary in Edinburgh, living in the college settlement in the city; my mother returned to Oxford. In the midst of all these distances my father applied to my grandfather for permission to marry my mother. It was granted, provided he did not take her to China, and the couple announced their engagement in December of 1915. Early the next year my father went to France with the Y.M.C.A. to join the front, but when he was found to be an American he was retained in Le Havre for three months, leaving only to greet Dr. Kelman in Oxford as his future son-in-law. Returning to Scotland, he continued at New College, and became Dr. Kelman's assistant.

It was March before my father's parents in China heard from others of his engagement. His father wrote, coyly, that he had heard that my father "had been taken prisoner in a certain engagement," and later "that she is a good, sensible girl I do not doubt—if she was not she would be an exception to the general rule in Scotland." He noted that the engagement took place while Dr. Kelman was away: "Will this affect your future seminary course?" His mother wrote, "we have proof that you have succeeded in persuading a certain Scottish lassie to join you in your life's work. We know nothing about her...but I feel when you have chosen her for your life's companion she must be fine, and I hope you have the truest and most beautiful life together and may God's richest blessing rest on you both." His father concluded his letter with "best wishes for a noble, useful and happy life." The telegram sent on July 6th, the wedding day, was stark: "Proverbs 18: 22." The text, "He that hath found a good wife, hath found a good thing, and shall receive a pleasure from the Lord," was not spelled out. For Grandfather Hayes the acquisition of a wife was to be for the benefit of the husband and of his work.

My mother had left college, much to Grandmother Hayes's relief. What was Barbara doing studying moral history when she should be taking up cooking, "&c."? My parents were married by Dr. Kelman in his church, and after a brief honeymoon in the Scottish highlands sailed for New York. There my mother had to register as an alien. With her country in a war which America had not yet joined, a war to which her friends went daily to die, she had to vow "to support the United States against all enemies, domestic and foreign" in order to become a citizen of a country which just over a century before had been an enemy of her own.

She and my father rented a house in Princeton, where my father enrolled in Mateer Theological Seminary, and they then went off to

My grandfather's brother Will Hayes and Mother in front of the Hayes farm, western Pennsylvania, 1916.

visit relatives on the family farms. My mother, with a trousseau appropriate for the only daughter of a well-known minister and his socially conscious wife, felt shy and frightened of the competent, direct, affectionate farm women she was surrounded by. Used to the blackfaced sheep of the highlands during summer holidays in the Scottish hills, she was awed by the herds of cattle, the big barns and the daily hard work. She was by then pregnant, often sick—in her words, "a great disappointment." However, the farm folk approved of her shyness and eagerness to please, and she found support, especially with my father's Aunt Lillie, his mother's sister. Aunt Lillie had raised a family of teachers and doctors in the market town of Mercer, Pennsylvania, in a comfortable frame house with a deep shaded porch, two blocks from the county court house, and had a special welcome for her nephew's anxious Scottish wife.

Back in Princeton, my mother welcomed her first American springtime, with its apple blossoms and soft wide breezes.

*　　　*　　　*

I was born in the middle of one of those juxtapositions of the unlikely that I later recognized as the usual condition of our family's life. A few days before I was born a crisis had developed; my mother contracted German measles. No maternity hospital would accept her with a contagious disease, and no contagious-disease ward would admit a pregnant woman. It happened that my mother's parents were in America. The British Foreign Office had sent my grandfather, Dr. Kelman, to encourage, by his preaching and lecturing, young men to enlist in the war. My mother had never held a baby. She accordingly sent for her own childhood nurse, Lena, to come from Scotland across the U-boat infested Atlantic and attend this first child. By April the cast was assembled; all that was lacking was a stage.

My mother possessed that universal solvent, connections. Henry Sloan Coffin, minister of Madison Avenue Presbyterian Church, who had known of Dr. Kelman and admired him, offered his ordered and elegant household at 129 East 71st Street in New York for the birth. My mother, equipped with her nurse, my father, and her parents, moved in. Sunday morning is prescriptively calm in a minister's house, but that Sunday, April 15, 1917, there was no peace for Dr. Coffin. A baby was due in his house, and inconveniently just before the 11:00

a.m. service. Maids scurried upstairs and down, carrying pitchers of steaming hot water, piles of towels, assorted basins, and other necessities. The doctor arrived, with his black bag. Varying levels of concern and expectation hovered in the air.

Leaving all this behind, Dr. Coffin set off for his church to preach

Mother, me, and Father, 1917, before leaving for China.

the morning service. Ascending the pulpit, he glanced at the sermon he had no time to review that morning, and read the day's text: "Oh that I had the wings of a dove that I might fly away and be at rest." So I started off as a general inconvenience and secular intruder into a household dedicated to the Lord. And I was also a setback to the world of sports. Back on 71st Street, my father, who had been crew captain at Merton College, Oxford, greeted his first child, a daughter, with the statement, "What a waste of a good pair of rowing shoulders." Years later, taking my place in a racing shell at college, I would exult in being so well equipped. But the word "waste" never left me.

My parents soon moved back to Princeton, to the little house among the blossoming apple trees, and Lena came too, but at first would not move in. A short, sturdy Scotswoman, with braids around her head, Lena seemed to bring with her the air of the gray Scottish streets and their stone houses. My mother would quote Lena's first words on her arrival in Princeton: "I willna' live in a stick hoose." Years later, in 1935, when I visited Lena in a little stone cottage in Glasgow, she told me that her fears of living in a wooden house were overcome because she thought that I would not survive without her. My mother would tell of the first weeks when I would cry and she didn't know what to do, until Lena would tell her, kindly, "Och, the bairn's hungry."

Finally it was time to set off for China, that far-off land my father had promised never to take my mother to. I was four months old. Mother told me of her panic at the door of the train compartment at Princeton Junction as Lena handed me to her, saying, "Feed her, Barbara. She'll be all right if ye do." My mother was eager, at that time very much in love with her husband, to make a success of what life with him required. For her, language and its uses supplanted experience, or perhaps constituted it. She accordingly decided to counter my grandfather's known reservations about a British daughter-in-law by greeting him in the Chinese language. Her memories of the long train trip up to and across Canada with its great mountains and forests, and of the four weeks at sea, were of diapers hanging across the cabin spaces and of me crying, interrupting her studies of the Chinese language. I have sometimes wondered if my lifelong addiction to language and my fear of its power were established in that closed cabin, moving across vast spaces of land and water, my mother desperately working for eligibility and acceptance by my famous and feared grandfather. In Kobe, Japan, they had to leave the boat because of an epidemic. Arriving in Tsingtao, Shantung Province, she greeted her still skeptical father-in-law in Chinese, establishing herself as the daughter-in-law every older person in China then expected to bring diligence and honor to him, to his lineage, to his achievements, and above all, to his son. The family moved to Tsinan, in Shantung province, where they had to stay for two months because of floods, finally reaching Peking in November of 1917.

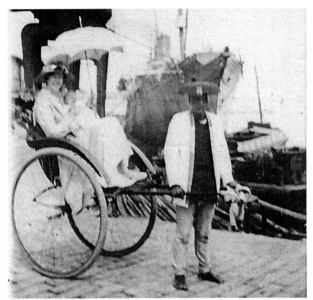

Mother and I exiting our ship in Kobe, Japan, 1917.

In those years, The Presbyterian Board of Foreign Missions owned the land that missionaries used, and housed them in what were called compounds. These compounds were set down among the low courtyard homes of city residents, with walls along the side of the streets they were on. A little gate house offered entry from the street, a gateman sitting at a wooden table, teapot and cup at his side.

In Peking there were two locations, the main one at Erh T'iao Hutung (Second Tier Lane) and a smaller one at Ku Lou Hsi Ta Chieh (Drum Tower West Big Street). Although most missionary families stayed in one location for the term of their service, our family moved between the locations.

Mission compounds, instant enclaves of a foreign culture, typically included houses for families, a house for single women (respectfully called the ladies' house), a church, a school or two, and a tennis court. (Rarely were there enough missionaries in any one location to accommodate any other sport.) In every mission compound I knew, there was either a ruined church tower or a plaque on a church wall listing those missionaries who had been killed in the Boxer uprising less than twenty years before we arrived.

Our compound at Ku Lou Hsi, Peking, 1920s. The ruined church tower on the left was a reminder of the Boxer Rebellion.

The Erh T'iao location was divided by the street it was on. The northern part held five houses joined by paths in a rough semicircle with a gate behind them, leading to a girls' school. The southern part across the *hutung* held a hospital, nurses' quarters, and a church, conveying a sense of care for body and soul.

The Ku Lou Hsi compound held two houses, a church, an engineering school, and the requisite tennis court. The compound was situated on the grounds of an old temple; three carved marble steles reminded us of the culture we were trying to replace.

Mother, Father, and I went first to the Ku Lou Hsi compound but moved soon to a house behind the church in Erh T'iao Hutung. Missionary family houses were bordered by plantings that attempted to reproduce the gardens people had left behind in their home countries. In front of this house a formal walled garden lay like an apron. English occupants before us had set roses, larkspur, and daisies between low hedges. Later, when I read Amy Lowell's poem "Patterns," this garden

Circa 1930: Dad's Oxford oar, and above it, his Leander cap, crew trials cap, and Chefoo school cap. Below the oar: boat race photo and school shields.

became for me an image of my childhood, planted by unknowns, patterned, and enclosed. A small square pavilion at the end anchored it in China, like a quilt.

When we returned from our first furlough we moved into the house on Ku Lou Hsi, the home most of my family remembers. It was big and two-storied, of clay brick, with a porch covering half the front. My father's study occupied the other half, a testament to the priority of its occupant. My parents' school shields from Edinburgh and Oxford hung prominently in the central hallway, announcing provenance, which was further signaled by the cutaway section of my father's victorious rowing shell from Oxford hanging on the wall nearby. The living room was on the right, shaded by the porch, and filled with the heavy upholstered oak sofa and chairs shipped by my mother's anxious parents from Scotland to this land of teak and tapestry.

Behind this front room, separable by doors that slid into walls, was the dining room, with windows looking out onto a side path leading from the compound gate. From there watch was kept for the usual unexpected guests, and rush orders sent to the kitchen. The sliding doors were the heart of our entertainment as we grew older. With no plays, movies or TV, we children provided our own theater in more ways than one, and for our skits the doors made an instant theater of the living room—a Bethlehem stable, a London apartment—and a staging area of the dining room. They also symbolized for me the power of artifice: strong definers of space and function, supporting fantasy, the sliding doors could reappear, restoring the rooms to proportion and purpose.

A swinging door led from the dining room to the pantry where shelves and a table flanked a large wooden icebox, tin-lined, which held blocks of ice cut from the imperial lake nearby, delivered by men with squares of heavy canvas across their shoulders. Behind the pantry was the kitchen, dominated by a large clay coal-burning stove, and a smiling cook. Chopping tables stood in the middle of the room and cupboards lined the walls. Doors opened from the kitchen onto a side yard, where goats and chickens wandered about during the day. Occasionally there would be a horse or two, or a donkey, and once an antelope, a gift to my father. Stables and goat pens lined the wall of the side yard that backed up against the street; there was a cistern for rain water, and a well.

Upstairs, gained by a parallel staircase at the back of the front hall, were four large bedrooms around a central hall. As young children we slept on a sleeping porch over the front porch, open to the air, the tree tops, and the sounds of the city. The front bedroom over the dining room was the nursery; steps led down to a small windowless bathroom with a bathtub and washbasin but no water. Behind them in a narrow little room was a toilet, which in my early childhood was a bucket under a wooden seat. The bucket was emptied daily into a pail, and at night transferred to a wheelbarrow, which collected the precious night soil, its operator bent over the two compartments, pushing the barrow along the dark streets, contents splashing out on either side.

Water was brought in enamel pitchers to the bathroom up the back stairs from the kitchen. In winter a kerosene stove provided heat, its perforated top throwing roseates of flickering light on the ceiling. A cupboard over the bath held first-aid supplies and a knife. After my second sister was born six years later, and the number of children in the family was uneven, I was afraid that if my parents separated, we children would be distributed between them, and that knife was there to divide a child in half—presumably me—to ensure a fair division.

Peking, circa 1918. My mother at center.

When I was about six, plumbing began to be considered a worthy addition to the religious life—and came first to our house, since my father was the chairman of the mission. Everyone in the compound was invited for the great occasion, which was to consist of the first push of the toilet lever, and a party to celebrate the wonderful sound. My father ceremoniously climbed the front stairs, the magic sound of running water filled the house, and then water itself cascaded down the front stairs and flowed out the front door. People in the living room watched the flood. So welcome was the sound, irrespective of the betrayal of its function, that everyone applauded. Standing there, I could think only of what a mess it was going to be to clean up.

In the Presbyterian Mission, husbands and wives were individually commissioned, so for the sake of the commissioned wives servants were needed to maintain their households. Provisions were daily bargained for and bought on the streets. My father's yearly salary ($1,200) provided wages for a cook, two man-servants, an *amah*, or nurse, for the children, a man for the livestock and the garden, and often, because public rickshaws could be lice-infected, a family rickshawman. For new families a Chinese tutor came every day. Father, raised in China, and fluent in the language, met with Mr. Chin, in a long gray silk gown, as his collaborator in revising a Chinese-English dictionary. I used to stand outside the study door, marveling at the efforts to match the English language and its meager string of letters with the thousands of beautiful Chinese characters and their myriad combinations.

Especially in Peking, there were real, present dangers that gave the ruined church towers a prophetic power. One time during the politically restless 1920s foreigners were suddenly evacuated from Peking, and our family's daily life took on an edge. Once my sister and I were in a rickshaw on the way to the American School in the city. We passed a military barracks and shots rang out, apparently aimed at us. Our resourceful rickshawman carried us to a nearby opium den, where, breathing the spiraling opium smoke around us, we got happily stoned until he felt it was safe to continue to school. That afternoon we went home a different way. My chief concern in the incident was the fear that my stern mother would dismiss the rickshawman for taking us to an opium den. She didn't, but my sister and I were prepared to concoct elaborate stories of his bravery if she tried.

Daily living, however, I remember with enchantment. The first sounds of the morning were the stoking of the furnace coals, then the choiring bands of pigeons, equipped with whistles, whose differing tones changed and faded as the birds circled overhead. Smoke from the coal fires of the low Chinese houses huddled against the mission walls drifted through the windows, mingling with the smell of goats assembling in the side yard for morning milking. Haze from the golden roofs of the Forbidden City reflected on the windows of my father's study, and on the walls of my mother's desk alcove. On the way to school we passed street vendors crying, "sweet-potatoes, chestnuts, persimmons." After school there were different sounds: our piano practice, my father's Chinese colleague's perfect pronunciation of the ancient sounds of our other first language, and in the evenings, over the compound walls the waning cries in the streets.

Finally, the last sounds of the night: the baa-ing of the goats being shut in their pens, my mother's voice reading English fairy tales over millet and milk, the furnace being banked. Then the Chinese night would settle over the big house, with the squat shadow of the church tower outlined on my bedroom wall, and the long lullabies of Chinese mothers to their children outside the mission wall, under my window.

My first memory is of running away, specifically from the Chinese *amah*, Li Nai Nai, who was assigned to my care. I was almost two, she was a hundred, with bound feet, so it was no contest, but being able to escape her was my first intimation that I should take care of myself. Her hands were gnarled and parched, the fingernails long and curved, and it hurt to be touched by her. She had been many years in the service of the mission, and came with the house my parents moved into when we first arrived. My mother was inaccessible, busy setting up a household in a new country, immersed in a new language,

Elinor and my mother, me and Dr. Fenn, and two ladies, Peking, 1922.

unfamiliar with a culture her husband had been raised in, and accustomed from her Scottish childhood to nurses caring for children. An elderly missionary, Dr. Fenn, also came with the house, and it was to him that at first I fled, only to be chided for being unkind to Li Nai Nai. He scolded me, which I didn't mind. At nearly two I was accustomed to it, but then he would send me back to her, which I did mind. I remember feeling that it was Li Nai Nai's job to be kind to me, since every one else was too busy, and perhaps she tried, but her kindness hurt. So I early wrote off external sources of support or understanding, and settled for discerning and then obeying the rules of survival.

Chefoo, Shantung Province, 1919. From the left: Grandmother Hayes, my sister Elinor, me, and Grandfather Hayes, at his mission in Shantung.

In a Chinese nursery school nearby I learned to speak the language well, and to sing "Jesus loves me" in Chinese, in a perfect Mandarin accent. For me, school was a welcome respite from home. Elinor, my sister, was clearly precocious. At one she could provide the last word for every line in the entire Santa Claus poem: "'Twas the night before Christmas." The grown-ups would say, "Twas the night before Christmas and all through the...," and she would say, "house." Her little treble voice enchanted my visiting Scottish grandmother, whose favorite she was, and for whom she was named. Elinor also resembled in astonishing physical detail the Kelmans' second child, a beautiful little girl called Daisy, whose mind never developed beyond the age of two. My mother told us that she lost her mother then. Mrs.

Kelman would spend hours combing Daisy's hair, holding her in a rocking chair, and was generally unable to perform her duties as the wife of a prominent Edinburgh minister, duties which increasingly devolved to my mother as she grew older. Mother remembered the humiliation of walking beside the six-foot-long perambulator that carried the twelve-year-old Daisy on Edinburgh sidewalks and the slightly embarrassed curiosity of passersby as they peered into it. It was years before I could persuade my mother to talk about this, and about her absolute conviction that school was the only place where it was possible to be alive, and where she could get attention and even what affection was possible in a Scottish educational institution of the early nineteen-hundreds. School was the answer to all her needs as she knew them, and we were the inheritors of that misshapen girlhood. Achievement was our job, and even our definition as her daughters. Once when I was in my teens she told me, "Margaret, what you have to offer a man is your mind." At one year old, Elinor had already made it.

In 1919, when I was two, my father was assigned to the International Famine Relief Committee and dispatched to the northwest provinces, warlord territory. A drought had led to a severe shortage of food. People were starving, owing to the failure of their crops, and also because most of what they could produce was preempted by the warlord who governed their territory, or by his men. It was therefore a trip made into dangerous territory, but my father was young and strong and above all, having grown up in China, was familiar with the people, the language, and the land.

There was no mechanical transportation in the northwest territories, so the expedition carried its supplies of grain in the open, in carts or on donkeys or camels, prey to bandits and starving peasants. The more serious danger, however, was from the warlords themselves. Far from welcoming supplies of grain for their hungry people, they saw food from outside as a weakening of their hold, and themselves as threatened by a foreigner riding in to distribute it. Since my grandfather had been revered as a scholar in the province of Shantung and had been given the status of a civil official, my father was accustomed to the Chinese traditions for dealing with those in power. Accordingly, when entering the territory of a warlord, first he would call on him, to let him know what he was doing, and to offer him whatever advantage the warlord might want to claim for himself in the distribution of the food. Several warlords he won over by showing how it might enhance their power—and economic situation—to distribute the free food without accrediting its source. Other warlords nevertheless felt threatened, and it was around them that the stories grew.

It was the custom in China to offer a meal immediately to anyone who came to your house. In fact, when I was young the standard greeting was, "Have you eaten yet?" Thus a warlord would offer a meal to my father and his party, which often included local people who had joined the expedition along the way. Some of these became attached to my father, and would warn him if the host he was approaching was likely to be hostile, or to sabotage the mission. They would make friends with the warlord's domestic staff and arrange to be in the kitchen when the food was prepared, to determine whether any of the dishes was poisoned. When they spotted one, they would stand at the kitchen door and send signals to my father about which dish he should insist that the warlord eat first. Once my father was indeed poisoned, and had to continue the journey ill, lying in a cart. A local man, En P'u, who had joined the party nursed him back to health and continued home with him. He became the chief servant in our household, bringing his younger brother with him and pretty much running the household. In this way those far-off, stricken territories seemed to move into our house.

Another time Father credited God with his survival. My father was not a drinking man. He had in fact made a name for himself at Merton College at Oxford University in the 1910s for devising a non-alcoholic punch and seeing that it was served at college celebrations—a first for that student body since the thirteenth century. Now he had come to call on a warlord who refused to distribute the proffered grain but invited my father to a meal. The host then offered him the potent rice wine that is usually served only with, or after, food, and in any case cannot be refused. The warlord insisted that drinking precede the meal, and father took it as a warning: whoever drank the other under the table would win. Father, however, suggested that they throw for each drink—rock, paper, scissors—and flung a quick prayer to God, the substance of which, he told us later, was that though he knew God disapproved of both gambling and drinking, right now it was God's responsibility to take care of His business. Although Father lost a couple of times, and had to take a quick swallow, it was the warlord who ended up under the table. To Father's surprise, a cheer went up even from the warlord's people, who rushed to help to distribute the grain before their ruler had time to revive. As a child I was accustomed to my father's skill in negotiating complex situations, but I remember being glad that God had also been on this job.

We all went to meet my father when he returned. He arrived through Peking's great main gate, dressed in a green leather suit, heavily bearded, riding a horse he had been given. A procession of animals followed him—pigs, chickens, donkeys, and an antelope— gifts from those who had received grain. People traveling with him rode behind, corralling stray animals that tried to escape in the little *hutungs* that led off the main thoroughfare, brought back into line yelling and squealing, braying and clucking. Father also brought stories that thrilled and scared us, and gave him a heroic cast.

All the animals moved into the side yard of the house. There wasn't much room for the pigs, which were soon eaten; the chickens took their places with those already there. The problem was how to accommodate the antelope in the same stable as our horse, Jack, who seemed to dislike the intruder. The antelope was beautiful, shy, and fragile; he would approach to be stroked. The first time Jack kicked him the lovely little animal had to be shot. I was sad, for I had become very fond of him. He had come all the way from a wild, desert country only to die in a small crowded side yard, brought down by an ungainly, powerful relative.

*   *   *

It was November of 1919 before our household settled down in one place. I remember a house full of grownups: grandparents, mother's nurse from Scotland, and other missionaries. We traveled to other cities in China, and to Japan, where beautiful sepia pictures were taken of my sister and me in silk dresses. Life was predictable but unstable; it seemed anything could happen at any time. World War I had finally ended, but not for my mother. Tall, anxious, beautiful as a young woman, she carried with her the aura of the lost generation of her home country; people were likely to disappear.

The back stairs of our house, steep and poorly lit, went from the pantry to a landing on the second floor, which led to the bedrooms. Along the side of these stairs, on the ground floor, was a narrow corridor, lined with books. Prominent among them were several years' worth of Punch, the English humor magazine. Folio size, bound in maroon cloth with gold lettering, they chronicled the British view of World War I. Long before I could read or understand the text, I would pore over the cartoons—cartoons of people dead and dying, of trenches and lines of men climbing from them to certain deaths, cartoons of empires and of emperors as enemies. I would think of my mother reading the casualty lists in her parents' home in Scotland, the young men she had known, rugby players, fellow students, dead. Death and destruction in a humor magazine?

I knew my mother and father had met as university students, so one cartoon in particular stays with me still. In it a group of young men seen from the back, dressed in academic gowns, with mortar boards, advance toward a gray, swirling cloud. Over their shoulders they carry guns, the bayonets extended. Later I would be able to read the title: "Graduating Class of 1915," but even to a small child it seemed predictive. Sitting in the dimly lit hall, curled up against the paneling of the stairs, I would handle the heavy volumes, looking for pictures I could understand, and for anything that would make my mother clearer to me. I would hear someone calling my name, and leave obediently but reluctantly, thinking that those volumes held a world far more real than the one I was summoned to. Those books held the world my mother seemed really to live in. I watched her efforts to transfer its standards and assumptions to an alien and resisting, though chosen, community.

Even our temporary feeling of stability was interrupted in 1921 when, one December morning, the house shook, waking us up. Mother and father were calm, there was no damage, and I put it down to one of the odd things that happened in the adult world. Although it was many weeks before we knew it, over 200,000 people had died that night in an earthquake and massive landslide in Kansu province, near the border of Tibet, over a thousand miles to the west. The quake, 8.3 on the Richter scale, occurred in an area with soil made of clay and loose quartz so that mountaintops slid into the valleys, burying cities and villages and the caves people lived in on the mountainsides. It was a month before the news reached the east. Chinese around me talked of the Chinese dragon twitching his tail under the earth, and that the "mountains walked."

Once again the International Famine Relief Committee in Peking called on my father to join an expedition to assess the need for food and other supplies at the site of the earthquake. Out came the leather suit, the high boots, the camel-driver's hat, the heavy gloves, my father's other self, going out to unknown danger to help people we didn't know. The last time we had learned after the fact about the danger, and certainly there would be no news of him for a long time, and no way of reaching him if anything happened to us. I didn't want him leaving us to go to a place where a dragon was twitching his tail under walking mountains.

From the May 1922 issue of the National Geographic Magazine: The Hayes-Hall Kansu Earthquake Relief Expedition, Kansu Province, western China, 1921. Father is fourth from the right.

Partings in that country at that time would often seem permanent, and they left a long legacy with me. Transportation was on ancient roads, subject to bandits and marauders; communication was usually by rudimentary telegraph from a post miles away from where the expedition might be. There were no telephone lines. In the political turmoil of the country during the 1920s, rail lines were not secure, road beds were often haphazardly maintained. Trains might be late in starting; they might not go at all. In times of plague, crews would often not come to work. Because of the fear of contagion, passengers dreaded the crowded conditions on trains that did run. One time I overheard my mother telling a story that she claimed was true. Crewmen were regularly employed to tap the iron wheels of railway cars to hear whether or not they were sound. A passenger, noticing that such an employee was moving along somewhat briskly, tapping as he went, asked him what he was doing. He replied that his cousin, the crewman, had recently died, bequeathing him the job. He did not know why he was doing it. As a little girl, whenever we traveled by train, I would jockey for a seat next to a window so that I would hear if one of the wheels sounded strange. I had no clear idea what I would do with the information, but it felt safer to have it.

Trains were often delayed by floods. Once, on a trip to the seashore, the train stopped in the middle of a flood, engine puffing, and waited for the waters to recede, while the dead bodies of people and animals floated by, bumping occasionally against the cars. Traveling, for me, was the ultimate in helplessness. It involved total dependence on other people doing their jobs reliably. Life in early twentieth-century China gave little assurance of that.

It did affect the seriousness with which I said goodbye to visitors who stayed with us. There were no appropriate or affordable hotels in Peking for missionaries in those early days, and we had many guests. It was standard practice in the missionary field to have a short prayer service before people left, especially if they were going into the interior of the country, asking God to protect them. Since I was never sure that I would see people again, I would stand on the porch afterward, waving until the rickshaws had turned the last corner in the compound and gone out of the gate. Sometimes I would run out of the mission gate, waving them down the street, tears running down my cheeks. Later, I would learn that the word "goodbye" derived from "God be with you," and implied the need for divine protection woven into the parting itself. When young I was an anxious traveler. We crossed the oceans on ships, and I used to watch nervously from the dock as the boat was loaded: could I trust the captain to be sure that the tonnage did not exceed the Plimsoll line?

Within our family the issue was further complicated. My mother, who came from a land where the *Flying Scotsman* train had run regularly from Edinburgh to London since June 1862, trusted neither Chinese technology nor its technicians. My father grew up in a time and place where Chinese families repeatedly tore up the straight rail lines Germans laid because the tracks often ran through family graveyards. He had a buoyant faith in getting anywhere any time, as long as the time itself didn't matter. Already anxious about traveling, I would listen to my parents arguing and retreat to a book, which took me places without any need to travel at all. Since we had to choose books to read on the trains anyway, there was usually one at hand.

Finally, when I was seven, we were going further than ever. We were going to America, a journey requiring two trains and two boats, a lot of packing, and from me the fervent hope that the train engineers, the boat captains, and the workers would have slept well the night before we climbed aboard. Everyone else trusted in God's care; I had no such anodyne. I knew perfectly well who actually turned on the switches, and watched for steam gauges and loading lines, and I didn't trust them. But perhaps things worked better in America. Everyone said they did, and I was ready to find out.

II

FURLOUGH

Near the Hayes farm, Mercer County, Pennsylvania.

Missionaries were given furloughs every seven years to go back "home," to catch up with relatives, to report to their supporting churches, to spread the word about God's work abroad, and, I came to think, to provide programs for Sunday Schools.

The first furlough was usually after five years' service, but our family did not go until the sixth year, in 1923, owing to the birth of my second sister, Janet. America had been for me a myth, a made-up country, a location for the childhood stories that my paternal grandparents, sitting in their living room in Shantung Province, told us of farms and front porches, aunts and cousins, farmers and lawyers, teachers and doctors. We would hear about horses hitched to wagons,

27

and about buggies taking my cousins to school.

Grainy photographs of our relatives—farmers and their wives dressed in field clothes, and formal photographs of college graduates in starched collars—perfectly matched the picture of "American life" in our first-grade primers. Solid American names—Aunt Sade, Aunt Lou, Uncle Plummer Thompson—lodged in our minds as people spoken about by others, in tales told.

On the Hayes farm, summer 1923. From the left: Plummer Thompson and his wife Sade Hayes Thompson (my grandfather's sister), Will Hayes (my grandfather's brother) and his wife Lizzie Thompson Hayes.

Yet America was the country my mother did not like, and that my father spoke of not as a country, but as a place where there were people who belonged to us. I don't remember when I first became aware that my birth in America made me the only member of my family qualified to be President of the United States, but it anchored me to a country that our family belonged to, but which didn't exist to us children as a known entity. To a six-year-old it presented the same confusing connection that being one of "God's little children" had. I knew who my father was. He could sometimes be found in his study.

It wasn't that we were people without a country. We had too many, and they didn't fit together well. My tenacious Scottish mother used to say that Britain's Thanksgiving Day was the Fourth of July. And whenever "My country, 'tis of thee" was played or sung, my mother required us to stand and put our hands over our hearts to salute the

King of England. I did this only as an obedient daughter, mindless of whatever loyalty and nationality might mean.

However, in 1923 I was excited. In our British-run, Chinese-staffed household, being American was unclear. Now we were going there. I wanted to meet the little girls who had sent us clothes in boxes which my sister and I hovered over as we opened them, to catch the first whiff of what America smelled like. In our ordered, restricted life, I wanted to know what a "sweet land of liberty" felt like. What would it be like to be with so many people of our kind? Would the people there like us? Would I like my country? I wanted to see the addresses to which we dutifully sent thank-you notes for Christmas gifts from people we didn't know. We had pictures of relatives—people standing in front of barns, beside silos, on front porches, but would those people actually be there? Did they live and breathe and move? Would they offer us food? Were there beds in those houses? I was glad to go to "my country" to see for myself what it was all about. In 1923, our careful, devout way of life was about to be interrupted, not only for a vigorous unknown, but perhaps itself to be tested in a market place, certainly to be on exhibit everywhere we went.

Uncle Will Hayes on his farm in Pennsylvania, summer 1923.

In the house behind the church we packed wooden, tin-banded trunks, sitting on them to force their locks to engage, careful that our fingers did not get caught on the tin hinges that held the lids open.

Janet, now four months old, had, with the wisdom of infants, gone to sleep in her traveling basket on the table in the nursery, which had been cleared of other furniture to be ready for the next missionary family. At last our parents gave the house key to the servants to lock up after we left, and we were on our way, past our curious neighbors to the line of waiting rickshaws in the street, and to the railway station. We were halfway there when my mother, in the lead rickshaw, looking back, suddenly asked whose rickshaw the baby was in. No one's. I was neither shocked nor surprised that the baby had been forgotten. I remember thinking how disposable we were. The rickshawmen wheeled around and my mother dashed toward the house, hoping that the servants had not yet left with the keys and that she could get in. She found the door unlocked, retrieved the basket, and we started off again, the neighbors even more curious, the baby still asleep.

I was wide awake; we were going to meet the people with the sturdy names, stand on their lands, go in their doors, and speak only English for twelve months. A week hence we would be sailing on the newly named American President Line.

We were to cross Korea by train and sail from Japan. While crossing Korea, an incident changed forever the picture I had of my father and of our family. We had settled into a compartment on the train, and my father decided to get a soda. Before leaving the compartment, he showed us the tickets for the train and trans-Pacific liner, so that if the conductor came to check we could tell him where they were. Father came back shortly, an open soda bottle in his hand. He said, calmly, "Barbara, I have thrown away the tickets." My world started to unravel. Had my father, always unpredictable, gone mad? No, he had been standing between cars, opening his soda, and tossed away what he thought was the cap. Instead, the tickets to Japan and to America had landed in a Korean farmer's field. The conductor, enjoying the crisis, pulled the cord to stop the train, my father climbed down the steps, and the train went on. I was stunned—my father in a Korean rice field and we on the train headed for Japan?

In Tokyo we were met by friends we were to stay with until the boat left. As we got off the train one of them asked, "Where's John?" I can still hear my mother's reply: "He's arriving later. He threw away the tickets." At that point, I gave up hope of ever reaching America, of ever trusting my parents again. Prematurely, it turned out. There are conflicting myths surrounding what arrangement my father and the farmer came to, and the story of the thrown-away tickets attained the status of legend in the missionary community, but my father arrived the next day, tickets intact, if damp. I now felt as if, instead of being ordinary people, we had become people in a story—as if, in fact, we had become the stuff of stories.

The *President McKinley*, at the pier in Yokohama, was beautiful, with long, sleek lines in the water, gleaming upper decks, and two black funnels—white dollar signs on them—from which steam rose as if the ship was conscious of her mastery of the sea and of the world beyond it. This was America's first offering to me, and I thrilled to it. I eagerly climbed the gangplank. Once on deck, I was in the majority for the first time in my life, my own language all around me. The groups of Japanese on the pier, the dockhands calling to each other, the muddy water slapping against the ship, all seemed to be part of a world I was leaving.

Enchanted by the signs, instructions, bells, and stewards who found our names on lists and directed us accurately, I followed my family toward our cabin. So this was the way Americans did things! Soon a whistle sounded, the engines changed gear, the ship lurched slightly as she pulled away from the pier, and up on deck I watched my first world slowly disappear. The restlessness of living in a land as a foreigner started to recede, and I turned toward this small microcosm of "my country" as a plant to sunlight.

The trip took two weeks, and I enjoyed it all. Meal times were announced by a steward walking along the corridors, striking a brass gong, summoning us to tables laid with linen and silverware. We played shuffleboard and ring toss and waited in deck chairs for 11 a.m. bouillon, served by stewards in white coats while we looked out to sea. We went to church in the ship's lounge. I remember how reasonable it seemed that services were held in a place that moved. I secretly thought of religion as a somewhat shifty enterprise. The slight swaying of the ship felt like an appropriate setting for it. And on this American ship I first became aware of my parents as members of my family, Americans like me, instead of being God's property, subject to His prior claim on them. In that crowded cabin, in that contained, ordered world, on a constantly moving sea, for a little time, my parents belonged to my sisters and to me.

For the first time, also, I met a secular world. In the dining rooms, the lounges, and on deck, I heard people talking about business, travel, politics, style, entertainment. These appeared to be as important to them as God was to the missionaries I had been living with. Apparently there was a whole world out there, untethered from the stern protocols of the religious life. I shied away from it; it seemed dangerous.

My mother's notes inform me that we landed in San Francisco, saw the Grand Canyon, and Lake George in New York. Puzzled that I have no memory of these most memorable places, I can only conclude that so strong was my desire to know who we were, and thus who I was, that my first memory of America is of the family farms. It was June when we drove down the lane to the first one, Plummer Thompson's place, and my farmer relatives stepped out of the first-grade primers and into my life. There were my grandfather's brother, Uncle Will, large, competent and "close spoken," Aunt Sade and Uncle Plummer Thompson, quiet, direct, and full of family curiosity. I soon fitted thoughts of my grandfather in China into this grounded place: there was the church down the road where he had worshiped and married, the nearby farms of his brother and sisters and their husbands,

Summer 1923. From the left: Mother, Aunt Sade Thompson holding Janet, me, Mrs. Hayes Thompson holding a child, Elinor next to me, and Uncle Plummer Thompson.

the county seat with relatives who were lawyers and teachers. He and my grandmother seemed like missing pieces, as if they had taken a bit of this seemingly non-portable life and carried it to China.

As we traveled among churches, I sang "Jesus Loves Me" in Chinese in endless Sunday school programs, often standing in front of supporting church groups wondering which little girl had sent the dress I was wearing. Slowly I began to form a sense of belonging to at least a part of this vast country.

Aunt Sade Thompson, me, and Uncle Plummer Thompson on their farm, spring 1923.

As children, we had lived next to animals all our lives. How quiet and stable these American cows were compared with the feisty goats that provided our milk in China. The calmness of farms seemed like an essence—a secular order conveyed in stacked corncribs, pantry shelves stocked with applesauce, strawberry and cherry preserves, their little blue-edged labels with spidery writing giving the date each was made. The orderliness, the necessity for producing and providing one's own food, became part of what I defined as belonging.

Instead of scattered relatives over several continents, here was a succession of generations, sustaining each other and the family land. I was awed, at the kitchen table, looking out at the corn tassels waving in the field that produced the corn we at the moment were eating. My own relatives were bringing it to the table, giving me a feeling of authenticity, as if we could take care of ourselves, instead of being

My grandfather's brother, William Reed Hayes (wrist circumference: 13.5 inches), and his wife, Elizabeth Ann Thompson Hayes, spring 1923.

served and maintained by another culture.

Their barns were large and dark and belonged to the animals. We were forbidden to go into them without an adult. Implements wrongly stacked could trip you up. There was danger in these great seminal buildings with their wonderful smells of animals, hay, and provender.

On a recent trip, the barn looked the same as it did in 1900.

Visiting the farmhouses, each with its sheltering grove of trees and its silo, I was aware of how different and individual the owners were. Compared to the houses the mission owned and assigned to different families—making us feel that we were all interchangeable—there was something firm and individually insistent about my relatives and how they lived. The place where they lived was theirs, and how they maintained it announced to the world the kind of people they were. Missionaries, however different individually, were hired employees, merged together by loyalty to God, by personal sacrifice, and by their difference from the community they served.

By September, America was confirmed for me. The people with the solid names, men in overalls, women in aprons—they were mine. I had eaten the food they grew, slept in their houses, kept still in their churches, sung in their Sunday schools, and listened to their stories about my grandparents and about my father when he visited them as a young man. Our life in China now seemed alien, something people were curious about, something we composed for them, and presented as a story. Accustomed to artifice, I began to see my life and experiences in China as something extrinsic, as America had been to me before. Now China was the story to be told. Was all of life simply a tale one told? I began to realize that I could make up my life as I went, a power that disturbed me. Did anything maintain?

Amish families now own our old farms. On a recent visit my family and I drove past small groups of children walking barefoot on their way home from school, satchels on their backs. It was if the years had made little difference—the same sober air lay on the country, the same thrift, the same righteousness, the same expected obedience.

*   *   *

But in 1923 there was more of America to discover, and it was so different from my experiences on the farms that I remember abandoning the goal of knowing what being American meant. My mother's father, Dr. Kelman, had been invited by the Fifth Avenue Presbyterian Church in New York to come from Scotland and be its pastor, and he and my grandmother were provided an apartment on West 56th Street. My father enrolled in theological studies nearby, and we moved in with my grandparents for the winter.

I was enrolled in The Spence School, an elite academy for girls, which I faintly remember as being a perquisite of belonging to a well-known grandfather, and at which I gained insufficient mastery of fractions. I loved the city, roller-skating on the sidewalks (sidewalks!) and going to church in the big Romanesque building where my grandfather had overseen the construction of a small chapel. The congregation was wealthy. It included stars of the Metropolitan Opera and prominent New York families. It was my first experience of knowing people for whom money was a tool and not a constraint.

At Christmastime, as grandchildren of a beloved pastor, we received one hundred and one dolls. My mother took immediate charge. We could each choose one. The rest must go to children who would not get one otherwise. I did not consider this just. The dolls had been given to us. Divided between us, the total would come to about thirty-three each. I wanted to be the one to decide how to manage my property, as the dolls' donors certainly did. We ended up, predictably, with one each. I called mine Henrietta.

In New York, we were less on exhibit than we had been in rural parts of the country. For one thing, many of my grandfather's parishioners had themselves seen China on world tours then fashionable and frequent, and had no need of secondhand reports. Also, New York City had other, more sophisticated forms of entertainment. We were now, however, as grandchildren of a famous minister, on exhibit for our behavior rather than for entertainment value. We had been used to this in China, where children's behavior reflected directly on their parents. I gave up any idea of a close relationship with my Scottish grandmother, whose attention was almost entirely on Elinor. Basking in people's affection for Grandfather Kelman, I would sidle up to him at every opportunity and reach for his hand so that people could see I belonged to him. I was in awe of this man, whom so many very rich and powerful people liked. But one Sunday that awe took on a new dimension.

Although the church scheduled Sunday school for children at the same time as the main service, my grandfather liked to have children in church for a little while. Dressed in Sunday best, we would take our places in the cavernous space, past the well-filled pews, at the front near the pulpit. There would be an invocation, an anthem, a prayer, a scripture lesson, and then, like a treat, a children's sermon, after which the children would self-consciously file out for Sunday school, where we would hear Bible stories and engage in improvement activities until the adult service ended.

One time, the Sunday school assignment was to draw pictures illustrating Bible stories. My sister Elinor drew a number of stalks of green grass underneath an empty blue sky. To the teacher's question about what story she was illustrating, Elinor answered that it was the lost lamb. The teacher then asked where the lamb was, and Elinor, with five-year-old scorn, replied that of course it was not in the picture —it was lost. This made a strong impression on the teacher. She then turned to my drawing, which was of a boat with two people on it, the American flag flying at the stern. Again she asked what the Bible story was. I informed her that it was Jesus and a disciple on the Sea of Galilee. She pointed out that America had not even been thought about in Jesus' time, and the class giggled. I was devastated. I had spent a

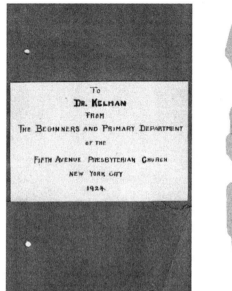
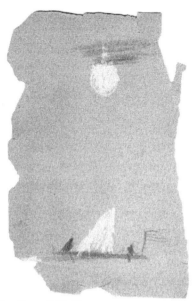

Jesus and a disciple on the Sea of Galilee.

good deal of trouble getting that flag to fly right.

The word quickly got out about the little girl from China who didn't know her history. My grandfather heard about it, but said nothing to me. I attended church the next week in shame, afraid that I had let him down, done him damage before his congregation. He started the children's sermon with a description of my drawing. I sank lower and lower in the pew, waiting for the scorn to come. Here is what he said:

> Boys and girls, I had a gift given me last Sunday morning by the Primary School in our Sunday School here, and it is a gift I prize more than I could ever tell anybody. It is this little collection of drawings in colored chalks which I hold in my hand, and there are many delightful pictures in it showing the children's fancies of the great stories about Jesus, but the one I want to say a word to you about today is this: Here is a picture that I am looking at of a boat that is like an Indian canoe with two men in it, one on the front and one at the back, and a Lake of Galilee to feed the five thousand people that were hungry on the other side, and on a small flagstaff at the stern of the boat there flies the stars

and stripes. Which thing I call a parable, and I will never, never forget, and I am taking with me back across the ocean that, as the memory of your great country that has been so beautifully told me in this incomparable little picture.

I have seen the stars and stripes flying at the stern of many a ship. I know that you have sent under your flag much food for starving people on the other side. I know that under your flag men and women have gone across far seas to distant places, where they have carried the bread of life to the starving souls of men and women. I know that in your hearts, you of this great land, there is helpful good-will, not for yourselves only, but for all who need it. And I thank God for America, for her vast resources and possibilities, and for her great and most splendid services. And I shall think of you, each of you, in his little boat, or her little boat, crossing some sea or other of life, with the American flag right in its place, true to your country. American citizens, believing in your land, understanding the meaning of the things that it has stood for, carrying forward the best of it that has been in the past into a still greater and nobler future. But I can see, also, somebody in that boat—Jesus. I beseech you, in the last of these many messages that we have had together, wherever your boat may be steered, whatever stormy or whatever sunny or moonlit voyage you may have through life, be sure of one thing: that beneath your flag there travels Jesus, the Savior, who makes the voyage of life safe and happy for us all, and will guide us, He alone, to the great haven on the other side.

How I loved him!

One of the members of his church was the Metropolitan opera star, Louise Homer, who was fond of Grandfather, and wanted to sing for him on his birthday. She had an understanding with the Steinway company that, if when accompanied on the piano she would use only Steinway pianos, the company would supply one wherever she sang. But the elevator to my grandparents' second-floor apartment could not accommodate a grand piano. So on the appointed day, June 20th, the Steinway Company built above the sidewalk on 56th Street a wooden platform outside my grandparents' apartment window, and hoisted a piano onto it. Mme. Homer and her accompanist then stepped through the window onto the platform. She stood by the piano and sang "Happy Birthday" to my grandfather and to the street below. I was for the first time completely proud of a relative. He had inspired affection in such a grand manner, and he was mine.

*　　　　*　　　　*

It was now my mother's turn to visit her country, and late in June, 1923, we sailed for England, where a beloved great-aunt lived in London. As the ship neared Southampton, I began to feel the tug of what I now think of as an ur-country. Of the four different areas that claimed my allegiance—China, America, Scotland, and the kingdom of God—Scotland was the only one that was not shared or diluted by a dual allegiance. My father was an American born in China, educated chiefly in English institutions; the kingdom of God was still a work in progress, insufficiently established for me to know that I was in it. Mother was entirely, permanently, and only Scottish despite her enforced oath to the contrary. Her country seemed the best defined of the four, small enough to be imagined, with an accessible history, contained and self-aware. I imagined Scotland to be a land of scones, gray stone buildings, and moors.

My great-aunt Janet received us in an old apartment in an old building in London. She had been a college president, and welcomed us with a college president's dignity, smiling but observant. She had illustrated books about nature that I had admired, and I thought of her as an artist, redeeming this ecclesiastical family. She and my mother caught up with the eight years since they had last met, during the Great War. England, devastated by the loss of a generation, was now struggling to regain its economy. I listened for evidence of her own deprivation, but she spoke only of her country and of the women of her college, almost all of whom had lost the men they cared for.

For all my life as a child, a picture of the Scottish moors hung on the wall over our piano in Peking. Framed in dark brown, the painting showed a rising slope in the foreground, covered with purple heather and low, prickly, gray-green ground cover. Bluish hills rose in the distance beyond; the sky was shot with mist. Often, coming home from school I would find my mother at the piano playing a Scottish song from a large maroon album called "Songs of the North," her head tilted back, her light voice drawing from the pages the tales of loss and defeat the Scots offered as their music. Now, approaching Scotland, I was ready for life in the minor key. The Scottish Presbyterian church, stern and unyielding, lay ahead, as did the tall gray stone houses of Edinburgh, and, on the border with England, the tower from which my Bell ancestors had flung burning oil and occasionally a flaming woman, onto invaders below.

Pictures from our visit show older Scottish relatives, in long black skirts and shawls, men in their wool sweaters and jackets—in summer—standing on lawns in the country near Aberdeen watching us children play. My mother had spent her summers in the countryside, and had told us stories of playing with her cousins, free of the oppressions of her life in the city. The one perfect memory I have of this Scottish summer is of the week we spent in a cottage set in the moors. It was called a ben-bar house: two rooms, front and back, with open fireplaces and a kitchen. My sister and I were responsible for providing fuel. We would run out of the kitchen door to a peat bog about a hundred yards from the cottage, cut squares of the moist, fragrant peat, and bring them back to stack against the side of the house to dry in the evening wind. We would then come inside to bask before the fire of peat dried the day before, enjoying our parents' acknowledgments of our virtue as the little house warmed in the long northern twilight.

It was in Scotland that I first heard the thunder of religion. The psalms in all their metric glory and tune took me captive. Religion in Scotland was not a subject for persuasion, as in, "Please listen, we have something you may want to hear." Even to a seven-year-old the difference was clear. "We've a story to tell to the nations/ That will turn their hearts to the right," sung in pleading tones before often indifferent groups was no match for a psalm sung by a full-throated congregation: "All people that on earth do dwell/ Sing to the Lord with cheerful voice." In Scotland, David's psalms were declarative and wonderfully assured. God was God, and in charge; this God of the Old Testament knew what He was doing. There was nothing plaintive, conditional, or uncertain about Scottish Presbyterianism. As I sat in my grandfather's church, psalms sounding in my ears, I thought for the first time that this might be a God I could believe in. I could not confuse this Father with my own father, nor did I have to remain "a little child." This was a God who expected praise and mirth and the assumption of His power.

But this was a God you could also think about. My grandfather's church, St. George's United Free Church, in Edinburgh, had earlier been one of the centers of a movement within the Church of Scotland to resist religious intimidation and become a "free church," and was thus a lively center of religious life. In addition, my grandfather's sermons had attracted young people, especially medical students from the University of Edinburgh, whom he influenced, I read later on, "to hold fast the faith of Christ without any narrow view of life or truth and without lessening their devotion to philosophy or science or business." Perhaps because I was proud to be his granddaughter, I attended his church, willing to explore what had been for me an illogical and unsatisfying system of belief mandated by my parents' profession.

Janet and I with Aunt Janet (Grandfather Kelman's sister), Scotland, spring 1924.

Moreover I preferred not to have God as a father because He had treated His son so badly. Actually, I had never really believed in Jesus, largely because of a prayer we children sang every night at home before going to sleep: "Jesus, tender shepherd, hear us,/ Bless thy little lambs tonight./ Through the darkness be thou near us,/ Keep us safe till morning light" How could Jesus be near everyone singing that prayer at the same time? Was he near Alice Gleysteen over on Erh T'iao Hutung at the same time that he was near me? We were a good two miles apart. I also wondered what he was keeping us safe from. How could he know all the dangers people might face?

As I climbed the gangplank of the *Patroclus*, the Cunard liner that was to take us to Singapore on our way back to China, I remembered our evening prayer, and was glad that it was God and not the tender Jesus in charge of the safety of my soul. It was new for me to believe, and I looked forward to His more reliable sponsorship of my life.

This new security was soon tested. We had been a day or two at sea when Elinor developed a sore ear. In those days infections were alarming. Without treatment, they could spread fast and become life-threatening. As we neared Gibraltar, the ship's doctor recommended that Elinor should get treatment ashore. The captain was unwilling to incur the charges or the delay required to dock at the harbor, so we had to leave the ship in the Gibraltar strait, at sea. The crew swung a rope ladder over the railing and our family, one by one, my father carrying Elinor, my mother holding the baby, and I, terrified but excited, climbed down the dark side of the ship and into a tug boat that carried us to the rock of Gibraltar, large, looming, and British. As we scrambled onto the pier, I turned to watch the *Patroclus* gather steam and come about and head into the Mediterranean. I concluded that God had proved to be an unreliable manager, and put my faith in my mother, who firmly believed that difficulties arising in areas governed by the British were likely to be solved in satisfactory ways.

We found rooms, Elinor found treatment and improved, but I never found the famous apes that reportedly roamed the rock. Soon another Cunard ship, the *Centaur*, picked us up and carried us to Penang, in what is now Malaysia, where we took a river boat to Port Swettenham where a close school friend of my mother and her husband owned a rubber plantation. A few days later we sailed for Shanghai. At seven I had been around the world and somehow recognized the irrelevance of nationality, since, after all, wherever I went I was still myself. I had found a God I thought I could believe in, and a way of thinking about my parents' profession that I thought I could support. At the very least I was going to try.

The *Centaur* anchored in Penang, 1924.

III

FOREIGNERS IN AN ANCIENT CITY

Inside a Peking city gate, 1920s.

B ack in Peking, we settled into the same house we had left, but I felt different. Possibly because I had heard others speak respectfully of the missionary enterprise, possibly as a result of representing abroad a missionary household, possibly from having contributed to the missionary enterprise myself, I began to enter the missionary world, to be conscious of it, and to evaluate it. I had seen the places and people that my parents had given up in order to spread their gospel, and I now knew more about the different reasons they had chosen for their decisions. So I began to identify myself as a "missionary kid"—in America we were called "MKs"—and to pay attention to the ways in which children of missionaries were different from others.

The servants welcomed us in the front hall of the house behind the church, and during the next few days, our family settled in for the long seven-year stretch before the next furlough, each of us to his own task. Janet, the baby, was handed over to the *amah*, Elinor and I registered for school, my mother started work with the women's programs of the mission, and my father resumed his work with Christian student groups and evangelical work in the countryside. We were all on assignment, immediately through the Presbyterian Board of Foreign Missions, but ultimately from God. Enough of all this loitering on the high seas, time to get to work.

How it looked going to school in a rickshaw.

Da Wong taking John to school, circa 1934.

I was to enter the third grade, and my job for God, and for my mother, was to get A's. The Peking American School was fabled even then. Founded in 1920, it was governed in 1924 by Miss Alice Moore, a tall, formidable American woman, whose presence intimidated. She presided over students of many nationalities, backgrounds, and interests. The standards of the school were high, since most of its students would be seeking to attend college in other countries. It served as the central school for the foreign community, although there were many Chinese students, often from families in the business world. Classes were in English and French. The red brick two-story building sat like a hen in a large yard on a small street branching off one of the main north-south streets of the city—Ha Ta Men Ta Chieh (The Big Gate Big Street). Exercise equipment filled one side of the yard; one that I remember especially was a set of iron rings hanging from a bar that had to be set swinging in such a way that you could progress from one ring to another. The contraption identified enemies; you knew you had one if the person ahead of you set the rings swinging away from you.

In 1924, still too young to bicycle the three miles to school, my sister and I went by rickshaw. One of us knelt against the back of the rickshaw, the other sat in the seat, a position preferred because it provided a chance to finish homework. The rickshaw man usually spent the day near the school and took us home afterwards.

Making A's had been no problem in the gentle, calm classrooms of Miss Spence's academy in New York. The Peking American School was a different matter. I had almost no background in arithmetic, especially fractions, so I went to school in a daily panic, but usually, after a hard evening's work, I had the homework done, if not understood. One evening I couldn't get the answer to a problem, and I dreaded the next day. Opening the front door to wait for the rickshaw, I was temporarily blinded by a bright shaft of sunlight and I immediately recognized a solution to my arithmetic problem. I turned around to my parents in the hall and said, "I can't go to school today. I can't see." I was known for truthfulness, often even exposing others, so my parents, after some inquiries, believed me, and Elinor went to school alone, triumphant in the rickshaw. My mother, now worried, made an appointment with the ophthalmology department at the Peking Union Medical College, and we set off. On the way I also began to be worried. The PUMC was founded with Rockefeller money, and staffed with well qualified physicians from all over the world. I did not know how to be believable to them. I decided the safest way was to be completely blind, and I could figure it out from there. The condition was considered serious, and I was admitted to the hospital.

Now I had a real problem. By the end of the first hour on the ophthalmic ward I was totally bored. How quickly could I stage a complete recovery? I looked at other patients' eye charts and listened to what they told their physicians. Could I plan credible progress? During the first few days I watched nuns giving piano lessons to little girls through the bare windows of a convent building about a block away, and noted their improvement. The worst of it was that I couldn't read. I was the subject of intense medical research; students and specialists gathered often around my bed. After a few days of slowly enlarging the field of vision on my chart, I could stand it no longer, decided that what was suddenly lost could be suddenly regained, and declared that I could see. If the doctors were skeptical they didn't reveal it to me. I have never checked the hospital record, so I don't know what the doctors concluded, or what my parents were told. I do remember the wonderful sight of books in my room at home. Of course, I was even further behind in arithmetic, so a tutor was provided to help me catch up, a providential arrangement, although I still have trouble with fractions.

*   *   *

The Board of Foreign Missions of the Presbyterian Church in the USA had been established in 1869, preceded by various Missionary Societies that operated in different regions. The Board was located on lower Fifth Avenue in Manhattan, was supported by the national church, and had world-wide responsibility and power. It owned and managed properties, assigned or recalled those who worked in them, and established strict standards. In return, it paid every missionary an annual salary. This money was supplied in part by individual churches, which served as home churches for their missionaries, funding and supporting them, and expecting regular reports of their work.

The arrangement made possible a household staff that freed missionaries to do their religious work, and allowed a standard of living much higher than those salaries would provide in the United States. Our household, therefore, ran on two levels: the level belonging to God, which our parents took care of, and the level of maintaining a household, which the servants administered. Wives, being missionaries, were expected to deliver full service to the mission station, often teaching in the girls' schools, supervising women's work groups, and overseeing the servants who maintained the house and raised the children. The rationale for this was that our entire household's reason for being was to do God's work, but I was never comfortable with asking grown men and women to cook, clean the house, empty the chamber pots, and in all weathers when we were young run between the poles of rickshaws to carry us wherever and whenever we went out of the mission gates.

I remember bicycling into our compound by the street gate, pausing by the "spirit wall" that kept out evil spirits and almost every one else, and looking at the silent houses, each house furnished, earnestly, as a fragment of a faraway culture: Iowa, California, New England, Holland. I would feel insulated, diminished, separated from the lively transactions of the streets, but, parking my bicycle beside our house, laying my satchel on the bench in the front hall, and pushing open the swinging door to the pantry, I reached the kitchen. There the servants would be, as in a picture by Brueghel, peeling vegetables, boiling goats' milk, polishing silverware, chatting in the language of my earliest childhood, smiling in instant welcome, and I was home.

A certain dignity attended servants' work. The year after we

Breakfast on the porch at Ku Lou Hsi, circa 1932: Janet, John, and Barbara.

Playing in the front yard at Ku Lou Hsi, circa 1932: Elinor, me, Barbara, and John (a blur at the far right).

returned from furlough, my father became chairman of the mission, and the year after that, chairman of the American community in Peking. Our servants thus had status among the other servants in the compounds, our cook K'e Ch'ang above them all. He had joined the family early as a young Mongolian "coolie," doing the yard work and assorted tasks. He was unhappy and, as my mother reported, "unsatisfactory," but honest, a rare characteristic in a local economy that depended on the ability to make two and two equal five. She asked him what the problem was, and he answered that he didn't like the work. What would he like to do? He wanted to be the cook. Had he ever cooked American food? No. Had he ever held a job as a cook?

K'e Ch'ang with Mother, 1948.

No, but he liked to cook; could he try? My mother famously had two answers to any question: "No" and "We'll see," and they both meant the same thing, but this time she'd thought, "Why not?"

Shih K'e Ch'ang was our cook for over twenty years, the most beloved person in the household. He took note of each person's favorite dishes, which on that person's birthday or return from boarding school he would bring to the table personally, beaming, lingering to enjoy thanks and congratulations. The birthday cakes he made were famous in the mission station: round sponge cakes with wonderful icings—delicate railings of spun sugar around landscapes of little animals, flowers, and trees. In my memory he is always smiling, even when, arriving late one day, he explained to my mother that his baby son had died that morning, which had delayed him. I knew that Chinese people often responded to bad news by smiling or laughing, as if adversity in their circumstances was absurd, but in my mind nothing bad should ever happen to this most loving and loved person, and, listening, I sobbed for him. At lunch time he came silently to the table, and laid my favorite dish upon it. To our knowledge, K'e Ch'ang claimed no religion, but for me he was the most "Christian" of us all.

He had a strong work ethic. My mother, ever alert to, if not motivated by, the task as a guiding principle, was always aware that her children would have to make their way in another country, and alone, and took care to see that we had experiences that would prepare us. With some other mothers she organized a Girl Scout troop where we were supposed to earn merit badges, which would prepare us for the rough times ahead in America. The requirement for one of these badges was to camp out for one night, preparing our supper and breakfast over a camp fire. We spent days assembling camping material, hard to find on the streets of Peking. We stealthily removed some pans from the kitchen, gathered fuel in the dark of night, and took from our well-stocked larder the sweet potatoes, eggs, bacon, and juice for the meals. We decided on the ruins of a prince's palace nearby in the countryside, outside the city walls, because the scattered marble would protect our campfire from the winds that swept down the hills to the west of the city.

We hiked out from the city gates in the early afternoon, pleased and excited by the prospect of providing for ourselves as pioneers. As we turned into the road leading to the ruins, we noticed a cloud of dust far behind us, which appeared to be raised by a couple of people and a donkey. Accustomed to curious countryside people, we paid no attention, and started preparing the campsite and the supper. As we were pulling out cooking utensils, the followers increased their speed, and soon we recognized K'e Ch'ang and a servant, accompanied by a donkey loaded with two large baskets. K'e Ch'ang stepped forward, and laid on marble near our campfire a fully cooked supper and breakfast. He told us that as our cook he could not let us prepare our own food—he would lose face with all the other cooks in the mission, and with his family as well. He stood by while we caucused. Should we sacrifice our ability to survive in the American wilderness to a prepossession of a 5,000-year-old culture?

The food he brought smelled delicious in the evening wind, and we remembered the scout motto: Be Prepared. We decided to be prepared to eat his food to save his reputation, and accepted his polite but urgent request to take all our food-stuffs and pots and pans back in the donkey's panniers. We gathered around the campfire and the delicious food and watched as the two men disappeared into the dusk, a lantern swinging in front of the donkey. As I lay in my sleeping bag looking up at the hills around, I thought that although the prince who had owned our campsite was dead, China was alive and would always be victorious. How futile were the efforts of a few foreigners to change a land with a face to save!

En P'u had nursed my father after he was poisoned during the drought-relief trip. He was short, stocky, powerful, a major-domo in the household, an excellent administrator, and completely devoted to my father. He served the meals, arranged transportation, saw to it that the house was clean, and discovered the undiscoverable, such as the time a train might be leaving. Above all, he kept my father's irregular schedule and sudden needs from disrupting the family. My father, turning from an afternoon phone call, would announce to my mother that fifteen extra people would be coming for dinner that evening. She would tell En P'u, and the problem was solved, even if the group did not arrive until 8:30 in the evening. My father went regularly to Shanghai to China Council meetings. One time the trains were canceled the evening before he was to leave. No problem for En P'u. Not only was there a train the next day, but my father was on it.

Sometimes I thought that En P'u made my parents' marriage viable. By the time we returned from furlough it was clear that their earlier passion for each other had found no stable form. There were silences, and "ask your father" or "ask your mother" would follow questions about family projects. Their discussions were about plans or emergencies. Except at the seaside, where there were no telephones, these two highly articulate people appeared to have little to say to each other. When they did not want us to understand something, they would speak in Greek, but briefly. In addition, mother was never comfortable in China, while father was wholly comfortable there. But En P'u made it possible to accommodate my father, so we turned over to him the practical difficulties my father continually produced.

Er Hung was En P'u's younger brother, brought from the great northwest plains where both had been raised. A man of medium height, slender, smiling, and accommodating, he was wonderful with the goats and with us children. He also worked in the garden, trying to bring forth my mother's image of a proper Scottish border: heather, lily-of-the-valley, roses, bluebells, pansies and crimson salvia. She would show him pictures from garden books; he would smile, get his tools, and plant among the Scottish borders peonies and small plots of bamboo. It seemed to me corrective, and Mother accepted them.

One afternoon many years later, my sister Janet, by now a doctor, sat with her husband and me in their sunny Long Island kitchen remembering my mother. I was remarking, sadly, how stern and cold she was, how she disliked being caressed, hugged, or even touched, and how her care of us seemed to be just a duty, an assignment. Suddenly Janet, herself sharp of tongue, turned to me and said, "I had a different mother than you had." I asked for the story.

She told me that when she was about nine, Er Hung and she started a sexual relationship, and she was cared for and caressed as none of the rest of us was. He hadn't wanted our parents told, because he didn't want trouble with his wife. When Janet turned twelve, however, she felt our mother had to know. Janet was taken immediately to Dr. Bash, the mission doctor. Mother told our father and the next day Er Hung was dismissed. Janet went on: "Thereafter she kept my secret, was tender and solicitous to me as to none of the rest of you, and did not send me to the boarding school where you sisters had to go."

Later, listening to my fellow workers in social service summaries labeling child abuse as inappropriate relationships between young children and adults, I would summon the courage to question their assessments; could we ever know enough to know?

Finally, there were the *amahs*, women who took care of the young children, did the laundry and the sewing, and provided the attention and often the affection our mother could not offer. My *amah*, Li Nai Nai, had been unable to deliver this to me.

Barbara, my parents' fourth daughter, was born in 1926. The mission hospital nurse who cared for her after her birth was a latent carrier of diphtheria. Within eight days the new-born had contracted the disease, in those days considered fatal for infants. Barbara and her nurse were immediately isolated from everyone else, and the family placed in quarantine. The nurse was devoted to her charge, and Barbara recovered, although the rickets which later developed left her with a thick tongue, which slowed her speech, causing my mother to believe that she was mentally retarded. In 1927, when we were evacuated from China, my mother hired Hao Nai Nai, who became Barbara's special *amah* and charmed us all with her gentleness, her firmness, her attachment to my mother and to us.

Janet, Barbara, Father, John, and Hao Nai Nai, circa 1932.

Hao Nai Nai became our emotional center. Like K'e Ch'ang, she watched over us, knew our preferences, corrected us—not for doing wrong, but for insufficiently preserving our parents' reputations. She muted our quarrels, and just plain loved us. She was also the occasional keeper of staff morale: through the swinging doors to the kitchen we would occasionally hear heated exchanges, slowly calming down before her quiet, mirthful voice, and then we would listen for the laughter that almost always eventually broke out. She had a room of her own, to which she returned every evening. She would never answer questions about her family or show us their pictures, sensing, I think, that we needed her too much to share her. She was with us until war separated us all in 1940.

So what was it like to be a missionary kid? Primarily it meant being good. There were no other options. Our parents had heard the call, and whether or not we had, we were all part of a system of service to an invisible God. Not only did we have to be religious, we had to demonstrate it. From the beginning I had trouble with this—how to demonstrate the invisible? The two people I most admired, K'e Chang and Hao Nai Nai, did not acknowledge the God my parents promoted. But that advocacy was our job, as individuals and as a family. And, as obedient children, we played our part. Thus being a missionary kid meant the assumption that you were a certain kind of person: religious, certainly; good, probably; and in America, a little exotic, depending on the country your parents were based in. Certainly different.

We learned to be far away from people we cared about in our home countries. Letters often took three weeks or longer to arrive, so that sometimes it would be six weeks before we received answers to questions of health or fortune. Every week my mother read the manifests for ships whose arrivals might bring news from America or Scotland, and we would scan departure lists to send letters or parcels so they would arrive as soon as possible.

We also learned to think of God in two languages. In Chinese the phrase for God was *shang ti*, the ruler or emperor above. The Bible was *sheng shu*, "the holy book;" hymns were "sung poems;" Christmas was *sheng tan*, "the holy birthday;" Gospel was *fu yin*, "the cheerful sound;" heaven was *t'ien t'ang*, "the sky hall;" and, my favorite, Jesus, was *yeh su*, literally the "mysterious revival," but probably chosen to imitate the English sound.

Having to use words other than those of the beloved King James Bible version we read every day cracked a code: Were there different ways to express the same faith? I doubted, though, that God the father, a personal god, was a transferable concept to so communal a society. When we lived at the Erh T'iao Hutung compound I would bicycle often to the Confucian Temple nearby, to take refuge—from anything. It was built in perfect proportion to a simple tablet on the altar, and devoid of clutter and trade. A great, dark temple building, it was surrounded by a quiet courtyard, with old trees, and small pavilions preserving the names of scholars who had passed the civil service examinations. Passing an examination had high value for me, and I would sit under the trees, calmed by the quiet, by the beauty, by the company of people who had passed examinations. Because the temple was proportionate to a man, a figure, and one for whom ethical behavior trumped ideology, it reset my restlessness, and I would bicycle back renewed.

Confucian Temple, Peking, 1920s.

Chinese mission churches tended to be of brick or clay; in the cities they were vaulted, with an altar and wooden pews. In the countryside they were often just small halls, with perhaps a squat steeple and wooden benches. The feeling they evoked was of a gathering. They were unheated; in winter people sat fairly close together, gaining warmth from each others' padded garments. Windows were of oiled paper, which, my mother pointed out, let in whatever was healthy in sunlight.

Sometimes there was a choir, in Chinese robes, with surplices over them—more often just a singer or two. The hymnals were of thin brown paper, sewn to form booklets made elegant by the beautiful characters in vertical lines from right to left, so that one saw and felt the hymn as a whole. No musical notation accompanied the characters; the congregation followed along with whatever produced the tune. Since there was usually no electricity, music was commonly provided by a pump-organ. These organs were highly eccentric, and often faded out, or wandered out of tune when the player got tired or forgot to press the pedal all the way down.

When my father made evangelical trips into the countryside, I would often go with him, taking a portable organ that folded into a suitcase and provided a great show when it opened up into a little keyboard and foot-operated bellows. The bellows wheezed, competing with the voices of village people who wandered into the area, and with the barking of the village dogs. I felt as if we were part of a biblical story, like the stories of Jesus gathering people around him and talking about his mission and his beliefs. But we were white, and looked and sounded strange, so it may have seemed to the villagers merely a show. Sometimes a few stayed after the service, watching us as we folded the little organ, mounted our bicycles, and left.

The routines of life in China differed from those in America. In the absence of affordable department stores, acquiring clothing was complicated. There were always the missionary boxes that arrived from the U.S., and beautiful patterned Fair Isle sweaters and skirts from our Scottish relatives. When we were small, *amahs* made our clothes, commenting ceaselessly on how fast we grew. As the oldest of four girls, I tended to get the newest clothes, and was the first to choose the images from the Sears catalog that was our style book.

As I got older my mother decided that better clothes were appropriate, and a new process opened up. The first step was the Sears catalog, as usual, but the next involved a visit to dark little shops in the "silk alleys," where we would wander among bolts of gleaming velvets and brocades until we reached the sober cottons and wools in the back, an attentive sales clerk hovering beside us. Once the choices were made, we would go to the cashier at the front of the shop, and the bargaining would begin, abacus clattering away. I hated this part, and would stand by while my mother pared the quoted price down, step by step, until she was satisfied. I knew that bargaining was the way shopkeepers maintained their business and their families, but I didn't like the clutter it added to buying useful or beautiful things, nor did I enjoy the feeling of being in a superior position. The shopkeeper was rarely in a position to decline an offer.

The tailor would then be invited to our home, to take measurements carefully supervised by my mother, who sharply monitored the process while he passed the measuring tape around my body. During spring holiday there would be fittings, and in the fall clothes would finally be finished, to accommodate changes that a summer's swimming and tennis would require. For shoes we would place our bare feet on a large brown piece of paper, proudly laid out by the cobbler, who then outlined our feet, always exclaiming how big they were. The Sears catalog would appear again while we chose the style, the cobbler remarking *K'e I*, it can be done, or *Pu k'e I*, it cannot be done. So the final choice was still made by a man who had never worn anything but cloth shoes all his life. These sessions reminded us of how much taller we were than the people who made our clothes. Finally, I always felt "made" by others, at the mercy of their skills, their generosity, and their views of what was possible, as if I was not responsible for how I looked. That fit the image of being only the Lord's property. We were not supposed to look too well-dressed. Our lives belonged to others.

I had felt derivative that way from the start. I was named for two dead aunts, both of whom died young, their lives ready for me to complete. My first name, Margaret, was that of my mother's younger sister, who developed mentally only until the age of two and died of pneumonia at age twelve, an unlived life. My middle name, Irene, belonged to my father's sister, the joy of my grandparents' lives. She died of pneumonia at eight at their mission station in China. So strong was their sense of substitution that as soon as I could write, my grandfather insisted that I sign a consolidated name: Margaretirene. It was as if my world was already formed—a template with an assignment for me, which I was obliged to discover and to complete.

This was reinforced by the important roles ancestors played in our family life, patterns of who we should be. My grandfathers were prominent ministers. My Scottish mother, perhaps more anxious than my father about destinies unfulfilled, would look sternly at us and remind us that "greatness skips a generation." It was never clear what to do about this. I learned early that it was wise to do what my parents expected, and to do it promptly, but being great was a stretch, and I settled for just being satisfactory.

As the capital, Peking was a city of occasions, and the foreigners' New Year's Day, January 1st, was one of the most spectacular. New Year's Eve was always sober, an occasion for remembering sins and unsatisfactory performances, duly rehearsed in prayer and hymn during the long evening services in Chinese and English. But joy broke out in the morning, as we laid out our best clothes and looked forward

Peking, 1926: Mother, Barbara, me, Janet, Father, and Elinor.

to the processions of the day.

After morning prayers, the day became gloriously secular. Our living room would be garlanded with flowers and red banners. Beautiful cloisonne dishes would be filled with dates, nuts, sesame candies, and various Chinese delicacies, and we would be sent upstairs to put on our best clothes. Then my father would come downstairs, resplendent in white silk scarf, long black overcoat, gloves, and the hat of the year, ready for the day's ritual of calling on all the embassies, heads of businesses, and other missions. My mother would follow him down the stairs, ready for a day of receiving the men, equally resplendent in national costume, who would come with their cards to lay on the silver tray inside the door, chat briefly, and leave as soon as they could politely do so.

Our servants received our visitors' outer garments, noting the rank they revealed, reveling in the fact that representatives of the world had come to their country. We would be allowed in the living room if we didn't say anything much more than Happy New Year, and I remember admiring my mother, in a beautiful silk dress and long crystal necklace, or in a Chinese brocade robe, greeting as many as she could in their own language. We did not, of course, serve liquor, but others did, and the room would soon fill with the social fragrances of the rest

Father and John in Chinese garb, out visiting on Chinese New Year's Day, circa 1932.

of the world. It was a wonderful way to start the year, the world coming through our front door, and my mother meeting it on its own terms, unfiltered through God.

Chinese New Year was also fun. Special food appeared: "long noodles," to encourage long life, and Chinese dumplings in celebratory shapes. Red banners fluttered along the streets, fireworks crackled in the evenings, and the shops were busy: all debts had to be resolved by the first day of the new year. In many Chinese households a "kitchen god" banner hung all year, monitoring the family's behavior. On the evening before the first day of the new year, the god's mouth was smeared with malt to sweeten his report on the family, and the banner was burned outside in the courtyard so that his report would go unhindered to heaven. The New Year was an important public occasion, with children in their bright new clothes flying banners and kites along the streets, people bowing to each other as they exchanged greetings; the city itself seemed to celebrate. In addition, in China when I was young, everyone became a year older on the new year (you were one year old when you were born), so that it was also an important family occasion, when presents were exchanged and children received new clothes. It was as if this huge nation, already over five thousand years old, rolled over, and accepted another year.

Every year on Washington's birthday, the American community held a ball to which all Americans, the diplomatic corps, and special guests were invited. It was held at the Peking Hotel, the grandest in the city, and was an elegant, black tie, unequivocally western affair. The Marine band played, the national anthem was sung. America was toasted in all the languages represented. Oil for the lamps of China burned bright. Before leaving for the ball, my parents, elegantly dressed, would come out to the sleeping porch to tuck us in, but we were not to touch them. As my mother said good night her long crystal beads would swing over my bed, catching the light from the sky—the shimmering light of a big city. When we heard the front door close we would leap out of bed in the cold night air, watching as my parents, stepping into the rickshaws, were tucked in under bear rugs, my mother's crystal earrings dancing, father's hat waving, the rickshawmen straining against the start-up of their run.

Christmas was the next big occasion in Peking, since on the Fourth of July most missionaries and their children would be out of the heat and cholera of the cities. At Christmastime the foreign community withdrew into their homes to celebrate the holiday as they would have "back home." To the Chinese the holiday must have seemed almost heathen: wreaths, trees, and candles—all in honor of a foreign god, and a baby at that. There was an expectation that services, concerts, and parties would be attended, a non-evangelical exigency. This holiday was for us as foreign nationals; with relatives far away we tried to come together more often and more intimately, but each household's observance looked back toward home.

Christmas for our family began in September, with the opening of the locked closet at the top of the back stairs. On one wall shelves carried primly stacked linens and household supplies. The rest of the room was a riot of gifts collected during the year, with wrapping paper and boxes. Mother would unlock the door, enter with her lists and lock it again, and we knew that Christmas was on its way. We were not allowed in, but occasionally Mother would be interrupted in her wrapping, and I would steal in. Lovely Chinese linens, silk jackets, gleaming panels of embroidered satin, jewelry, jade and brass ornaments, lustrous lacquer boxes and trays, with my mother's Scottish school writing on the labels—all for other people.

I would sit, surrounded by the forbidden beauty, thinking that this must be what it is to be a grownup—equipped with things in such quantity that they could be destined for others. I'd hear my mother's step returning, and slip down the back stairs into the kitchen, where the servants in their plain clothes and plain ways brought me back to childhood, leaving my mother sitting in all that locked up glory, tense with decision.

Next came the drama of her desk. Lists of people living all over the world would appear on it. She would have the story of our family doings over the past year printed on lovely rice paper, a delicate Chinese accented symbol of the season—in red, usually—placed in the top left-hand corner. I learned secretly to consult these Christmas letters to find out what she had thought of my behavior that year—who had I been to her? What had I done that was worth reporting across those great oceans? Since she usually described us positively, I read the reports as if they were a mirror.

She would consult the manifests of the trans-Pacific liners, and sometimes I would read on the address label of letters or parcels "via SS," and feel hopelessly divided: the country she was addressing the mail to was my country and I was here, hung between two languages, and three cultures. My mother was never more Scottish than at Christmas time.

On Christmas eve we lit the tree, literally. First, two large pitchers of water were placed under the tree. Then the grownups clamped little brass candleholders to the branches and filled them with small white candles. The tree seemed to be waiting, like one of us. My father would put the star on the top of the tree and that moment I remember as being the time when our family felt like a real family. We joined hands and sang "Star of wonder, star of night, star with royal beauty bright, Lead us to thy perfect light." Then my father would tell us children to get to the other side of the room. The circle broke; we became children and grownups. I understood why, but, as the eldest, taking my place near the doors, I used to plan what I would do if my parents went up in flames. The servants lined up silently behind us. The house lights were put out, and finally, starting at the top, my mother and father, on separate sides of the tree, would light the little candles, and Christmas was suddenly in the room.

Christmas Day was like a trumpet blast, all day. We children would get up early, dress hurriedly, and tiptoe out into the frigid morning air to the frozen flower plot under my parents' bedroom window and sing as loudly as the cold would permit: "Christians awake/ Salute the happy morn/ On which the Savior of the world was born."

Then we would rush inside and burst in on my parents, sleepy from Santa Claus work the night before, and remind them that time was wasting. Breakfast was a mere prelude to opening the stockings, which was permitted before the household prayers. These Christmas day prayers were a major production. The servants, having cleared the breakfast table, came into the living room, and we all knelt to pray, my father's perfect mandarin accent addressing *shang ti*, the god above. (As I grew older it reminded me of the emperor praying for heaven's cooperation with good harvests.)

Then we rose and sang "Hark, the herald angels sing"—all the verses, the servants in Chinese, and we in English. After the hymn, my parents, bowing, handed to the servants the little red envelopes in which gifts of money were given in China, and we children, bowing, presented our gifts to them. Then everyone bowed again, the servants left, and we turned and fell into the piles of gifts under the tree, Mother standing straight and tall in the midst of wrapping paper, notepad in hand to keep track. We were not allowed to play with anything sent by people overseas until we had written the thank-you note, a rule we didn't find restrictive, since those were usually clothes.

There was, however, for me a predictably dark moment. I would approach the present labeled "from Daddy, with love" with a mixture

The Hayes family assembled at Ku Lou Hsi, April 4, 1931, for my brother's christening. Mother and Father are standing. Seated left to right: Grandmother Kelman, Barbara, John, Grandfather and Grandmother Hayes, and Janet. Seated on the ground: Elinor and me.

of sadness and curiosity. For I knew the handwriting: it was my mother's. I would go up to my father and show it to him. He would look at the gift and say, "That's nice; who gave you that?" I would say, "You did, Daddy," and he would say, "I did?" and look gratefully up at my mother. What was I? An arrangement between them? No, the assumption was the worst part of it, that our parents, dutifully providing, seemed never to think of us as individuals worthy of imagination or singularity. And, amid all the celebration of that morning, my father was listening for the telephone.

Then it was the children's turn to produce. The sliding doors to the living room were shut, and the room transformed, usually, to a stable scene. Usually, too, we produced a play that Elinor wrote, cast, and staged. The only problem was providing for the baby Jesus. We always wanted to use the latest baby in the family, but it was prohibited. In 1930, however, when John was born in November, the temptation was too great, and my sister, Janet, as Mary, emerged on the stage, carrying him. She approached the sofa, converted to a stable bed, and as she sat, dropped him—on the sofa, fortunately. Sitting at the piano, my usual place, I saw my mother blanch; it was, after all, her first-born son. A true Scotswoman, she steeled herself to the occasion, but she was the one to lift him when the play was done.

The rest of the day tilted toward the service in the late afternoon, at the community church in downtown Peking, when the foreign community met for an English service, adequate and restrained after the long day. We rode home, rickshawmen leaning against the icy north wind, to a coal fire in the living room, waffles and creamed chicken on the kitchen stove, and paid the rickshawmen a few extra pennies to celebrate the day.

My mother's caption on the back of this picture, taken probably in the 1930s: "While her mother looks on, the child is feeding in the corn to be crushed through a hole in the upper stone. The family makes its living by crushing out vegetable oil in a most primitive way, which they sell to the postal buses."

In between holidays our strict, Western lives unfolded soberly on the bright and busy streets; shopkeepers displayed their wares on tables or cloths laid on the streets, and potential buyers would be asked to have a a cup of tea while the shopkeeper weighed the goods on a little tray, balanced on a long rod with weights on the other end against which the price was calculated. The abacus with its clicking beads would be brought out, and everyone in the vicinity would come to watch the transaction, largely, it seemed, to enjoy the drama of purchasing. We were not allowed to buy from the alluring, colorful displays of candy—especially *t'ang hu ler*s, narrow sticks strung with fruit (oranges, cherries, dates, and apples), all covered with a flavored syrup, which attracted swarms of flies, batted away by the vendor, all the time saying, "Hurry and buy; see, there are no flies on them now." Long beige twists of malt candy, sugared dates, mandarin oranges dusted with coconut were laid out on bamboo mats; we considered those less likely to consign us to bouts of diarrhea.

Traveling the streets was a challenge. Streetcars ran down the middle of the street, clanging continuously, and claiming the right of way, scattering rickshaws, donkeys, mules, and the carts and drivers aside; even the rare car had to veer quickly, to shouts and curses from

Typical Peking cart, 1920s.

those it barely missed. For health reasons we were discouraged from riding the streetcars; spitting was not prohibited—in fact, widely indulged—and tuberculosis was everywhere. One day on the streetcar I sat down on the bench seat beside an elderly man who was slowly picking off pieces of his finger. I asked why, and he answered that he had leprosy, and preferred the privacy of the street car to dispose of the loosening flesh.

I usually bicycled, dodging carts, wagons, horses, mules, rickshaws, dogs and camels, the occasional car, and other bicycles, my bicycle bell ringing continuously, ignoring the cries of *yang kuei tzu*, foreign devil, as I went past. I enjoyed the excitement and fun of being part of the city, outside the sober, confining mission walls. Bicycling was easier in the winter when kitchen and household refuse in the middle of *hutungs* froze and provided a firm surface.

The *hutungs* sometimes provided drama, since sounds within them often reverberated between their walls. Coal for heating and cooking was often brought to the compound by lines of camels tied by ropes to each other, sacks of coal between their humps. One time they arrived in the *hutung* outside our gate just as my father was starting an itineration to the countryside on his motorcycle. As they stood waiting to be unloaded, he started up his machine. The camels did what camels do—they acted in their own interests. They burst from the ropes, coal scattering all over the *hutung*, and galloped back to the northwest they had come from, the camel driver running after them, shouting curses alternately to them and to my father. Residents of the *hutung* soon gathered up the coal, discoursing on their luck. The Mission paid for the coal destined for the compound, and for a missing camel, and thereafter my father started up his motorcycle inside the compound.

The chief problem with riding bicycles was the dust. Peking was near the Gobi Desert, which sent its sands frequently over the mountains on the north wind. Fine, stinging dust driven by the wind would fill every crevice of face and clothing, so we would arrive home gritty, exhausted, covered yellow with dust. During dust storms dust would cover the house as well, entering through the window frames, under the doors, even down the chimney. With no vacuum cleaners, it took days to remove, and meanwhile it got into the bathrooms, the beds, the kitchen, even the food. There was a dessert called Peking Dust, a delicious concoction of pureed chestnuts and cream which K'e Ch'ang sometimes served.

It was, however, largely because we were in Peking that there were no deaths in our family. A hospital was on the grounds of the mission; the great Peking Union Medical College was downtown. Twice I developed a double mastoid infection which required immediate surgery and hospitalization. The excellent care we had spared us not only from death, but from the fear of it, which missionaries in isolated stations had to live with, and which further underscored the depth of their dedication and the bravery of their faith.

Chinese stages were often small islands surrounded by water, to purify the sound, and to enhance the necessary distance for plays and operas. Music was my water. Our piano was a Baldwin, of dark brown mahogany, and upright, as befitting a Presbyterian household. It had ivory keys, worn and yellowed, and stood against the wall of the living room, opposite the hearth, matching music to fire. The only reliable source of harmony in a contentious household, its very presence seemed to set a key. It was in all of our ceremonies and performances, whether as prelude, accompaniment, or program.

For me our piano was the essence of privacy, wealth, and welcome. It stood ready, factory tuned, music rack built in, the lid easily opened, and attended by its matching music bench holding the sheet music. As I sat down and lifted up the lid, centuries opened up. The piano held all I could play of any composer, but above all, of Bach. I took lessons early, and later I played fairly well, thanks to a wonderful Canadian house mistress at boarding school. At home, the hubbub of the house and the pressure of homework would fade away, and I was alone with this generous piano and its famous tenants, the composers whose music formed such an important part of my life.

One day I decided to find out how the music was made. My mother offered to play, and my sister and I clambered up along the side and opened the top lid. I was horrified to find that this nurturing instrument essentially was percussive, that the music was produced by hitting. It did not change my loyalty or my delight, but made me realize how complex those feelings can be.

The piano was a foreign instrument, part of our Western culture. Chinese music sounded unnatural, misshapen, and toneless when played on it. So this piano held our culture, our sorrows and joys. When we gathered around it, we felt, briefly, like a family, obeying a sturdy instrument's foreign, familiar voice. It had within it the music and songs of "home."

We had brought back from furlough recordings of Mme. Homer in operas she sang, often with Caruso: "Aida," "Carmen," "Il Trovatore."

My father, in one of the few times when he seemed vulnerable or even still, would listen to them as if they were sacred, calling on an inner sensitivity we were otherwise not privy to. Especially in the aria—*Ai nostri monti returneremus*—he would seem far away, above the world he was so skillful in managing. At these times we would tiptoe around, careful not to break his spell, since this was a father we did not know.

Prayers were sung four times a day if we were at home—a different grace for every meal—holding hands as we sang, lest someone reach out when our eyes were closed to capture the largest piece of bread or fruit. Then at night we went to sleep with "Jesus, tender shepherd," sung in wavering, sleepy tones, clutching teddy bears or dolls in case Jesus was busy elsewhere that night.

I was the musician for the children in the family, playing for our skits and pageants. Mother played for household occasions and when we gathered for Scottish singing. She played like a conductor, staccato, rhythmic, keeping us all up to speed; my mother did nothing slowly. When I went to boarding school and became the organist for daily chapel, I would linger on the organ before and after the hymn was sung, erasing the memory of those commands she had forced on the music. Students in chapel took a dim view of these strolls, and I finally had to adopt her strict tempos, and leave lyricism to Chopin in the student concerts we produced. Music became part of my self-definition. It was a private world I made, all too publicly as I plowed sturdily through Hanon and Bach, but it was mine to produce, to love, and to own.

One of the most difficult parts of being a missionary's child was the knowledge that one's parents belonged primarily to God and to His work, and it was our job to help with that. Growing up we did on our own, or with the servants. We were of course to be beyond reproach both inside and outside the house, and never, never, never to let our parents down, which was also a requirement of Chinese society. The parts that were most difficult for me were the actual contradictions of our lives.

Doctrinally I had many doubts—especially about the virgin birth, when from En P'u we learned why the goats had to be taken to the hills in the spring, and what went on there. I was an attentive reader, and carefully parsed the hymns we sang:

I asked the little joyous bird
Who taught him how to fly.
And sing his songs so sweetly in
The bright blue morning sky.
He told me it was God above,
Who gave to him his wing
And taught him how to build his nest,
And taught him how to sing.

God seemed impossibly busy: "A little tiny bird/ With sweet and cheerful song/ God watches, thinks and cares for/ All the day long." Then there was the summary hymn for God the creator:

All things bright and beautiful
All creatures great and small
All things wise and wonderful
The Lord God made them all.

Each little flower that opens,
Each little bird that sings;
He made their glowing colors
He made their tiny wings.

How could I, who took nine months to draw the American flag to scale to qualify for Girl Scout membership begin to have any relationship with so prolific a creator? Finally, there were contradictory images of God and of Jesus. "Jesus, tender shepherd," which we sang at bedtime every night of my childhood, was also the leader of soldiers marching "beneath the cross of Jesus." The ultimate contradiction, of course, was between the way we lived and the reasons for our living. Almost every winter morning, sitting in the rickshaw, wrapped in rabbit fur and bear-skin rug, I would be pulled by a thinly clad rickshawman, sweat running down his back, past the frozen, right-angled bodies of people who during the night had huddled up to the mission walls for the warmth that came through from the straw-filled goats' pens. If we were in China, as I understood it, to improve the lives of the Chinese people, and working hard at it, something was going seriously wrong.

When I was older, I bicycled to school down one of the great north/south axes of the city, past the hill under which emperors buried coal for the court, with its little temple on top to camouflage the storage, so the coal wouldn't be stolen by those freezing people. I would turn onto the path beside the moat around the Forbidden City. There, daily, in the winter, girl babies lay frozen in the ice. In the summer their bloated bodies floated, lapping against the walls of the moat. For all the commiseration that greeted the births of four successive girls in our family, we were fed, clothed and schooled, while those we came to serve lay dead at the foot of the crimson walls of the imperial palace. My belief in the legitimacy and efficiency of the life available to me began to weaken, although it was many years before the collapse came.

The moat around the Forbidden City, Coal Hill to the left, 1920s.

I felt the arrogance of our presence in China. What prerogative did we have to introduce anything beyond the schools and science this country wanted, the health care that it welcomed, and better and more humane methods of growing the food that the starving people begging at the mission gates were desperate for, while we rode in for supper? I didn't see why it required a God to organize these services. But our pattern was that of a closed religious universe, and in those days I knew only to obey. I did not talk to my parents about this. It seemed disloyal to their sacrifices and ideals, and I still wanted our family to work.

These feelings were mitigated by my direct contacts with the work of the mission. My mother and a few other missionary wives supervised a workshop called a *kung ch'ang* for Chinese women. On fine linen place settings, table napkins, runners, and table cloths, they sewed exquisite cross-stitched pictures of Chinese life: wedding processions and beautiful scenes of bamboo and peonies, with lovely patterned edgings. These were packaged, tied with ribbons, and set aside to await the arrival of the next trans-Pacific tourist liner. The day after it docked, my mother would arrange space in the most elegant hotel to display the linens, and my sister and I would be asked to help sell them. Dressed in our best, we stood behind the piles of beautiful linen, anxious to explain to the tourist ladies in their 1920s finery, beaded handbags brushing the packets, what the designs represented and the good cause their purchase served. The money was paid directly to the women who made them.

I was evangelical about this; I had seen the robes my grandmother and grandfather wore when he taught at the court of the Empress Dowager, and knew that the eyes of the women who had sewn the patterns of golden thread used only on imperial robes had been cut out when they finished them, to prevent duplication of the design. This was our mission's answer to this terrible fate, and I was proud of what we offered.

I was also proud of mission work every time I came home to the southern compound at Erh T'iao Hutung where we lived during the early years. A path from the gate led to the mission hospital, a low, two-story building with a central corridor and wards on both sides. Almost every day, but especially during epidemics, families filled the steps at the front of the hospital, baskets and bundles beside them, waiting to help care for a relative inside or to find care for themselves. Dr. Bash was the mission doctor, a short, busy, compassionate woman with a brisk manner and a perfectly calibrated sense of humor. She was also a good doctor. Somehow the flannel bands she prescribed to wrap around an aching stomach worked. Above all, she understood the Chinese she cared for, and I was glad to be associated with what she did and how she did it. I wanted to volunteer at the hospital, but missionaries' children were discouraged because of the wide variety of diseases against which we had no inoculation or vaccination. Every day I would look at the little groups on the steps, and be glad that whatever the source of sponsorship, Douw Hospital, at the Presbyterian Mission, was there.

And yet, because of the conditions extracted from China after the Boxer rebellion, foreigners were governed by extraterritorial law. We were not subject to Chinese law, and the exemption further increased my feeling that we were visitors in a culture that had not invited us, which we nevertheless refused to be governed by.

There was also, however, the sense of being part of a world-wide, heart-supported community of like-minded people doing the right, difficult thing. At breakfast prayers every morning in our house, we read from a little book that listed all the Presbyterian missions across the world and named the people in them, so that as we sat in our dining room we could hear not only the names of places no one knew, much less visited, but also of people who were doing there what our parents were doing where we were, and we prayed for them. This lent intimacy and scope to what often seemed a mysterious and baffling enterprise. There is a hymn that expresses this:

> As o'er each continent and island
> The dawn leads on another day,
> The voice of prayer is never silent,
> Nor dies the strain of praise away.
> The sun that bids us rest, is waking
> Our brethren 'neath the western sky
> And hour by hour fresh lips are making
> Thy wondrous doings heard on high.
>
> So be it, Lord, thy throne shall never
> Like earth's proud empires, pass away;
> Thy kingdom stands and grows forever,
> Till all earth's creatures own thy sway.

This was what my parents had dedicated their lives to; how could it be questioned by a child?

IV

PEITAIHO: NEAR TO HEAVEN

View of Baby Beach from our house.

Summers in China were famously hot. In Peking, the desert winds scorched the city, and cholera and diseases spread. So foreign dependents were encouraged to leave their stations and spend the summer elsewhere. Most foreigners in northern China went to Peitaiho, a resort on a small peninsula in the Gulf of Chihli off the China coast.

My parents need not have worked so hard for heaven. In 1922, they bought one. It was a two-family house in Peitaiho. They bought it together with my father's Princeton roommate, Lawrence Mead, and his family, and for the next seventeen years it was the closest to heaven any of us children wanted or expected to reach. In fact, "near to heaven" is a Chinese alternative name for the place. The formal name, Peitaiho, means "bearing the north river." The river came down through a village to the sea, ending in an extended estuary of sand flats. To the south were communities: East Cliff, Lighthouse Point, and Rocky Point. To the west were low, wooded, templed hills called Lotus Hills.

We lived in East Cliff, composed of small and medium-sized cottages owned mostly by foreigners and clustered around two main beaches: a shallow beach, called Baby Beach, and a longer, deeper beach, Big Beach, which adults and older children used. There were other special-purpose little bays: Whooping Cough Beach and Impetigo Beach, for those who faced quarantine.

We left for Peitaiho as soon as possible after school was over. The goats usually left early in the morning on a freight train, with the servants. Later we piled into rickshaws in the stifling dawn, down through the familiar streets to the gaunt open station outside the city gate, and to the train, already steaming. We gave my father a wistful, empathic embrace and climbed on the train. One servant, En P'u, stayed behind to take care of him. We chose "hard seat" cars because of their relative absence of lice, thus joining most knowledgeable travelers, mostly Chinese. The train began to move, and my father ran beside it, finally stopping at the end of the platform waving his Panama hat until the curve of the rails hid him from sight.

The six hours it took to cross the north China plain was for me a torment until we reached the other side of the high, rickety Lanchow bridge over the Yellow River. The train had to slow down to cross the bridge, and both the train and the bridge rocked sidewise, which seemed to me a bad sign. Once we were over it, all I could think of was that first glimpse of the sea. At Peitaiho Junction we left the train and boarded a little, puffing "Yes, I can" narrow-gauge train that carried us to Peitaiho. From the rickshaws and donkeys that crowded around us at the little Peitaiho Beach station, we chose several and started towards "near to Heaven." The unpaved path went through the staid and expensive village of Rocky Point and climbed a ridge from which we could get glimpses of the coast and the longed-for sea. We took the road toward East Cliff, turned left, then right, and there it was, the first wide view of the sea, darkening against the evening light.

**Arriving at Peitaiho Junction, 1929. From the left: Hao Nai Nai
with Barbara, Mother, Janet, me, and Elinor.**

Our house topped a slight hill, its wide front porch facing the sea. A low stone wall enclosed the grounds. A path fringed with spirea and small mimosa trees led downward from the front steps past a tennis court to a small opening in the wall onto the main path leading down to Big Beach. At one end of the tennis court was a small guest house. By the side of the court sat a little pavilion, called a *t'ing sze*, of stucco, with a red-tiled roof. From north of the house, a path led down across open fields to Baby Beach. The western part of the house was a sunken courtyard where the goats were kept, and where merchants came by daily with vegetables, fruits and fish. A cistern collected rainwater. There was also a well.

We waited especially for watermelon, which we never had in Peking. They were sold by weight. We would visit the pails of

The front of our house at Peitaiho in the 1920s.

potassium permanganate solution in which the servants immediately submerged the melons after buying them, watching the fruits opened to see if the pulp inside was purple, meaning they had been injected almost certainly with polluted water. There would then be long and loud arguments with the sellers, who soon learned to bring only untainted watermelons to our house.

The house was divided only by sliding doors between the living and dining rooms, each of which had a front door leading onto the porch, which extended across the front and along the sides, with access to two bedrooms on each side. The porch was wide, of smooth concrete, with low stone railings. An interior corridor ran along each side of the house, leading to the bedrooms and a toilet in the back, a bucket furnished with a wooden seat. There were no bathrooms and no running water; a basin and water pitcher served each bedroom, and large pitchers of water stood outside the house for us to empty over each other to wash off salt water after coming up from the beach. Such living was high maintenance. The corridors also gave access to a big kitchen, where the two staffs provided food separately for their families. The servants lived on a lower level under the house, and would often meet in the courtyard in the evening, sitting around the well, chatting with servants from nearby courtyards.

Both sides of the house were the same, with the exception that from the dining room on the south side a narrow, winding staircase led to a second floor, which ran the width of the house, an enclosed bedroom at one end. At both ends of this floor steps led up to balconies, with a chimney and a flag pole for each. The two families alternated sides each year so each would have access to the treasured view of the mountains on the north.

One of the joys of Peitaiho was being with the Meads. Our families had the same number of children at ages that approximated each other. Any given summer there might be ten children, four adults, and assorted guests in the house. So benign was the setting and so stable the pleasure of being there that conflicts were rare, and those that did erupt were usually solved by the eldest Mead child arriving on the scene and famously announcing, "Calm down, everybody." Mrs. Mead and my mother admired and enjoyed each other. In the winter, the two families alternated Thanksgiving dinners at each other's houses. So even though at the seashore we maintained different schedules, staffs, and food, the feeling was of an extended family on holiday, enjoying each other and our common house.

As the house with the largest porch in the community, it was for some years the place where community meetings were held, including church services every Sunday afternoon. We would fill the space with folding chairs, but as the porch was open air, people would sometimes sit on the railing, looking out to sea as the service proceeded, giving it the feeling of a gathering, rather than a formal service. It was formal enough, however, to prevent the porch being used for Saturday night dancing, so teen-agers were among the most enthusiastic supporters of a move by the community to build a house for the meetings and services. Missionaries were people of conviction, and, with wide varieties of points of view, the issue of a dance floor flared often. Ultimately, the meeting house was built with a dirt floor. Our porch was consequently liberated, and when Elinor and I were teen-agers we happily spread talcum powder on it every Saturday night, stacked the records for the hand-operated Victrola, strung lanterns between the supporting columns of the porch, and danced until midnight while the twinkling lights of the naval base across the gulf came on like a diamond necklace.

For most of us, Peitaiho was freedom. After a few cautious days to toughen the soles of our feet, we went barefoot for the entire summer. Shoes were required only for church. With no electricity, no plumbing, and above all no telephone service, life was lived blissfully on its own terms. Eventually, however, as a community of home-owners, some sort of association was needed, and the East Cliff Association was formed. For communication, the Association depended on door-to-

Church service on our veranda.

door delivery of news, a wonderful way for older children to make money. We would each be given a message text, and lists of houses to take it to, called chits; we were paid ten Chinese cents a signature. Usually in the cool of the morning, we would start our assigned routes, acquiring signatures, collecting and spreading gossip and news, and be back in time for eleven o'clock swimming, informed and enriched.

The Association also arranged classes in anything anyone felt like teaching: sewing, singing, art, piano, cooking, swimming, languages, tennis, and drama. For the last one, we often produced a play. It required a sloping yard, a copse of trees for costuming, and a cooperative cottage owner. One summer we produced "A Midsummer Night's Dream." Another year, my sister Elinor adapted and produced a skit about Jeeves from one of Wodehouse's novels. The Edwards's cottage, to the north of ours, was the library. How I envied Anne Edwards. She could sit at home and read anything she wanted any time without being restricted by library hours, cards, or fines. We were, however, mainly there for the beach. The men volunteered to be lifeguards between about ten-thirty and two, but you could go down to the beach any time. Most families went to the beach in the middle of the day. A raft was tethered about a hundred yards from the shore. In order to use it, you had to prove that you could swim to it and back, and show that you could handle yourself in waves, which sometimes rose swiftly if a wind came up. A Chinese junk provided high sides for diving; a lifeguard was assigned to it.

There were programmed water sports from time to time, but most

Elinor's production of "A Midsummer Night's Dream," summer 1929.

of the time we just swam and dived and splashed in the waves. At one o'clock, a red towel was run up on the southern flagpole of our house to inform members of our household that it was time for lunch, and the other swimmers that it was one o'clock. We would tramp up the bouldered path, empty the pitchers of water over ourselves, slip into dry clothes, and after lunch curl up with a book for the house-scheduled quiet time. Occasionally, after an especially hot day, if the wind had not picked up, we would go to the beach again in the long

August 1925. My sister Elinor (with cap) and me (in the dark sweater).

The raft at Big Beach, late 1920s.

evening, enjoying it almost alone, floating on the quiet sea, watching the moon begin to rise.

In our family, Mother wanted Sunday to be different. We would go down to the beach for an early morning swim, the water still cold, coming up the path while everyone else, including the Meads, was going down. While the others frolicked, we would spend the time quietly reading or writing, and pointedly move inside before the Meads returned. Then it was time for lunch, quiet time, and setting up for the church service. At first, I strongly resented being set apart so conspicuously, but as I grew older I developed a respect for this adamant Scottish woman and her conviction that religion should not be dissoluble in the sea.

The other major activity was tennis. At Peitaiho, we played tennis every afternoon except Sunday. Grownups almost always had priority, so we were often ball boys and girls. But there was a magical interlude when the grownups paused for refreshments in the *t'ing zse*—cool grenadine juice and light cookies—and we could take over, playing fiercely competitive games to show the grownups that if someone didn't show up for the doubles games, we were eligible to substitute. Our court was near a cliff that went abruptly down to the sea. If a ball sailed over the high fence surrounding the court, we raced to retrieve it, stopping just short of the cliff to watch the little white ball sail off on the blue afternoon sea to Korea, a strangely poignant moment.

Tennis was for many of us the game that defined us, and we hated to lose any part of it.

Summer, 1932. Our tennis court overlooking the ocean. Father and Mother on the far side of the net, Uncle Ernest and Aunt Dorothy on the near side.

There were tournaments for almost every age group, and anyone with a tennis court was expected to offer it during tournament times. We did not feel deprived. Missionaries played at a fairly high level; one player later qualified for the Olympics, and we watched him avidly, our chance to learn the game of our choice.

The men usually tried to be at Peitaiho for the Fourth of July. First on the agenda was the annual donkey polo match. Donkeys were hired, goal posts erected, polo sticks produced, and almost everyone in the community came. The donkeys, of course, never got the idea. The ball was of no interest to a donkey. It might be a foot away from the goal posts but the donkey would just balk, braying loudly, refusing to move. Sometimes one of them would sit down, tipping his rider off, and just rest. At other times, a donkey would wander away on his own to nibble some grass and refuse to return to the melee. Sometimes a donkey would gallop off completely, carrying his rider and flailing polo stick out of sight. When riders and audience were finally weak with laughter, the game was called, and the donkey drivers collected their pay, corralled their now docile animals, and walked off, exclaiming that these foreigners were indeed foreign devils.

July 4, 1927. The balking donkey on the left is throwing its rider.

It was then picnic time, and tablecloths were brought out and laid on another large patch of grass. We opened picnic baskets, with much observation of who had what might be hoped for next year. The men brought news of the cities and the programs there, and those who wanted to organized a soft ball game. As the afternoon wore on, we gathered to sing songs of America, or favorite songs a family would start, until we all rose for the national anthem. This was followed by silence. Tears were often in people's eyes, and "home" seemed far away.

After sunset, under darkening skies, people picked up the tablecloths, stashed the picnic baskets where they could find them in the dark on the way home, and moved toward the little rocky bay where fireworks could be set off over water. Those in charge of the display climbed to the end of the rocks across the water, and the rest of us found places among the rocks facing them. Parents called out to be sure their children were nearby, and suddenly the first rocket went up to cheers, setting the sea aflame. After about fifteen minutes, the show was over, there was one last cheer, and families collected their children, tablecloths, and picnic baskets, and set off for their cottages, flashlights and lanterns lighting the way, sometimes the moon rising over the water behind them. Slowly the lights flickered over the fields and paths, then lamps shone from porches and bedrooms, until finally all the scattered lights went out, and only the diamond necklace from across the gulf shared the darkness with the moon.

Peitaiho was a wonderful place for birthday parties, and some, especially those from inland stations, planned them for the summer when they could invite friends they saw only yearly. At some of these parties, after the gifts and refreshments were attended to, entertainers were hired. Sometimes it was a Chinese magician, sometimes a story teller. My favorite was a traveling artist who would arrive with his tray of brushes, rice dough, and paints. Beginning with the birthday person, he would take out a stick, wrap a fingerful of dough around it, and shape a head and body. Then, glancing frequently at his model, he would paint a likeness of her: hair, complexion, dress, shoes and socks. When he had finished, he sprayed it with shellac and handed it to her, bowing low. We would all crowd around while he made statuettes of each of us. Some emerged with a faintly Chinese cast. These figures never lasted; they would dry up and crack, and sometimes the dough would turn sour. But for a little while, they were what we looked like to someone else. They seemed to me similar to what the summer itself did for us: furnished a new self to carry away.

Janet and Barbara (third and second from the right) with friends on the dunes at Peitaiho, 1934.

There were also excursions, to the sand dunes beyond the estuarine flats, and to the Lotus Hills. The sand dunes trip required tidal research. We would wait for the earliest moment the tide left the flats passable, then run to the sand dunes on the other side. We climbed them, then leaped, ran, rolled, jumped down, to climb again and again. Someone would be posted to listen for the slight sound of the sea starting to return, and we would sit on the dunes watching the tide come in, calculating how long we could stay before the tide might catch us on the way back. There was a delightful element of danger in this: if a wind came up, hastening the tide, we might have to run fast across the damp sand, watching the waves approach. Usually, however, we were accompanied by a sane and conservative adult, who

Off on a trip to the Lotus Hills, 1927.

would start back long before danger was possible, prompting objections, and eventually relief.

Trips to the Lotus Hills involved donkeys, always a welcome element in any project. We would gather at the foot of the house steps, picnic baskets ready, mount the donkeys, and set off westward, up the hill toward the crest of East Cliff, then down to Rocky Point, and on to the templed, fragrant slopes of the Lotus Hills. There we would explore old shrines until it was time to sit on one of the terraces under the pine trees, the wind soughing through the branches, and eat lunch, looking out to sea. Returning, we would stop at Kiessling's, a famous German restaurant and the only safe place to have an ice cream cone. Then up and along the crest again, back to the front porch steps and fresh bargaining about the price of the donkeys. East Cliff, being newly developed, had few trees, and the visits to the Lotus Hills brought fragrance and shade to the summer.

Often Ms. Mead, a slender woman of Latin descent, would sit on the railing in the evenings on the north side of the porch, guitar in hand, silhouetted against the deepening shade of the mountain range, and sing Spanish songs. It was my first experience of longing—to be

The Mead and Hayes families, 1931. Father and Mother are at the top right, the Meads top left. I'm holding Kanga, Mother is holding John, Elinor is to Father's right, Barbara and Janet are to my right and left.

able to provide beauty simply and immediately, as part of an evening, without preface, program or piano, part of being a self.

Eventually it was time to put away the shell collections, store the bathing suits—whom would they fit next year?—and start to think of

Leaving Peitaiho, circa 1934.

the year ahead. There were the annual pictures on the steps of everyone who had stayed in the house that summer, the last swim, the last walk along the night sea.

The next morning, donkeys saddled, we took a last quiet look at the sea in the golden sunrise, and turned westward. For me Peitaiho was an essential stillness, the stillness of moving waters, the stillness of things done with other people voluntarily, the stillness of no electricity, the stillness of the outside. Back we went through Rocky Point to the little train chugging at the station, to the long, noisy ride back, across the rickety Lanchow bridge, to the dusty Peking railway station with, again, my father and En P'u on the platform, waving us home.

V

EVACUATION

Evacuees on the deck of the *Saarbrücken*, April 1927. I'm standing at the back holding Barbara. Elinor is to her left, looking down at Janet, who's looking to her left.

In the spring of 1927, Chiang Kai Shek moved to rid his army of communists, and on April 3, 1927 an explosion went off in the army barracks near our house. With chaos in the armed forces, anti-foreign sentiment that had been building since 1919 now became threatening, and word went out from the US Embassy that dependents should leave.

My sister Barbara was now a little over a year old. I was ten, Elinor eight, and Janet four. My mother decided to take the four of us to Scotland where we could wait out the crisis with her parents. Along with many others, we left on the railroad, going by way of Tientsin to Shanghai, where we booked passage on the *Saarbrücken*, a German passenger liner. Shortly before the ship was to sail, we went to the dining room for lunch. Elinor, not feeling well, was in the cabin and I was sent back to check on her. On the way, I encountered the captain striding through the dining room, followed by the ship's doctor. They marched—it's the only word—directly to my mother's table, and the captain thundered: "Mrs. Hayes, your child has the German measles. Leave the ship immediately." I was puzzled by this. What more efficient procedure was there than to have German measles on a German ship?

In front of all the passengers in the dining room we trailed out and hurriedly packed our bags. A steward wearing a surgical mask escorted us by back passageways to a gangplank at the back of the ship, and we were quickly deposited on the dock, evacuees again.

Fortunately, we had an uncle and aunt living in Shanghai, and we were offered their empty second floor. I was moved by their hospitality; I knew they were trying to have a child, and, having been born while my mother had German measles, I had been told how lucky she and I were that the disease had occurred so late in the pregnancy.

On the second floor of the house, my mother had a small room. Elinor and Barbara, who had the disease, shared a room, and Janet and I took the third. I had had German measles and was therefore immune, and Janet showed no symptoms. We stayed there for the incubation period—two weeks—never leaving the rooms, in order to protect Aunt Dorothy from exposure. Meals were brought up and set outside our doors, with Mother calling, "bowls, girls" when they were delivered. Books and games appeared from time to time. Elinor and Barbara recovered, Janet didn't come down with it, and when the incubation period was over, we left for Peking. Aunt Dorothy and Uncle Ernest waved us away with affection and relief, doubtless in equal measure. They never had a child of their own, but later adopted a little Chinese boy.

We were delighted to be back in Peking, especially since it meant that we would be spending the next few months at Peitaiho, instead of shivering through a chilly Scottish summer. In Peking, Hao Nai Nai joined our household, and in June we all went to Peitaiho, as beautiful as ever and even quieter since most missionaries had successfully evacuated.

Although the evacuation order still held, the resort was considered safe, especially after a US cruiser, the *Marblehead*, was assigned to Chinwangtao harbor, across the gulf water, to protect us. On a clear day, we could see the ship, low in the water with two black funnels and, in our excited imaginations, powerful, deadly armor swarming over its decks. For the Fourth of July festivities, however, its presence posed a problem. It seemed unpatriotic not to ask the sailors over for our celebration. But the more conservative missionaries, especially those with daughters, were unsure whether the *Marblehead* sailors were here to protect us, or we needed to protect ourselves from them.

My mother, with her British love of a navy that had preserved her island nation just ten years earlier, was a champion—despite having four daughters—of inviting the sailors for the entire day, including the after-dark fireworks. The sailors came over in a launch, bringing picnic lunches with them, and they seriously energized the donkey polo match. Navy people knew how to give orders; the donkeys seemed to get the point, and we had the most raucous donkey polo game ever held at East Cliff. They also brought assorted refreshments, sodas, candy, and celebratory foods not easily found in the small shops in Rocky Point. They knew and loudly sang several songs with which

On board the US Navy cruiser, the *Marblehead*, summer 1927.

missionaries were not familiar, and they knew all about fireworks.

After it was over, everyone was sad to see them board their launch and return to the ship. A few days later, our sadness was alleviated when the East Cliff Association received an invitation to visit the battleship. There was much discussion among the parents, and agreement that the invitation could be accepted if girls wore dresses sufficiently long and dowdy. It was a great day. We swarmed the decks and the gun mounts, ate real American food, and were each given a genuine *Marblehead* hat band as a souvenir. After that sailors would sometimes come over to spend Sunday afternoons with the families that had become friends. They'd stay for church services and supper and row back across the waters, we girls watching every dripping oar.

Since we were not going to school in the city, we stayed at Peitaiho longer, this time going to Tientsin again and then to Shanghai, where, as luck would have it, we boarded the *Saarbrücken* on the unused tickets of the last attempt. To our delight, Hao Nai Nai came with us. Mother found the fine print on the evacuation order, and saw that families with four children were now allowed to take an *amah* free of charge.

One of our evacuation ships.

This time we got as far as the port of Belawan, in what was then known as the Dutch East Indies, now Indonesia. The ship stopped there for a day, and most passengers went into the capital city of Medan for sightseeing and shopping, a diversion from the long journey by sea. A train station for people going to Medan lay across the road that ran along the docks, and my mother crossed first to monitor us as we crossed. Elinor ran after her, and was instantly hit by a truck. Hao

Nai Nai and the rest of us children stood in shock as an ambulance was called, and Elinor, limp and unconscious, was lifted in.

Mother summoned Hao Nai Nai to come with her and then, climbing into the back of the ambulance, called to me, "Do the best you can, Margaret." I was ten, and had Janet, who was four, and Barbara, at twenty months, to take care of. We watched the ambulance disappear and turned to get a suitcase from the ship. The stewards, hearing of the accident, had unloaded our baggage and moved it inside a storage shed on the wharf which was locked. The person with the key had already left for Medan, for the day.

Mother had given each of us some money to buy gifts, and I used it to buy a ticket on the next train to Medan. It was now nearly dark, and the first order of business was to find a place to stay. I started with hotels that seemed affordable, Barbara growing ever sleepier in my arms and Janet certain that everyone would surely want us. We had no money, no baggage, not even a toothbrush, and were routinely turned down. It was now night, and in desperation I turned to the biggest hotel of all, figuring they had enough margin to put up three children for a night.

The Grand Hotel de Medan was brightly lit, the dance floor full, the lobby packed with people in evening clothes, and I was about to leave before trying, when the radio came on announcing the accident in Belawan and asking the public to be aware that three children might be needing overnight shelter, since their mother had to be with her unconscious daughter. Suddenly people started looking at us, and I stepped right into their conjectures. I was delighted to fit the part of someone who needed shelter. We were fussed over, provided with food, toothbrushes, a room right across from the dance floor and best of all, a telephone, so we could let my mother know where we were. Elinor was seriously hurt, in a coma, and my mother cabled my father to come if he could.

It happened that the chief neurologist for the Queen of Holland was on the island, caring for the wealthy owner of a rubber plantation who had had a stroke. When the doctor heard about Elinor's condition, he requested and received permission from the Queen to offer his services. Initially the prognosis was grave, but after about two weeks Elinor began to rally, and by the time my father arrived, she was conscious. My mother and father joined us at the hotel, and one night they went dancing. The tune was "Valencia," and for the first time, crouching at the tall window of our room, I saw my parents as they must have been early in their marriage, enjoying each other and the dance, smiling at other couples.

My father had to leave after a few days. My mother spent every day, all day, at the hospital. We stayed at the hotel for seven weeks, wandering about the city, finding parks to play in while Elinor slowly improved. We could eat in the hotel if we went before the dining room opened for each meal. I remember once going alone into the huge empty dining room and ordering *rijsttafel*, not knowing what it was. I was provided a bowl of rice, which I promptly ate. I turned to leave to find 21 waiters lined up, each with a different condiment for the rice I had dispatched. The waiters and I walked out of the dining room together, and I vowed to myself that some day I would eat during regular hours, order that dish, and gloat.

In November I wrote a letter to my father.

Dear Daddy,   Nov. 27, 1927.

Isn't it perfectly wonderful that Elinor can walk? I think its perfectly beautiful. She walks all round the hospital now. She walked all the way round the back of the hospital without any one's help! Wasn't that nice? I think its so nice to see her up and around again.

This afternoon was a very beautiful afternoon for us. Mummy borrowed a Church of England prayer book from the Joneses and she read it to us, Elinor and I, I mean. There was the most wonderful confession of sin and altogether the whole afternoon was a real pleasure to me. Mummy ended it up by going to the call to prayer. She went the other day but she just missed it and so she went to-day, Nov. 27. Why I didn't write Wednesday was not because of just carelessness as is my habit nowadays, but I missed the mail.

I ended with:

> The valley isn't so very wide or so very deep and we can look over onto the range of hills beyond. We are crowned with blessings, Daddy, we aught not to grieve but it is hard sometimes you know. Your loving daughter,
>> Margaret

After Elinor was nearly well enough to leave, we visited my mother's school friend, Tats, in her plantation that, with its spreading lawns, palm trees, open porches, and columned porticoes, thereafter provided a colonial setting for any book I read about the Raj in India or for any novel set in Southeast Asia.

At the end of November Elinor was cleared for travel, and we boarded yet another boat, the *Fulda*, bound for Rotterdam, where we planned to meet my father, now also evacuated. This time, we got as far as Genoa before Elinor fell on the deck, hitting her head on the railing. Again an ambulance was called, again we had to leave the ship, but this time with our baggage. My mother had by now come to the not unreasonable conclusion that travel by sea was not what our family was doing best, and as soon as Elinor was able to travel, we boarded a train for Rotterdam. As I stepped onto the train I remember thinking that all this train had on its mind was getting to Rotterdam, where my father had already arrived, also by train, on the Trans-Siberian railroad.

There was one more sea-borne trip, across the North Sea, and the most magical sea voyage of them all. It was Christmas Eve. We had been unable to book passage in advance. A small Dutch freighter was about to leave for Scotland, and we boarded it. We were the only passengers. Inside, a few cabins were arranged around a central space, with a rough wooden table and some sturdy chairs; the ship's small galley was off to one side. A lamp hung over the table; the corners of the room were shadowy. A little unadorned Christmas tree, with unlit candles, stood in a wooden barrel near the end of the table.

We went to stow our baggage in the cabins assigned to us, washed up, and emerged for supper. The room was empty while all hands got the ship under way for the usual rough trip across the North Sea to Edinburgh. Once the ship was moving, the crew gathered in the room, greeted us, and carefully lit the candles on the tree—little white ones, such as we had at home. They then sat down around the table and started to sing Dutch carols, passing around Christmas cakes and cups of hot chocolate. Gradually the room quieted. After the long day of loading the ship, the sailors slowly turned in. Tired from the trip, and from being the eldest child, but unable to leave the magical sight of a lit tree at sea, I sat in a chair to the side and watched, as if I were in the middle of Dickens' "Christmas Carol." As the ship hit the strong winter current, the tree would move and the candles would falter, as if acknowledging the sea. A sailor would move closer, but the ship steadied, and the candles resumed their unflickering radiance.

Aboard ship, 1927, on the way to Scotland.

At last we reached Scotland. How stable it seemed! We moved into a little house in Edinburgh, on a quiet street at 33 Grange Loan, a small yard behind it, a prim path in front. After the year of chaos and travel, my life seemed suddenly something I could trust. Elinor and I were enrolled at St. Trinnean's School for Girls, which had been established as a boarding school by a teacher from my mother's old school, St. George's School for Girls. Most of the students were children of civil servants based abroad, so even as day pupils we had immediate common ground. Everything else was different: uniforms, the setting, the organization of classes, the way subjects were taught, and I gloried in it. Uniforms provided an instant identity; everyone on the street knew not only that you were a student but also of which school. Our uniforms were dark blue tunics with boxy pleats and a belt. With them we wore white blouses, long black wool stockings, black shoes, small dark blue wool caps with the school emblem on the front, and a dark blue blazer, the emblem proudly displayed on the upper pocket. I had been accustomed in China to looking conspicuously different from my neighbors. In Scotland, I felt secure in a uniform that hid who I was, but proclaimed an affinity, a belonging, an identity that told enough.

Father (in the cap) starting Trojan touring car outside Merton College, Oxford, 1927-8. This is the car we used to get around England and Scotland.

The school motto was *Virtute et votis* (By virtue and vows). The school itself was housed in an old mansion which reputedly had belonged to one of the families loyal to Mary, Queen of Scots, whose palace, Holyrood House, was nearby, on the other side of Arthur's Seat, a low hill in a park behind the school. A story, which I instantly believed, claimed that the building was linked to the palace by a secret tunnel. Indeed, there was a small dark opening behind the tuck cupboards where we stored candy and supplies. The entrance was locked, but could be opened, and led to steps downward, to a cobwebbed darkness.

St. Trinnean's School for Girls, Edinburgh.

A curved driveway led up to the school's massive front door, which opened on a long, wide central passageway, with rooms on either side. In the middle, on the left, wide stairs ascended to the second floor, separating into two flights under mullioned windows. There were several wings to this ambitious building, and a turret or two. The school was divided into "houses," named for Scottish clans, each containing all levels of instruction, and each with its own designating color of school tie. I was assigned to Kilninian. My tie was green and my loyalty absolute.

Miss Catherine Fraser Lee was the headmistress of what to me was paradise. A tall, formidable woman—a former pupil of hers said no ruler in Europe was more of a dictator—she founded a school based on sheer learning. There was no formal punishment, no individual reward. Students were expected to do serious work on subjects of their choice; she used to announce that the only discipline was the discipline of learning. I fell to it as to a natural habitat. A spacious, high-ceilinged, raftered room at the rear of the house, windows giving out onto the lawn and cricket field, was a study space during the day and later became a dining room, with a beautifully-set long table and candles lighting the shelves of bound books that had been used during the day.

At the end of the school year, I wanted to remain in Scotland so that I could stay at St. Trinnean's. My subject was history, and I had chosen for serious study the history of clan Kilninian. I was deep into the thirteenth century, among the Scottish moors, with a young, enthusiastic mistress. I considered Elinor, now nine, old enough to take on the responsibility of being the eldest sister. And I loved my grandfather, Dr. Kelman, who, though he was not well, I used to visit in his tall, gray, and gloomy house, listening to his stories of Australia, and, with equal interest, to his preparations for the week's sermon.

I loved the wools we wore, the way the language was both warm and brusque, the brogue, the food, and even, to be truthful, the oatmeal and the scones.

Father recuperating on the Scottish links, 1928.

As to my father, he had for the past year been in uncharacteristically poor health, and he took advantage of this forced absence from work to get a thorough physical check up. He was found to have a chronic and disabling form of amoebic dysentery. To his delight, it was considered curable, and to his further delight, the prescription was—what else in Scotland?—golf. He took happily to the links, where Elinor and I joined him on weekends, taking turns caddying. He also bought an old car, a Ford Trojan, which he loved to drive, and, when it could be persuaded to move, took us on trips all over Scotland.

In August, school over, we went to my mother's favorite "local habitation and a name:" Clachaig, a village in the Western Highlands at Glenchoe. Surrounded by mountains jeweled by lochs, it was the Scotland of story and legend, and for us suffused with my mother's delight. But staying in Scotland was not an option. We were already feeling like local Scots, acquiring a slight burr, and enjoying it, when the telegram came: We were to return to China as soon as possible. Chiang had established control, and my parents were needed back at work.

Barbara in Clachaig, Scotland, August 1928. Mother is standing in the doorway

So we left this efficient, beloved country and started for Europe. In Berlin, Elinor became sick with something unknown, and we romped on the beds in a *pension,* incurring imprecations from our parents and extremely vigorous German from our landlady. Finally we were on the Trans-Siberian railway, moving through the great forests near Irkutsk. Leaning over the top bunk to look at a spectacular forest fire in the distance, Elinor fell and hit her head again. My mother weighed the options: uncertain medical care at the next station, or careful and constant scrutiny by family members for the ensuing seven days. She settled for family care, which irritated Elinor. This care was difficult to maintain, but by now destination trumped caution, and we stayed on.

In those days, the Trans-Siberian Railroad was still on a single track, and trains often had to wait on sidings until the train from the opposite direction went by. At those times we could walk around the train, listening to the silence of the forests and the great spaces. At stations we got out and visited stalls offering hot water, Russian breads, and roasted chicken, but during this trip we usually ate in the dining car, getting our exercise walking the length of the train, listening to the unfamiliar language, trying to make friends with Russian children, whose parents discouraged them from encounters with capitalists. It was near the beginning of the first Soviet five-year plan.

At Mukden we changed trains for the southern branch of the great railway, and in October arrived in Peking. My sister Elinor and I had been together constantly during the ten months away from home, and our differences had intensified. My strict Scottish mother did not abide quarreling, a problem for her with five children just a few years apart. She had an instant solution: when the level of dissent became unsupportable for her, she would ship the older child off to a boarding school.

I was accordingly packed off to boarding school, the North China American School, at Tungchow, a city about 15 miles from Peking. I was eleven years old. The explanation given to me was that the dust in Peking was dangerous for my ears, although it had been two years since the mastoidectomies I had had while younger, and there would be none for three more years. We marked the clothes: "Hayes, 101." I felt it was ironic that everything I wore now carried my name, just as I was leaving the family. I never lived at home again for any length of time, except for the summers.

In addition, we were now assigned to Ku Lou Hsi compound,

which was our home in China ever after. We shared the compound with an older couple, the Johnsons, who had no young children, so it felt even more isolated. Someone gave us a perfect dog: a combination of police and shepherd who tied the family together as the only one that everyone loved. His name was Donny, a name that aroused fear among our Chinese neighbors. In Chinese, *da ni* means "hit you," which, when heard over the mission walls, caused people to wonder about the Christian ethic. But for us, he joined K'e Ch'ang and Hao Nai Nai as the most beloved members of the family.

Elinor, Barbara, Mother, our dog Donny, Father, Janet, and me at Ku Lou Hsi, 1929, standing in front of a stele from an old temple. The dark area over Elinor's head is from scholars taking rubbings of characters on the stele.

I now felt like an outsider within the family. I never believed the explanation based on health. I felt evicted, though not from the family responsibility toward God and the furtherance of His will. NCAS was a school founded for missionary children and was overwhelmingly attended by them. My doubts and puzzlements were now simply on a larger, potentially more exposed, and therefore more hazardous, stage.

VI

EXILE TO BOARDING SCHOOL

Boarding schools seem so categorical. Defined and imperious, they claim the total life of every student. Framed by rules, which provide the shape, if not the essence, of life in them, they build a one-size-fits-all world in which it is difficult to experiment, to test, to challenge authority. I ended up in a system where independent behavior was even more restricted than it was in my family. In both cases the result of experimenting was severe: in the case of my family, eviction; in school, punishment.

Missionary parents from the interior of the country sent their children to the North China American School (known as Tungchow, for the town it was near). Often coming from isolated mission compounds where there might be few, if any, American children, these children found in each other the comfort and companionship of others raised in a foreign land. But they also found customs and requirements that were foreign to them. There were no *amahs* at Tungchow. Life was rigidly ordered. Bells announced bells—there were bells that told us another bell would be ringing soon.

Missionary life teaches you how to be flexible, how to adjust to other customs and expectations. So these children, for the most part, learned quickly how to live the prescriptive, designed life. As a result, for the six years of my life spent in boarding school it was as if nothing happened there—beyond four ecstatic years of Latin and Bach, and some wonderful tennis. I felt laminated, my I.D. fixed as someone who obeyed.

I arrived at Tungchow in October 1928, and after the year of travel abroad and the long vistas of Siberian forests and plains seen from the returning train, I felt immediately a sense of being enclosed. Since the school year had already begun, I rode out on the train alone. Someone from the school met the little train, and as we walked toward the school compound with my green baize suitcase, I felt myself approaching a cocoon. The four school buildings were part of an American Board Mission compound; two of them faced a semicircle of missionary homes. The path that connected the missionary houses and that ended at the school buildings, was exactly a quarter mile in length, and that quarter-mile was the boundary of permitted school ground. As I stepped onto that path it was as if my world changed. Gone were the busy, noisy, crowded, brilliant streets of Peking that had been the way to school before. Under my feet was this prim path, the physical limit of my school life.

Peking, circa 1931, while I was attending Tungchow. From the left: Elinor, Mother holding Barbara, Janet, Father holding John, and me.

I had never lived away from home before and, as I entered the long corridor of the girls' dormitory, I heard in awe the hum of voices belonging to people more experienced than I in being distant from their families. The matron, Mrs. Outerbridge, tall and formidable, acknowledged my arrival in her no-nonsense Canadian voice, took me to my room, announced me to my two roommates, and told me to hurry and clean up; it was nearly time for supper. I walked down to the dining room with my roommates and faced the entire school—about sixty boys and girls, from seven to eighteen years old—standing behind their chairs, waiting for grace before sitting down. My name, grade status (seventh) and seating assignment were broadcast. I found my seat, bowed my head for grace, and sat down, reminding myself that I was there so that I wouldn't have to get any more mastoidectomies and had better make the best of it. That night, unfolding my sleeping bag on the bedframe in our cold sleeping porch, I listened to the chatter of those who had spent the day in my new world, trying to learn all I could of how one made it in boarding school.

I soon discovered that one of the requirements was to pay attention to the bells. There were twenty during the day—ten for prescribed events and another ten five minutes prior to them as warning that the affecting bell was going to ring. And that did not include the bells that rang between class periods. The weekday inspection after breakfast of beds, rooms, fingernails, and appearance gave me an idea of what was to be expected of me personally. I took enthusiastically to the expectation that people should take care of their living space and tried never to let my roommates down by anything untidy on my bureau. As we walked to chapel that first day, and later to class, I listened carefully, again to try to pick up the expected. At home I had been the eldest, setting standards, and had been treated by my mother as the one to be a responsible model. Suddenly, at school, I was nearly the youngest, classified as a lowly "grader," as the grade school students were called, and looking for which models I myself should admire and emulate.

The schoolhouse was a large, square three-story building with four columns in front over a flight of wide steps. It looked intentional, even forbidding, and the first time I climbed its steps, I wondered if I would make it to the college it was clearly built to deliver me to. Once inside, however, my anxiety and tentative ways disappeared. Thanks to the schools I had already attended—Peking American School, with its assurance that everyone was going to college from its hallways, and St. Trinnean's in Scotland with its punishment-free enthusiasm for learning—I knew, or thought I knew how to deal with school. The school building provided classes from sixth grade through high school, and the curriculum was designed to prepare us for college entrance.

Graders were taught in the basement, the first floor contained teachers' offices, a library, and a study hall, and the third floor was for the high school.

I loved the building. It had been built in 1915, with beautiful hardwood floors and elegant stair railings. Two staircases went up from the lobby, one for girls and one for boys, only to deliver us all together in the lobby upstairs. Windows in all the rooms gave views of the compound and of the countryside. With books and teachers, pencils and paper, and above all, things to learn, I felt more at home in the schoolhouse than in the dormitory, with its long halls and rows of rooms and their chatting inmates.

Chemistry lab, early 1930s. On the left, Winnie Hemingway and I.

My two favorite rooms in the schoolhouse were the second-floor Latin classroom and the first-floor study hall. From the window in the classroom, studying Caesar's wars, I could look out on a sunken road, which had been used since Caesar's time, and, with its carts, peddlers, men and women with poles across their shoulders carrying straw and clothing, evoked a Roman period frieze. Sometimes a string of camels, sacks of coal between their humps, came along, and I would think of King Solomon's mines. It seemed natural to translate an ancient language in this ancient land; I enjoyed activating the inert. Uncomfortable with my peers, I took solace in the company of people who had vital, consequential, and beautiful things to say to each other two thousand years before. And it was fun building—with a boyfriend's help—any bridge Caesar described.

Though the other classes—taught by women from the compound or young teachers from America—were small, serious, and lively, my other favorite room was the study hall. This was a large, oblong room where the entire school was required to do homework every weekday evening. Graders left early for their earlier bedtime. High school students worked from 6:30 - 8:45 p.m., occasionally allowed to visit the library next door or to go to the bathroom. Monitored by a teacher or by a senior student, study hall was, for one thing, prescriptively quiet, and I loved being among a group of people, seated at individual desks, learning.

When I had a boyfriend, in high school, there was an edge to studying. One was aware of someone important and near. If either one of us left the room during study time, we would glance back from the door quickly to the other—a signal of possession, perhaps. After the 8:45 bell rang, we would put away the books under our desks, walk slowly to the door, out to the lobby, and silently join each other. We would walk down the wide steps and take the path that went around the tennis courts in front of the girls' dormitory. We would turn left under the part of the path shaded by trees, quickly and briefly find each other's hands, let them go, and emerge in front of the dormitory steps where the matron waited. Then my boyfriend would go to the boys' dormitory across the field, which lay on the other side of the sunken road, and I would turn to the company of girls preparing for bed, gathering for prayers, during which I secretly reviewed what he and I had said to each other around the tennis courts.

There were lively, merry times also. Rehearsals for dancing with streamers around the maypole provided humor for weeks in April. We staged "frolics" on Saturday evenings in the social hall, with skits, concerts, and games. A beloved cook, Chu Shih-fu, provided special foods for birthdays and holidays. His carrot cake was the pride of the school, served to visiting sports teams. And there were sports. With only sixty students in the school, nearly everyone could be on a team, and there was fierce rivalry with teams from the Peking American School. When they visited us, they enjoyed our carrot cake; when we visited them, we enjoyed being in the city. Strong programs for boy scouts and girl scouts gave us chances to take hikes, visit temples in the hills beyond Peking, or tour the city our young American teachers wanted to see.

There was also skating. On the grounds of the Lu He school for boys run by the American Board Mission was a pond that reliably froze over in the harsh north China winter, and on which we could skate. These were festive occasions, skating freely outside the rules of sports, breathing undedicated air, on our own on the ice. Occasionally boys and girls would skate in pairs, which in Tungchow was considered daring and the sign of a serious relationship.

Although the territory of the school was otherwise restricted to the ground within the quarter-mile path, there were other places in the area we could visit with permission and supervision. Behind the mission houses that faced the school a path led to the bank along Tungchow city's moat—a favorite, forbidden place where sometimes we were permitted to ramble and gather bunches of violets.

Outside the Tungchow city wall, circa 1930.

The ground from the moat led up to the old city wall, with its round tower at the corner, and to the story it kept. In China, patricide was considered the worst of sins. If in any city a son killed his father, a corner of the city wall was torn down, a round tower built, and the son buried alive in it. If a city had four such tragedies, the city itself had to be abandoned. As it happened, a city near Tungchow had already had to erect three round corners, when a fourth son murdered his father.

The city of Tungchow offered to save its neighbor from being destroyed by presenting one of its own corners for a round tower, in which the son from the other city was accordingly entombed. I would sometimes sit by the city wall, my back against the old gray bricks, thinking of the tower and the body buried alive within. Looking across at the mission houses and the school beyond them I too felt smothered, rules piled like bricks around and over me.

Part of the problem was of my own making. I was a prisoner of doing what I considered to be the right thing, and intolerant of anything else. Once while I was captain of the girls' tennis team I chided Helen Adolph, the best player on the team, for beating a Peking American School opponent 6-0, 6-0. Helen didn't care—she was too good a player to be upset, but the team members were angry with me. The coach took me aside. "Margaret, it's not just that you should never take a risk of deliberately losing a point that might turn the game around. You must not deprive a sport of its dignity." I had the reputation of being kind to younger or weaker people, and now that was no longer a safe specialty.

Except for sports and music, I was physically inept. Like other younger girls, as a grader I ran errands for, and generally served, an older girl. The one I was attached to was Joan Long, a tall, dark-haired daughter from a Tientsin business family. Once she asked me to change the water in a flower vase, which I dropped, and it broke. "You are such a clumsy girl," she said. "You can't do anything right. You are a veritable jinx." Even with the alternative spelling I insisted on, Jinks, the name stuck. At alumni meetings I hear it still. I was devastated then, not least because I believed it of myself. It caused me to retreat into studying and sports, the latter of which required equipment, racquets, balls, and bats, extending my reach and masking the awkwardness of my fingers.

Shortly after Joan Long named me, an urgent call came from Peking. In November of 1930 the longed-for son had arrived in our family. My mother, now 37, had difficulty with the birth, and I was summoned to her. As I approached the mission hospital in Peking, I saw in the first floor hallway my father standing outside my mother's room, talking with a hospital attendant. As I came near, I heard the attendant greeting my father in the Chinese way, congratulating him on his "first-born." I understood that; it was the culture. But then I heard my father, without correction or amendment, accept the statement. Standing there as his actual first-born I felt extinguished, along with my three sisters. The damage was all the more acute, because until then I had been called the first born by the servants who cared for us. Forty years later, in conversation with my brother, I remarked on the impact of his birth. He turned to me in surprise; by the time he was born I was already out of the house. He had always thought of me as sort of an aunt.

Music was my joy. Miss Wickson, a gentle but firm teacher, gave music lessons on an out-of-tune piano in the social hall, a bare, pillared room in the basement of the girls' dormitory. She was always there for the lesson, welcoming, but focused and serious. We started with scales, so introductory and hospitable, then moved to Hanon, a classic exercise book, repetitive and tuneless, delivering everything needed to play anything else. We would sidle through a melody or two, and finally, after a year or so, reached Bach. Miss Wickson loved Bach, and so did I. She told me that I would never be lonely as long as I could play a Bach prelude. She was right. Sometimes at school when I was restless with loneliness, I would request permission to go down to the social hall to play outside my regular practice time. Approaching the silent, bare room, all feelings of alienation, awkwardness, and loneliness fell away. I opened the instrument, then the book of preludes, and lost all notion of time and longing. The prelude would end, and I would shut the instrument, close the door of the room, and climb slowly to the chattering upstairs.

Because Tungchow was a school primarily for the children of missionaries, daily morning chapel was required. There was grace before meals, nightly prayers in the dormitories before going to bed, and on Sundays, a full church service with members of the mission compound attending. The formal nature of these ceremonies required no devotion—they were attended, like classes. Only the hymns stirred me and troubled me for my lack of faith. Should I sing them or not? I did. In boarding school, conformity trumped any alternative. In addition, while singing hymns I could shift over from the words to the tunes and enjoy their rhythms and harmonization, while mouthing words I had to disbelieve. It became easier when I was a senior and played for chapel services, enjoying every note on the wheezing little organ and not having to sing.

I also tried to believe. It seemed to me that belief in God would make it somewhat easier to be good—a missionary child's primary job. By my senior year I contributed a poem to the school year book, titled "To a Poplar Tree."

Have you no soul, that rear your head so high
Your gleaming trunk so straight in line, so true,
Your tinted branches through the azure blue,
Your stately crown flaunting against the sky?
You have fulfilled the high ideal that I
Did set before myself with purpose true,
To grow up straight. How, while I toil, do you
With small endeavor top the aim so high?
Perhaps I have bethought myself too much
Of crooked, earthly things, and worried how
I doubted, planned, and gave myself to such
Through which God vainly tried His will to show.
Oh, let me grow like you, so true and straight.

"Gave myself to such/ Through which God vainly tried His will to show"? Had I ascribed "vainly" to God? What did that imply for the underlying doubt that always attended my attempt to perform religiously in school, in my parents' world, and in their legacy? As an admirer of the poplar, had I become an animist? No, I was flailing about for something external to believe in. Occasionally I slipped into belief as an accommodation to expectations, but it never lasted long. Although I was considered deficient in common sense—"It was just left out of you, Margaret," friends kindly said—God, Jesus, and the Holy Spirit simply made no sense to me. Their stories were incompatible with each other; they required a cosmogony that was not believable. The religion delivered a judgmental God who offered no comfort and a personal God who, even in human form, was transparently impossible.

On Sundays the school took on a slower pace. We had waffles for breakfast, went to church, had dinner, and then settled down to write the required letter home. The dormitory was still on Sundays, heads bent over paper. The younger ones sometimes blurred their paper with tears. The letters were collected by the matron, who would sometimes ask about families back in the mission station, or about older brothers and sisters who were in America. After the letters were gone, we would reach out for each other. Brothers and sisters would get together; others would read, or go for a walk with friends. It was also a time when one would walk with a boyfriend around the quarter-mile. From the dormitory steps we would go past the school house, then proceed on a dirt path that bordered the sunken road and offered a slight shielding of willow trees, and finally emerged in front of the semicircle of missionary houses with their occupied porches. Then we would go back to the dormitory steps and round again. It was a time when relationships were formed, strengthened, and enjoyed, and sometimes ended. Sunday afternoons were feeling times.

Life at Tungchow was otherwise Spartan. In an area the same latitude as Moscow, we slept lined up in rows on sleeping porches summer and winter. We laid sleeping bags on single-spring metal beds and would often wake to find frost on the edges of our sleeping bags. In summer, the screened porches sometimes let in mosquitoes, and we would hoist nets over our beds, leaping out of them to gain the inside of the dormitory before we were bitten. We cleaned the dormitories ourselves, sometimes using dirt for cleaning the bathtub when cleaning powder didn't arrive. Squares of cloth served for menstrual supplies, which washing women picked up and returned, along with the weekly laundry. Meals were served on bare wooden tables, and were prompt. If you didn't make it to the dining hall by the time the bell rang, you did without. Discipline, especially for the boys, was harsh. Mr. Lund, the headmaster, maintained a cane, with a prescribed number of blows for a range of sins, and sometimes boys would have to stand to eat. For girls there was a tough session with the matron, followed by a good deal of sympathy from the rest of the dormitory, but we were not physically threatened.

The school had what seemed to me an institutional stubbornness, in which I took pride. During the years of political unrest in the 1920s and early 30s, when fighting broke out in and around Tungchow, there was a determination that the school should continue. In the spring of 1933, when there was fighting close by, much of the school was evacuated, but the graduating class stayed to take their final examination in mathematics, on schedule, under Mr. Lund's unwavering eye. At the end of the allotted time, he told them to sign their notebooks, pack their belongings, and be out of the school within half an hour because soldiers were gathering for a battle outside the schoolhouse. At other times that year, mattresses were stacked inside the windows to interrupt bullets. Secretly, I was proud of my school for its determination to continue, however much our lives might be at risk. After all, we were the children of missionaries, who had risked everything to come to this country.

I left Tungchow feeling as I had entered it, incompetent and unsure. I had made a close friend, Edith Galt, tall, calm and devout, who became a nurse, went back to China, and died too early, of tuberculosis. When we were in high school, she was popular, though reserved, and for the last two years of high school, I felt near to someone, and thus potentially near to others. I had a boyfriend, a senior, who left the year before I did, and was in college. There was talk of marriage, and I corresponded eagerly with him until he found someone else. I had managed to maintain my religious doubt in six years of conformity. I was ready to exchange my Tungchow-laminated self for an unknown one.

Commencement, 1934. From the left: Dr. Adolph, Wells Hubbard, Winnie Hemingway, Frances Evans, Dorothea Smith, Hubbard Ballou, Edith Galt, me, Julia Connolly (my roommate), John Lair, and the American ambassador, Mr. Johnson.

Most of the nine members of my graduating class were going to college in America, but our family, being larger than most, could not in

1934 afford tuition in the States. I faced with delight the prospect of going to a Chinese college nearby—Yenching University—and looked forward to summer hours with a Chinese tutor on the windswept porch of our house in Peitaiho, to learn, and in some cases, to refresh the *ch'ien tze k'e*, the thousand characters needed then for entrance to higher education in China. The beautiful characters, their meanings defined by tones—the flight of an arrow, the bowl of a spoon, the dipping of a bucket in a well, the fall of a camel's foot—seemed to float in the breeze from the sea, as if tempting me to catch them and put them on a paper that would open the future for me. So to Peitaiho I went, that future beckoning.

Graduation from Tungchow, June 1934. I'm talking to Dr. Adolph. The American ambassador, Mr. Johnson, faces the camera. The girls' dormitory is in the background.

VII

YENCHING UNIVERSITY

Front gate of Yenching University, 1934.

The Yenching University campus was a jewel set in a fold of the Yen Shan mountains west of Peking. It lay at the base of the foothills, from which temples and pagodas looked down, seeming to watch over it. The grounds, called Shu Ch'un Yuan (Garden of Modest Gaiety) had been the property of Ho Shen, a minister of state in the reign of the Emperor Ch'ien Lung. When the emperor died in 1789, Ho Shen was condemned to death. His estate was confiscated by the new emperor, but was neglected. It had man-made hills, with a lake, fringed with willow trees, which dipped their branches into the water. Bamboo grew everywhere.

A beautiful old 18th-century-styled courtyard house was the

115

Administration Building. Water tower to the right.

residence and office of the president of the university. Winding paths with carved marble bridges linked the buildings; fierce marble lions guarded the university's front ceremonial gate, and the university buildings themselves honored the traditional imperial style, built with tiled roofs that curved up at the corners, and brilliantly colored pillared facades. The university's water tower, near the lake, was in the form of a pagoda. "Cloud pillars"—tall columns with marble clouds attached near the top—and the lion sculptures at the main gate had come from the Old Summer Palace of the emperors, by permission of the last Emperor, Pu Yi. The builders of the University had wanted to preserve the best of Chinese architecture, and indeed, as I entered the university gate, past the lions, between the cloud pillars, and amid all the new buildings, I felt the presence of a 5,000-year-old culture of reverence for learning—and for more than learning. I quote from Dwight Edwards's *Yenching University*: "Before it [Yenching] was built there was considerable debate whether it was seemly for a Christian institution to adopt a type of structure brought to China by Buddhist missionaries. But a study of the function of pagodas revealed that they had very wholesome associations and that, when the breeze stirred the little bells hanging from the successive pent roofs, the listener was expected to turn his mind to pure and exalted thoughts."

Yenching University was founded in 1916 from four other institutions: North China College, North China University, the North China Union College for Women, and Peking University. It was supported by four mission boards and affiliated with other

A campus pavilion in winter. Water tower in the background.

organizations: Yale, Harvard, and Princeton Universities, and the Missouri/Yenching and Rockefeller Foundations. It had an international faculty and board of trustees. Yenching operated as a private university until it came under Communist control in 1949. In 1951 the name was changed to The National University, and it is now known as Bei Ta.

Winter view of university buildings.

When I was a student there, the president was John Leighton Stuart, who later became the U.S. ambassador to China. Most of the approximately 800 students were Chinese, came from all over the country, and represented many different faiths. Some non-Chinese students were permitted to enter each year. As a private university, it attracted students whose families could pay tuition: mine was the equivalent of about $150 for the first year. Yenching was an ancient name for Peking, and meant "the city of swallows," since the profile of the mountain range to the west of the city supposedly resembled a flight of swallows. I thought of myself as entering a vibrant, beautiful center of learning, set against mountains, on which temples and shrines watched over us and beckoned us to rest from our learning on their terraces and under their pines.

I had applied too late for foreign-student status and entered as a Chinese student, which meant the obligatory entrance essay, for which

The mountains near Yenching.

you had to be familiar with at least a thousand characters. So I entered Yenching through the elegant, evocative Chinese language. My entrance essay was written beside the sea, on the porch in Peitaiho, under the eye of my intensely concerned tutor. He would lose face if his student didn't succeed, so I never doubted my admission.

I arrived on campus in mid-September and was assigned to a dormitory room with a woman from Shantung. She was a gifted pianist and spoke English fluently, although at my request, we spoke mainly Chinese. The dormitories were low, two-story buildings, arranged around three-sided courtyards, with a wall and gate on the fourth side —much like a traditional Chinese home. Each courtyard, as a dormitory was called, had its own common room where we could play Ping-Pong, visit, and study together. We did our laundry in the bathrooms. In one courtyard, a dining room common to all of us served Chinese meals three times a day. Breakfast consisted usually of cold boiled peanuts, boiled eggs, dishes of salted cabbage, and, if the supply held out, wonderful *shao ping*, a flat bread, sometimes baked with sesame oil and seeds.

It was the first time I had been among Chinese young people, and

I spent a lot of time watching and listening. I had roomed for the last six years at Tungchow with my best friend, Edith Galt, a tall, calm, and organized person, who could be counted on to get everyone in her vicinity to meals and classes on time. I missed her; we had helped each other negotiate our world. My new roommate, Mamie, was a tiny, pretty, popular young woman, always friendly and willing to help me with things I didn't understand. But as I lived among those whose country it really was, I felt increasingly like a stranger in the country I grew up in. Most of the women students were shorter than my five feet, nine inches. I felt conspicuous among them, while longing to be one of them. The women would sometimes look up at me and giggle. When I noticed this, I would say in Chinese, "Too tall, yes?" and they would nod, and giggle some more. Often I would say how convenient it was to be so tall, and to be able to offer to get things from any upper shelf for them. Then we would all laugh and separate.

My family was very much involved with the university: Father was on the board of trustees, there were many family friends on the faculty, and my father's work with students, a prime interest throughout his life, brought him into student circles. I didn't feel completely independent there. It was as if I still had to justify my family's reputation, while at the same time starting my own career. I had begun to feel the tension of starting the rest of my life.

Archery class. I am third from the left.

I enrolled in the required English course, and in philosophy, psychology, economics, music theory, choral singing, and biology. I played on the tennis and basketball teams and took archery as a specialty, partly because I had seen the little windows on the Great Wall designed for archers. I also registered for piano lessons, and learned to play the *erhu*, a stringed instrument for which the bow is placed between two strings, making, as I heard it, a somewhat plaintive sound, as if its tone were imprisoned somewhere between the strings. I also joined the choral group, conducted by a charismatic, enthusiastic music director, Dr. Wiant, who brought to our concerts an interest in many different kinds of music, as well as a wife with a glorious voice.

In my English class we were required to keep a journal, which was then reviewed by the teacher, Mr. Rugh, a young American who seemed primarily interested in the experience of being in China. He encouraged us, therefore, to report observation rather than private experience, but inevitably there was plenty of both. My first entry, for September 14th, 1934, describes the fear of being thrown into the lake, a ritual the sophomore class enthusiastically carried out on freshmen while the weather was still warm:

> What a warped outlook fear produces! It does no good and yet does infinite harm. I don't know how many selfish things I did today could have been avoided had I not been scared of the Sophomores and their threats.... There must be something else involved as well, for who would be so scared of getting wet? A certain amount of disgrace goes with it, however, for the persons are quite definitely chosen and even warned. Perhaps it is an unconquerable and partly unreasonable desire to keep my self respect that makes me fear anything that would make me so conspicuous as that. If I ever get to be a Sophomore here, it will be very strange if I ever threaten a Freshman, or try to scare her in any way. Freshmen are lonely enough without the help of fear.

The next entry was four days later:

> Since it is the anniversary of Japan's entering Manchuria, assembly was called for 11:00 o'clock today. We got there barely in time and there wasn't a seat left. All the windows were pasted with green paper, and the room was quite dark. The gray curtains were drawn across the stage with an opening in the middle. In this space there was a map of China at the top with a red splotch over the part Japan had taken. Below this, spyrea was arranged and candles were lit almost like an altar. Indeed the whole effect was something like that of a church

At Yenching, 1934.

without the organ or the cross. Five minutes' careful thinking in silence followed, and the eleven o'clock bell rang. This was ended by the playing of "Ase's Death" behind the curtain. The speaker of the day— a Mr. Hung, one of the Profs of History spoke about China's three great enemies: poison, officials and Japan. By getting rid of these three in the order mentioned, he felt we could free China. Then another silence followed, broken by the playing of Chopin's Funeral March. Everyone was silent all day—the Chinese seem very impressionable and emotional in cases and incidents like these.

I have chosen some journal entries that reflect what that first year at Yenching was like for me, keeping the original phrasing and form, but grouping them and adding headings.

UNIVERSITY LIFE

A Reflective Moment

9/14/1934

Some days seem to go by with one thing right after another, almost automatically. You have no more finished one thing than another is directly on your heels.

> "What is this life, if, full of care
> We have no time to stand and stare?"

There are times when I agree with that and times when I don't. Going from Sage Hall to Miner Hall today I was conscious of very rich beauty right before me. It was clearing over the mountains, and the sky seemed to shine. The willows made a lovely frame for the brilliant colored flowers, red, white and orangey brown that glowed against the green. The two buildings with their cream walls and reddish brown pillars made a lovely frame. It was all so perfectly balanced, so lovely in every corner, and yet so real, so living, it took my breath away for a moment and though I had no time to "stand and stare" it left a colorful, rich, peaceful impression on my mind that somehow lighted it. I did without my supper to get to Mr. Wiant's concert tonight. There are some things worth a dozen suppers (and some suppers worth a dozen things)!

Rainy days

9/28/34

A cold, gray rainy day—one which leaves a perpendicular impression on my memory—not unpleasant, not joyous. Bright colored umbrellas bobbing along the tops of hedges, the squeak of rubbers along cement sidewalks, trees drooping amid the long gray lines of rain, everyone with sweaters on, the raindrops glistening on sleeves and shoulders, gasping into classrooms, comparing one's state of shoes with every one else's, wet, glistening puddles, the stones of macadam surfaces sparkling through the mud, wet umbrellas, raincoats and galoshes dripping on the floors outside classrooms, lamps shining over glittering cement walks between the dripping leaves of willow trees, barely lighted roads with streams of muddy water gleaming, and lots more—a rainy day.

9/29/34

What is more dreary than a dormitory the second day of rain—and Saturday to boot?

Cold and the poor

10/2/34

The second of October, and yet it's so cold that everyone is wearing a winter dress or coat, or both, and everyone's hands are blue and cold! There's no frost in the morning, and the trees are still green, but the grass is shriveling up. A cold north wind blows ripples of red in the leaves on the dormitory walls. A woolen blazer, long-sleeved blouse, wool skirt and long stockings were not too hot today. It must be awfully hard on people who have calculated their clothes and heat for November, as many people do. And the trouble is, those who have to calculate are usually those who don't have enough anyway. This must be a bitter time for an awful lot of people. We, wrapped in our snug coats and sweaters and stockings grumble enough about the cold to make up for those who, far less adequately fitted to bear it, rarely say a word about it. The injustice and inequality of human life and adjustment strikes you every time you really think into ANYTHING.

North China weather
10/24/34

A very typical North China autumn day—clear baked blue sky and a warm bright sun. The flustered, powerful wind, tearing around corners, whistling in the roof, tossing the branches of the trees and bushes, whirlings of dust that envelope you and swirl around you and give ingenious twists to your coat that make it entirely beyond control. The sun is glinting on the window panes, while shadows darken the paths, deserted because of the darker chilliness. The sun is enriching the autumn colors on the maple trees decked in exuberant delicacy, rioting with russet and gold while the wind whirls the old, withered, colorless leaves and the dirty, dry dust in its swing as it sweeps along in its way. Dusty, cold, sunny, bright—this day is so common that one does not realize it is a very particular kind of day until it has gone.

A gymnastic exhibition, 1935.

Basketball

11/1/34

The Freshmen women lost the first basketball game. The gym was crowded, people blocked the doors, and bulged over the lines of the court. The place was filled with energy, light and noise. Cheers and yells were incessant, studies left behind in the peace and quiet of our rooms, or in the busy stillness of the library. Everyone was not himself, it seemed. The court was so much bigger than I was used to, the lights were so strange, the people so different, it didn't seem as if basketball was the same game I played in high school, when we played in the open air, laughing and bouncing after the ball, shivering with fun and cold, and running over uneven ground, while little groups of Chinese children stared with wide open eyes and round mouths as the ball wove its way in and out, back and forward.

Why do we ever leave middle school?

Owen Lattimore

11/20/34

Mr. Lattimore spoke in Assembly today, and I was glad to hear him. He speaks with clear, interesting expression of his thought and with such a pleasant English accent. He evidently has studied to some extent the art of speaking in public, for he spoke for a whole hour, yet hardly was I aware that the time had passed. He also "speaks with authority" and from personal experience. I wish I could learn as much about China as he does. I guess the only way is to keep eyes and ears open and mouth shut! One would think that this would be a perfect place, but there's so much else that is compulsory that anything that isn't absolutely necessary jolly well gets kicked to the side.

A Chinese entertainment

11/30/34

Preliminary statement—I always like writing the 30th or 31st of any month. It feels so encouraging, and as if a cubby hole were about to be filled up, or a box finished and put away, or a page written and folded. These are none of them discarded, the past is indestructible....

We went to an entertainment given by the premed club of 35 last night. It was great fun. There were many musical numbers and two very interesting Chinese plays at the end. But the thing I liked best was the *t'i chien'erhs* [kick the shuttlecock]. The stage was bare except for a little table at the back upon which were arranged several different colored shuttlecocks. Two stately gentlemen, each clad in a long wadded blue silk gown with a short black jacket on top, came forward and bowed. One of them made a short, half-apologetic speech and then they both retired to the back of the stage, where they took off their big outer garments and gave them to two little helpers, who carried them off the stage. The performers then came forward, dressed all in black with short jackets, long cloth trousers bound around the ankles with black cloth, and the usual Chinese shoes, of black cloth with stitched padded soles.

Then the fun began. They kicked the little shuttlecock in perfect rhythm, each slapping it with the side of his foot. They turned around while doing it, they switched it to their knees, still in perfect rhythm. Then they did a few tricks together, batting it from one to the other, always catching it in some peculiar place—on the feet or knees and other places. They would circle each other, continuing fantastic stunts. Then each performed alone. The younger man twisted his body and legs around, keeping the shuttlecock always rhythmically bouncing. The older man did tricks with his arms and made the little toy come up his back, shoulder, head or leg. They had great fun catching it on the soles of their feet—in fact each caught it in almost every way you could think of. They kept it up for over fifteen minutes. The agility, neatness and solemnity of the performers, combined with the rhythmic plat, plat, plat of the shuttlecock combined to make a permanent memory.

Bus ride to Yenching
12/3/34

I caught the seven o'clock bus this morning and rattled out to Yenching. The day was fine, the sun had not risen when we left the city walls and the massive gates behind. My eyes were gradually drawn toward the west—riveted on the foothills in all their solidity and strength. Then it happened. Even while I was looking, they changed. The soft, bright colors of the rising light played over the hillsides. The curling mists of the morning along the sleeping valleys lifted slowly, and the air around the hills became clearer. Pink, orange, light reddish brown, diffused pale purple, the light shimmered over their sides. They seemed unreal, too wonderful to be there. They were exhausting in the intensity of mystery. I turned for relief to to the high, still, clear peaks of the cold blue north, where the range cut the dome with jagged line. How wonderful these were, and how restfully impersonal and quiet. And then when I turned my eyes back to the hills, the intensity was gone from the near ones. They were soft again, welcoming their lord sun with steady slopes and windblown grasses, bathed in the quiet glory of the morning light.

Lab thoughts
12/7/34

Yesterday I spent from one until five in biology lab. I got my lesson through as soon as possible and spent the rest of my time squinting at spirogyra shriveling up when treated with a strong sugar solution. Now the question is—why should one colony shrivel up completely as it's supposed to do while another colony once in a while of the same species, lying as far as I could see on the same plane and in the same zone as the first—why should the second one show no reaction?

There is no "chance" in science. There must have been some law somewhere there that has to do with it, or that connects it with some other phenomenon about whose behavior we are familiar. Why do these problems trouble us? Why can't we "pursue the even tenor of our way" without bothering about all these disturbing and in some cases theoretical or else too specific to be of any general use questions? Perhaps it was because God made us in His own image, and He was not willing that we have anything but the most abundant joy or be tempered to anything but the finest steel.

CHINA AND ITS CUSTOMS

Lecture notes on Mandarin marriage customs
2/13/35

One day before the marriage, mandarins used to invite the future bride to the house of the mother-in-law, who, with her husband, the bridegroom, and his brothers and sisters make the bride's bed in the mother-in-law's home. Dates, chestnuts, lotus seeds and nuts are put on it, while saying lucky sayings: an early birth, the birth of a son, giving sons continually, and that the marriage is precious. Bride's gifts from her own mother, a vase, silver, or a watch are presented. A clock is never sent, since the sound might be the same as the clock already in the household.

These gifts must be arranged according to betrothal arrangements on a table. The bride's room is decorated for her. She then returns home in a red sedan chair, decorated with embroidery and tassels and returns in it the next day to the wedding in a restaurant. All wear red; concubines are not allowed. The bride is not allowed to step on the ground in the restaurant—the sedan chair is carried to the room used. The bride is given an apple; she takes a bite, and the apple is then given to the mother-in-law, who should refuse it, indicating that the bride still has freedom. The bride must then *ch'ing an* [meaning salute or greet—literally, "request peace"]. This she does by stooping on one knee, with her hands on it. She must then stand all evening to serve tea, first to her mother- and father-in-law, then to the aunts, uncles, brothers, sisters, and relatives of her husband. Her own father and mother do not come to the wedding.

Every morning after she is married she must go in early in the morning to her mother- and father-in-law, and repeat the greeting of *ch'ing an*, bringing tea.

Lecture notes on ancestor worship
3/27/35

Ancestor worship, connected to religion, was to establish a relation of the dead to the common life. It took place in a special area in the house, and was carried on by the laws of a controlling group, the *ssu t'ang*. In many families it took the place of government; there were books containing many regulations. Its function was no less than the administration, education and regulation of the whole family. Difficulties within a family must be brought to the *ssu t'ang* before lawyers were consulted, or arbitration called in. When a child is born, a lamp must be hung in the worship place. If this is not done, there is a curse on the family, which is obliterated.

The regulations are usually formulated in the negative. Some of the important ones follow:

Concubines can never have the safety or authority of the *ssu t'ang* and are not allowed to go out of the gates of the house.

The family must not allow children to steal chickens.

Don't adopt a boy; should he become illustrious, there is no blood relationship the family can claim.

Don't listen to wives' talks; don't dance, play, or sing, except in autumn and springtime; don't resist the government; don't be a lawyer; don't be friendly with officers; don't marry a bad girl; don't be an actor, actress, or slave; don't have concubines; don't use monks or nuns; don't learn Chinese boxing; don't believe in a religion; don't have meetings at night. If a child came to believe in another religion the family can drive him out, or let him die within the family. When a child is 12 years old he must recite 39 regulations while burning incense.

The lecturer gave an example of *ssu t'ang*, management of disputes. Two families live near each other, energetic farmers, who haven't fought for a long time. Huang sends his ox into Hsiao's field and much damage is done. There is fighting—several people are killed; the families employ others to fight for them. However, it is all arranged before they fight; the number of people to be killed is pre-arranged by *ssu t'ang*.

A road in the country
10/26/34

The *ma lu* [horse road] to Tsinghua is known as a good road—no doubt about it—*pu tsuo* [nothing wrong]. Two deep ruts mark the way leading through the village of Ch'eng Fu over a stone bridge crossing a stream in which the women squatting in their faded blue jackets and flowered cotton trousers are batting and rubbing the clothes. Then bumpity, bump, bump over the knobbly surface in the middle of the road, or else riding nervously on the side of the road, skidding over large flat paving stones with the treacherous ruts between them. The willow trees slightly swaying in the wind, the sloping shallow ditches filled with coarse grass and weeds at either side, and the fields, laced with little paths beyond. And last but not least, the travelers: stolid carters, saucy goat boys, cocky apprentices, with black silk wadded *k'u tze*s [pantaloons], long gowns wound around their waists, swaggering by on bicycles in the recognized intended-to-be-noticed manner, soldiers in groups of twos or threes, ambling slowly along, and groups of girls, their little charges blinking sleepily over their shoulders, stopping to turn and stare at the *yang kue tzus* [foreign devils]—these are so familiar, delightfully so.

Search for a phone
10/27/34

In a hurried search for a telephone, I threaded a narrow little alley at the end of which I knew there was a small Presbyterian mission school. Every school, methought, should have a telephone, especially Presbyterian ones. Leaving my bicycle at the narrow end of the alley, I found a small courtyard, a curious crowd of small children, a schoolroom with wooden benches, a scrappy blackboard, blue and white flags on the walls, and a placid janitor who, after listening with patience and some well-purposed but unsuccessful attempts to suppress his humour at my earnest pronunciations of *tien hua* [telephone—literally, "electric speech"], with much cooperation from the young fry around, told me that there was no telephone, but wouldn't I come in and have some tea instead? I said that I was very grateful, but had had some, and could he tell me where I could find a phone? While he was trying to remember, the youngsters produced many suggestions, from Hsi Chi Men [the west gate of the city], to Tan P'ai Lou [a street arch several miles away], but all seemed suddenly to agree, jumping up and down, to the suggestion of one of them that the "the little tea shop" had a telephone. All claimed that it was just around the corner, and all offered to escort me to it.

With many profuse thanks and smiles I bowed myself out, only to find I couldn't turn my bicycle around, so had to return and reverse direction, much to the amusement and amazement of everyone. The author of the satisfactory suggestion about the tea shop followed me out, telling me all the time that it was just to the north, and suggesting that he help me find it. By the time I could get a word in to say that really, with all his kind help, I felt quite capable of finding it myself, we had arrived at the shop, and a phone at the foot of the rickety stairs was offered to me. I made my call, while my gallant escort held forth to the interested crowd that had gathered in front of the shop on the subjects of bicycles, tea shops, and the helplessness of foreigners who did not have young men of intelligence to guide them to telephones.

A village impression
10/29/34

A village dump heap—piles of dirt, torn bits of paper and cloth, old tin cans with ragged rusty edges. Bright-colored fruit peel, pieces of red paper torn off the doors and purple wrappings and string from ancestral altars. Then a stream of dirty water, steaming from a housewife's skillfully tipped basin, running into the center of a shallow ditch, carrying dirty ashes with it, stirring the sluggish stagnant pool in the middle. Two old women, poles and baskets across their shoulders, dexterously picking out the bits of paper or wood that might be useful, with long sticks hooked at the end.

Pigs wobbling and grunting in the sticky dumps and waste, and gaunt yellow powerful dogs stealthily eyeing promising bits of rubbish. Little children, their aprons and trousers grimy, chubby fingers to their mouths, pause in their play to watch us go by. We eye the familiar dump heap with a new idea—that of finding out of what things it actually consists, and what it means to those who use it.

Trip to the mountains
[undated]
The foothills of mountains to the north and west of Peking were only five miles from the campus, and we often went to the temples in them, which were frequently tucked away in sites considered favorable, protected from wind and vandals. These temples were active shrines, often beautifully kept, with courtyards and pine trees, tall marble tablets, and buildings around a main temple, with its gods and altars. The Buddhist monks welcomed visitors, but there were no formal accommodations—we brought our own bedding, which we laid on whatever floors or *k'angs* [low brick platforms used for sleeping, often with stoves in them] were offered. Sometimes these were in the shrine of a lesser god.

A weekend trip to the hills
11/10/34
Packed into an old truck, the "windy sky" above us, the dusty white road beneath, we bumped and banged our way to Ment'oukou [a mountain pass—literally, "door-top-pass"]. There we burdened the patient donkeys with our bundles, boxes, and bedding, and tramped the dusty, dirty, hot path up the valley, through the coal mines where little villages clustered around great heaps of coal. These villages swarmed with men and boys, their dusty faces gleaming with sweat; slow, leisurely camels, patient strong mules and quick-trotting little donkeys, all bearing the inevitable sacks of coal strapped over their backs.

We paused for lunch on an old threshing floor above the valley, then wound our way up to the pass along a stony narrow path, rough burnt grass on either side. Over the pass we went, and down into the misty splendor of the setting sun, and the quiet ranges of the hills with their soft valleys. Then the arrival at the temple, the lighting of lamps, tugging of ropes, bending over bedding, spreading mattresses on the *k'angs*, setting fruit and sandwiches on the table, the little stove always in everyone's way, the friendly, courteous call by the prior and his assistant, and polite, but merry talk with much gesticulation and articulation. Later we settled down to sleep, tired but warm, the friendly stars peeping through panes of glass set in papered windows, and the straight, gray-green bamboo stalks gently rustling nearby.

Near Yenching.

Sunday, ll/ll/34
Some notes on T'an Che Sse, the temple we were in. Nice, quiet
monks. They eat three times a day, rice, vegetables, soups, *mant'ou*s [a
steamed bread], no eggs, no meat, no wine. Their life consists of
reading four times a day—when it begins to grow light, 11:00 A.M.,
4:00 P.M., and 10:00 P.M., accompanied by the banging of gongs,
drums and bells. They burn incense before the temple guardians twice
a day, meditate, and tend and light the lamps. There are many buildings
and terraces, a separate court for the treasury, which has a round
yellow and blue roof. There are long quiet meditation halls with
wheels of life on the walls, very dark and dusky, quiet and cold. Above
these is a terrace with a beautiful incense burner, the loveliest I have
ever seen, of polished bronze, about ten feet high. I stand in front of a
large and lavishly decorated hall in which autumn services are held,
and from which we could not go in peace until we had placed two
grimy and ragged *mao p'iaoer*s [paper money, worth about one
American cent each], on either side of the altar. The monks appear
contented and kindly, wearing long, loose black garments, tied at one
side, and heavy black cloth shoes. Their heads are closely clipped and
their teeth appear to be in terrible condition.

A spring to the east and on a level with the highest part of the
temple runs out of a cool dark little cave with brown, green, and
brilliant bracken; as we knelt to drink, the dry autumn leaves cracked
under us. Coming back from the spring, I meet farmers and country
folk with huge baskets on their backs going to get leaves for fertilizer.

Cheerful, with wadded blue, black, or gray clothes, some with coolie cloth blue napkins around their heads, they sat and talked to me, as did the carriers of rice straw, starting out on the long trip to Ment'oukou. Many fires on the mountains, where people burned grass, flamed around their path.

Temple in the hills.

On the hill opposite and a little to the side of the temple you could see how the temple lies cradled in the hills, with paved stone paths branching out all around it to the little shrines that perch near and above it. You can also see how the great paved highway between T'an Che Sse and its sister temple, Chieh T'ai Sse, dwindles into a small country road, and finally to a mountain trail before sweeping into the valley again. And there are the trees, the glorious ginkgoes with seven-leaved shoots from branches—Buddha's hand. Their golden leaves gleamed against the early morning sky; the tree near the meditation hall had been raised to the rank of duke. Little stairways everywhere led to unexpected alleys and courts, beautiful terraces and stately temples.

Monday, 11/12/34

Today we went from T'an Che Sse along the river bed, up a little stony, dusty path to the pass, from which we could see the great plain in its dusty stillness. Here our party divided, some of us going up Ma An Shan, which was no child's play. Up the face of the mountain we scrambled, clinging to bushes and shrubs until we reached the "big road," a little pebbly path which wound like a white ribbon under the cliffs. We had hoped to get to the top, but after much scrambling around, only one of us reached the summit. Back we raced to Chieh T'ai Sse, coming upon that beautiful and sacred place from above. We ran down the uneven steps leading to it, gobbled our lunch at one end of the great terrace and peered curiously at the gilded gods towering behind the pewter vessels in the dimness of their tapestried coverings. Here there were many gods—he who is god of ever-climbing fire, he who controls the place where he is, as well as the smiles of happy children, he who holds in his hand the little red ball, which, if thrown at a human being, reduces him to helplessness, so that the god may crumple him under foot.

Then back we went out by the big bronze bell, down a paved highway which led out and away from the hills. Down into the dusty valley, through villages where people crowded to the doorways, little children with pink cheeks and bright red spots on the foreheads, young girls, little children in their arms, their feet new to the tightly bound lacings, mothers with soiled aprons, autocratic old mothers-in-law hobbling on their tiny, shiny black cloth shoes. The men, strong and dirty with unexpressive faces stared at us as we asked them the way, and old grandfathers, sitting in doorways with the little children seemed pleased when we remarked how nice and fat the little boys were. And so, crossing the river on the old wooden bridge, behind the leisurely, soft pads of the camels, we found our truck. It took us swiftly under the long lines of the hills, the swaying branches of willow trees and the stars, back to the lights, the books, and most of all—the beds of home.

I loved these trips. They took me to the beloved hills, to the over-arching sky, to the people for whom, presumably, we were in this country. But we were a privileged group, who had alternate lives we could come back to, while the farmers and the miners endlessly carried the heavy burden of the coal and food that made our lives so comfortable.

Chinese dining arrangements
12/4/34

I learned something lately about the Chinese seating system at a table. The father and mother sit side by side, father on the left, mother on the right. The guest of honor sits at the father's left—the next highest opposite him, the next highest near the guest of honor, the fourth opposite him, and so on. The children are down at the end of the table. One cannot invite one's aunt's daughter-in-law (your own married cousin) and the aunt at the same time—there is no place for both of them. The honorable part of the table is the end opposite the one from which the food is served, i.e., the one farthest from the door.

The whole arrangement is very carefully planned. There must be no complications or embarrassments; everyone must be correctly placed, or ill feeling is bound to result. "It is good to avoid controversial combinations with potentially explosive possibilities."

Mamie and I, 1935.

After six months of rooming together
3/13/35

Mamie says that she would never think of going into the city without staying with her "auntie," therefore can never come to my house for a night. It seems to be the way with the other girls also—they apparently don't spend nights in other people's houses. Mamie said that it was partly because Chinese girls always had lived at home, and rarely went out, and partly because the clan influence is still so strong that they didn't dare not see their relatives when going into the city. Mamie said that she always stayed with her auntie rather than her grandmother, because she had another grandmother older than this one! Chinese girls are certainly saturated with the knowledge of the intricacies of what is and isn't done.

Another trip—more personal
11/2/34

Miss Burtt [a teacher] and I decided to bicycle to Wofusse [another temple], and went along a big white dirt road across a stony river bed to the bright gateway of the temple. Along the way we passed many people—some with shallow panniers of persimmons set on blue cloth in the bottom of the baskets. Others, and there were many, balanced huge bundles of grain over their shoulders. Old women, wrapped bundles in their hands, stumped along the bypaths. It was a joy to ride or walk among them, though we had to be careful of pigs, hens, and children on the road.

That evening I took my mattress out of the temple building, and lay under the pine trees in the courtyard. The brilliant clarity of the stars overhead spread my thoughts out, to the rims of the dark hills and beyond to the sharp mountain peaks piercing the softness of the night. Above my head the pine leaves wove their lacy patterns in the star-studded dark. The temple bell rang sonorously and evenly in the still air. A little breeze stirred the poplars, and their leaves moved the air. Then all was still.

In the coolness of a November dawn I woke, and quickly dressed. Stepping out of the temple court, I wound my way up the hill and tramped along the ridge. Soon I changed course, and scrambled up the mountain, scuffing my shoes, tearing my skirt. Up and still further I climbed until the sun tinged the grass at my feet. But my goal was the top. Up, over two boulders, around the thorns and into the full fresh blast of the wind, into the spaciousness of the plain, into the long blue line of mountains, and into the presence of God. Lying at full length among the waving golden grasses I gazed up at the sky. It seemed to shine in its clarity. The hills opposite were bathed in the soft glow of sunrise, their sides curving in molded precipitation to the valleys. Little paths led to the villages already distinguishable by the blue haze over each one. Steadily the sun was becoming the master of the day, as his creator was leading us into the paths of peace. Everywhere all around me absolute stillness lay like a clear, transparent mantle. The mountains were still, the valleys were quiet, the plain lay calm waiting for life to waken and move over it, the little villages were barely awake, the day was radiantly peaceful, and the wind whispered.

"The mountains shall bring peace to the people, and the little hills, by righteousness."

Another bike ride, but in the city

11/24/34

My way home led me through the northwestern part of the city. As I swerved off the wide road with its blazing lights and clanging trolleys, I just missed a rough cart drawn by a horse that had no interest in speed. I apologized to the driver for scraping his wheel, and got a turn of the head and a look of sleepy surprise as he took his long pipe out of his mouth and, sitting cross-legged on his empty sacks, pondered over this forward young foreigner.

The street was dark, the electric lights that tinged the clouds on a dark night had not penetrated these rutty streets. Here and there a large lantern swung from a pole which supported the white four-squared umbrella that leaned over bright persimmons, little yellow pears, steaming brown and yellow breads, twisted crisp rolls and big bowls of soup. Farther back, dingy window panes glowed with the yellow, oily light lamps give out, as men sat around the table, sending smoky clouds into the air as they drew on the pipes. Now and then the glow of a fire would show hot roasted chestnuts, and the chink, growl, chink, of the shovel would draw hungry and cold customers to buy some, and chat with the brawny, voluble proprietor. Little paper lanterns hung by the side of empty carts as they bumped forward, lanterns swung along the sidewalks as servants, shop keepers and apprentices jostled each other on their way home. The twinkling stars canopied these human dots of light, and under them I rode home to the fire and the shaded lights of home.

Chinese children
11/21/34
I think little Chinese kids in the winter are irresistible. They waddle along in their bright cotton padded jackets, their wadded trousers wound around their ankles, with the slits that make toilet training unnecessary, their padded shoes scuffling over the ground. The little tiny ones, with rosy cheeks and chubby little hands perch on their sister's shoulder, big brown eyes opening wide. Then there is another

I'm wearing a Chinese quilted outer gown.

one whose apron, tied on down the rear, keeps flapping at the backs of his legs in the wind as he stoops to pick up an old corn cob. There are the girls, their hair braided into shaggy pigtails tied with closely wound strips of cloth or string, their soiled blue gowns telling of work in the house, hands clasped behind them at their backs, supporting the curious, round-eyed little brother, both gazing curiously at the strange-looking foreigner who is looking at them, but trying so hard not to be doing so.

Fixing the bicycle

12/9/34

It was very early morning—about 6:45—when I left Yenching. My tire was flat—I had to get to a bicycle shop before I could start the ride to the city. The little town the university is in, Haitien, was still. There were occasional blurs in the opaque window panes, suggesting sleepy merchants fixing things up for the day. Now and then a drowsy apprentice pulled down heavy shutters, or swept or sprinkled the "pavement" before a shop. The only stores that were open were those outside of which clouds of steam arose from twisted fried breads, or steaming bowls of hot soup, inviting the shivering, garrulous rickshawmen to come, eat, and chatter. It was to them, my fellow travelers, that I finally went in desperation. They crowded around the front wheel, exchanging and debating diagnoses of the problem, assuring the *ta chieh* [big sister] that it could be fixed by any bicycle shop; there was one six miles down the road. One of them, however, had a bicycle pump he was taking to his brother, who had told him not to use it before he delivered it to him.

There was then a discussion of the ethics of the situation; I believe everyone, including the proprietor of the shop, delivered an opinion. Sadly, I must report that the ethical problem faded in the presence of several yuan I produced as I sensed deadlock, and the bicycle was wheeled to the back of the shop, where no one would see me use the pump, and the tire restored.

New Year customs lecture

[undated, but probably early 1935]

Thin glass lanterns are in front of shops, with colored pictures and red paper banners pasted over the shop door. "Open business with great luck." "Greet you with good luck." "Loyalty and sincerity promote clan." "Learning and books will make dynasty long." There are many traditional foods, especially steamed breads with red dots of bean paste on top, sticky sweet rice buns, and balls of malt candy.

There is in many family kitchens a paper image of a Kitchen God. At the beginning of the New Year celebrations, the whole family gathers in the kitchen to ask the kitchen god not to say anything bad about them. They paste his lips with malt candy to ensure this, then burn the image of him to speed his way to heaven. In his absence they cook all kinds of good, special food, so that there is no report of too much good food or too little philanthropy. At the end of the week of celebration a new kitchen god poster is installed, and behavior, at least in the kitchen, is again monitored.

MILITARY MATTERS

Japan had invaded Manchuria, a northern province, only four years before, in 1931. The Red Army was already marching up from the south, in the mountains along China's western provinces, and Chiang Kai Shek's Kuomintang army was fighting the communists in the east.

Communists in the university
3/11/35

Today Lie Li Jei, a girl in the Third Dorm, was arrested for being a communist. Mamie [my roommate] told this story. She said that early this morning a friend called her up over the phone and told her to hurry and go over to Ts'ing Hua [a nearby university] where they could escape together. This girl hurried out, took her bike and off she chased. On the way there she saw her friend with a policeman and a plain-clothes man. She was badly upset by the shock, and fell off her bicycle. The policemen, upon arriving in Yenching, went straight to Li Jei's room, and, finding it vacant, went to the dining room. They found her in neither of these places, but did not stop looking until they had found her. Mamie said she thought she was at Miss Speer's now [Miss Speer was the Dean of Women], denying that she is a communist. The other girl escaped, and is back again at Ts'ing Hua. It is a tragic story, isn't it?

Perhaps some later day people will wonder at our persecuting people for their political ideas, as we wonder now at people who in the 16th and 17th centuries were persecuted for religious ideas.

They say there are a lot of Communists at Yenching, and even more at Ts'ing Hua. Even in this *hu ting* [part of a dormitory] where I live, there is one, and I think I know who it is. It certainly is a shame. It seems strange that we live ordinary, common lives while such things are going on twenty feet away. Surely our right hands know not what our left hands are doing.

I think the woman in my dormitory was the one who asked me to join Mao's Long March, and who eventually went "over the mountains" to do so herself.

The Japanese question
2/13/35

What attitude should we foreigners take here on the anti-Japanese question? Is national spirit a good thing, and worth fostering, and dividing into the good channels, recuperative ones? Is it possible for China to unify in other ways than the common hatred of Japan? What can we do to prevent silly measures like the maneuvers in the Pacific? What is at the bottom of this rickety situation? What and where and why are we?

Does religion explain the universe? If so, why isn't man pure and good and true as his creator is—as he was made in his image. How did the world get into such a mess? How is it going to get out?

Does belief in God do any good to help? Is there the kind of God I have been led to believe? Is Christ "with us always?" How did we get where we are then? What is the purpose behind all this? Where are we going to?

Personal problem
2/12/35

In psychology class today we were discussing final wants and ways of satisfying them. Dr. Sailer asked Ms. Wang to say if she would give up opportunity for study for anything else. Yes, she would—to travel. These two were to satisfy knowing the world. Would she give that up? Yes, for a million dollars. These two were regarded as ways of satisfying her want—to enjoy life. Would she give that up? Yes, and guess for what. To drive the Japanese out of Manchuria!

How very difficult it is! One day I offered my roommate some oranges of a particularly soft and pungent kind. I noticed that she didn't receive them with open arms, but thought no more of it. Later, she made the remark, "These are probably Japanese oranges." I said I was sorry, and she said, "That's all right, you didn't know. That's what the Japanese are good at."

My roommate is very Christian and lovable, and sees that her attitude is wrong, but she asks, "What can you do about it?"

Giving medical aid to soldiers
12/5/34

A long argument in discussion group about whether we should give medical help in time of war. To tell the truth, it had never occurred to me that there was ever a possibility of dissension on this point. To give medical help had seemed as natural to me as to make food for the soldiers.

The arguments against it—and the majority of the group were of this opinion—were as follows:

1) That all you were doing in giving medical aid was to heal soldiers so that they could go back and fight.

2) That if medical help were definitely stopped, men would not go out to fight, realizing they had very little chance of getting well, once hurt, and therefore war would be stopped.

My answers to these would be as follows:

1) The point of medical aid is entirely missed. The main purpose of medical aid is to relieve suffering. It is definitely a fact that many of the men that are healed do NOT go back to fight. They are just saved from complete wreck of body, that's all, and [given] possible reduction of pain. In the question of whether or not it might be more humane to let them die, the law is prohibitive. We are not allowed to kill people in misery; to sit back and let them die would be nearly the same as killing them.

2) Stopping medical help so that men will be afraid to go and fight may eliminate the possibility of war as such, but it will not destroy the spirit of men that rushed to war in the first place. That is the cause of this frightful thing we call war, and that would find its expression in other results, possibly worse, if possible, than war itself.

We are faced with human nature. Few people can think of brothers, sisters, friends, or very dear relations of any kind fighting and suffering without doing a thing to help them. We are up against a very fundamental emotion of people which cannot and will not be suppressed.

Therefore I feel that the solution lies elsewhere. Medical aid is not the incentive for going to war. Cessation of this will therefore not affect the cause in any effective way.

STRUGGLES WITH RELIGION

Since I was a literal-minded child, I was skeptical about the claims of religion. But upon starting an independent life, I found myself in need of faith, and also unwilling publicly to differ from the convictions for which my parents were well known. The following excerpts illustrate the conflict precipitated by this.

Thoughts on Religion
3/2/35
Now, it's all very well to speak of putting God first in your life. It's what all Christians are expected to do, and so on. But when you come right down to it, you find it is well nigh impossible. People aren't that way. They don't seem to realize you're trying to put God first into your life. Our social, economic, political systems are not built on that supposition. We get out of sorts with life, and everything goes wrong.

Before we go any further, perhaps it would be a good idea to define our terms. What do we mean by God, anyway? Do we mean the God of the "Thou shalt nots" as applied to our modern life, or do we mean the God who designs? God can be both a way of choosing an interpretation and an attitude.

If we are to put the highest first in our lives, we must first find out what the highest is. And how to find that out?

Simply, no one is more anxious that you should act according to the highest than God. What did He make us for? What is more important yet, no one is more anxious to tell us that than God. And this is where we slip up. It is so very easy to mumble a few words as you slip into bed, and say a little about the good night you have had when you wake in the morning. But it seems to me that we do too much of the talking. We give God an either/or and then say, "Thank Thee for the strength Thou hast given us to make this decision," and let it go at that. The part that is hard to do is to be sure you wouldn't mind doing exactly what God wants you to. Trust this—for it is true—God will never give us something that is humanly impossible. But this may be said—why bother about talking to God at all—why worry about Him, always pulling me up to things that are hard to do? I'm getting on mighty well by myself. Why make all this extra fuss if one can live all right without it? I'm having a perfectly good time and enjoying myself thoroughly.

My father's Sunday
11/18/34

Daddy had a full day today. Breakfast at 8:00—Bible class at 9:00—Church (Chinese) at 11:00—dinner at 1:00 (right after church) and short nap—student retreat (the first in the North city) from 2:00 until 6:00—church session meeting 6:00-7:30 (when we sent Janet to call him), then supper, a short nap, preparing his talk for chapel at 7:00 the next a.m., and bed. Sunday is a heavy day for Daddy for the very reason that it is a light day for others.

I think one of the hardest things to give up is a quiet and peaceful Sunday. It rubs the wrong way when things "have to be done" on Sunday. By this, I do not mean making tea—getting Johnny down and up, into and out of bed. I mean those messages that ought to be sent—those proofs that must be sent back, those papers that must be written.

Most people wouldn't agree but I really believe that 6:00 a.m. on a cold winter Monday is better for doing business than any time on Sunday—quite apart from religious motives, which of course are the most common bases of arguments. There is a certain stability and poise to steady and direct the week in a quiet, reverent, gentle Sunday.

Chinese church service
11/25/34

Daddy was speaking at the Ku Lou Hsi church today, so I decided to go to hear him. Our church was a gift, and is a large brick building, with a front that goes up like a triangle facing the street, and a tower above it, in which there hangs a bell that disturbs the Sunday morning peace every week at 10:30, 10:50, and 11:00. The church was but sparsely seated when I entered. A few women sat with stolid faces, their hands bound in long knitted scarves they unwound from their necks. Wadded garments caused them to walk slowly as they waddled up the aisle. On the men's side there were a few who seemed to be sleeping, judging from the hardness of the bench and the angles of their backs. The rest were mostly servants or young students.

I sat down, piously, by some girls, their brown sweaters falling loosely over their shoulders, and their gaily bound jackets covered with calico of florid design. With amused charity they watched me find the place in the Chinese hymn book, and with eager curiosity would talk to me about the most irrelevant subjects with apparently no guilty feelings about doing so in church. The old lady to my left considered us a giddy and forward bunch of youngsters during the service, but was congenial later.

How does my father feel about this audience? He had no time to be asked, it was on to the next one.

Rituals [I had requested permission to receive Episcopalian communion.]
10/13/34
I wonder whether rituals and services may be forcefully invested with a meaning or whether it's a case of "serene I fold my hands and wait" before a rich deep meaning will come to me.

The candles on either side of the dark altar, the great cross, the gleaming white altar cloths, the shining vessels, the full red of the wine clearly quiet in the bowl of the silver cup, the richly embroidered cloak from the priest's shoulders touching the soft rugs on the altar dais as the holy man kneels and the soft and harmonious organ music all help to invest the Holy Sacrament with a very beautiful meaning, but the actual partaking itself is only an action amid these surroundings, instead of being the central thing around which these beautiful things are placed. A quiet, sunny clear sky and the far off hills seem to draw me much nearer to God than this very different and solemn rite, although very reverent and beautiful. I expect it must grow to mean, or we grow to be able to receive its meaning, or else not only would it have died out long ago if it didn't mean very much to people, but I doubt that Christ would have started it at all.

Sunday, October 28, 1934
I know of very few other things more helpful throughout the week than the knowledge that Sunday is a day of rest. And I know of very few joys comparable to that of waking up on Sunday morning with the satisfying assurance of a whole day in which you may think about just what you please, in which it is not necessary to hurry to anything, in which you may look around you and find where you are, and what is more important, where you are going. Sunday has a charm all its own —that of going to communion in the crisp morning air, glorious with fall colors, that of a lazy, enjoyable long rest after lunch with the sun streaming through the window onto the foot of your bed, that of writing letters with the feeling of your friends right near you, that of going to church and the music ringing through the air, the long dark

line of the hills and the colorful autumn leaves against the soft blue of the altar curtain. Then coming back to the quiet room to read a little, write a little, ponder a little, and through it all a sense of joyfulness, rest and peace, which radiates through the presence of Jesus Christ, our great companion.

REFLECTIONS

10/13/34

What a unique feeling one's first return to one's school is after graduation. Pure joy is in the anticipation—to see everyone again, to be greeted by people you have lived with for so long—to see the places you used to work, play, eat and sleep in with so much seemingly careless thought. With beating temples the school buildings came into sight as the train rushes by. Gladly you get off the train and eagerly look around each familiar turn of the path. You enter the dormitory. "Why, Jinks," "Hello, Jinks," "Well, when did you come?" "Do come to our table." Gradually amid all these questions you find yourself pushed a little away from your former relationship. Up in the room where you once lived, the full poignancy of the emptiness of the whole place now that the special friends are gone, sweeps over you and though you may enjoy yourself thoroughly as you probably will, never will the full satisfaction and wholehearted feeling of the school be completely yours again.

Men's gymnasium.

12/1/34

Depression is one of the surest blights I know. I was moderately happy all day, considering that I had been unable to go to Tungchow to watch the games. Even when I received an indistinct telephone message that both the boys and girls had lost, I said, "Well, there really is another chance, you know, at least for the girls." But when Mother came back from Tungchow and told us how all four games had been lost by terrific scores—how 18-11 was the nearest approach to an even score, I nearly cried. It wasn't acute enough for that, it was a dull, depressed attitude that dampened me all evening. I thought how I wished I had been there at least to comfort if not to praise. I thought how I might have been there. I thought how those poor kids, entirely trodden upon, were feeling now, beaten, and thoroughly beaten, by their greatest rival. And through all this, I felt I was doing wrong to be so miserable, it was my job to be cheerful, and to encourage the others to be so. But my own attitude nipped every spontaneous effort. This generates more depression and altogether I was glad to see my bed where I could lay myself and my troubles aside

9/26/34

Another one of those days when you wonder how and if you will ever in all your life have free time, sanctioned by conscience to do anything you want! I suppose that is selfish but just listen to things I could do if someone gave me four extra hours a week that could not be filled with anything else. First of all letters—to everyone! Then copying poems, reading poems, catching up with the magazines, knitting, reading Mansfied Park, mending, thinking, and last but not least, sleeping! Then there are all the hundred and one things to be done at home which would seem to do so much more good by their being done than sitting around in classrooms. Perhaps sitting in classrooms will do some good later on—who knows?

I wish Egglet [Edith Galt] were here. I guess I do miss her and Julia [also a long-time roommate at boarding school] although I tried not to give in this year. I hope Eggie's happy. Since this is the first year for 6 years that I haven't roomed with her, I feel a little lost without her to be sure that the light is turned off and that we get to chapel on the dot.

9/25/34

How nice it is to have books of one's own! I am sure everyone else has the same material in his King James Bible as I have in mine, but how thoroughly glad I am to possess my very own—one that becomes a part of me. As with other books, even those associated with much less intimate and personal affairs, I am thinking of a copy of Jane Austen's novel that I was given for a birthday present. I love to take it down from the shelf with a feeling of ownership. The book seems almost a part of me. My music also seems like that—even in a stronger way for it is emotionally bound up in my expression of myself, as well as fulfilling a sense of pride in ownership.

A person likes to keep his books nice-looking—especially if they are well-bound. I used to treat my Bible comparatively roughly—so that it would look as if I had used it! I'm beginning to resent my unrestrained treatment of it now—and look ruefully on the recklessly used cover! Every time a surge of affection for my books comes over me, I am sure my hobby is book collecting, and every time I straighten my accounts, I'm just as sure it isn't!

11/13/34

To go or not to go—that is the question. You see, I think I had better crystallize my thoughts on the subject of going to America next year. I will put down the pros and cons as Benjamin Franklin recommends, and see if that helps any. We will take the arguments against going first. I could be near home another year—the year that my sister will still be at home. It would solve the problem of my going home by myself—and connected with that, of my activities in America before college opens. It would certainly be cheaper. Having once gotten into the life at Yenching, I really hate to leave it and my friends. There would be more chance to live with Chinese and learn more about them. I could take some courses in Chinese philosophy that I very much want to take. Any more? None, I think, except for elaborations of these.

The arguments for it are of overwhelmingly strong quality. Most people advise changing college before your junior year. Under that heading are such topics as taking the extra courses Wellesley requires that are not given here, starting a continuous study of my major subject, getting into the life of the college in order that I may get used to college life before my upper classman years, making sure of all my credits before starting full work in my major, etc. Some other reasons would be that I could have one year to get used to being without my family, and then could see them the next year [when they would be coming on furlough] which would make it less hard. There is also the probability of a scholarship this next year. I would like to see Edith (my roommate in high school) if that were possible (but that can hardly be counted as a reason for going next year. It would be an effect rather than a cause). Well, I can think of no more reasons and yet I seem to be no further on to my decision than I was before I started. Bother Benjamin Franklin! I guess it's my own fault, though, and not his. Anyway, it doesn't have to be decided tonight.

11/14/34

I must get into Wellesley if I bust in the attempt! I wonder if it will be worth all the plays I'm not in, the concerts I don't attend, and the energy spent each day! …If I didn't spend half my time worrying about "getting into" Wellesley, I might stand a fair chance of being admitted! But there is something about the kind of things that Wellesley stands for, about the quality of work expected there, that makes me feel as if anything I could do now would be worth all the energy if it achieved my entrance into Wellesley.

11/28/34

Discussing co-ed colleges at the Ritters' [faculty couple]. We started with the question as to whether this should be a factor in determining or influencing the choice of a college. I think it does only in that it is clearly connected with the reason for going to college. People differ in this fundamental aspect of a choice. After all, the way in which you accept and interpret your college life and work is the thing that is going to determine its value for you. Some people frankly state that their main purpose for going to college is to develop their personalities. I am not here to criticize, but it seems to me futile to have to spend as much money as a good college probably requires in order that people may "develop their personalities." I could think of several less expensive ways. But that is not an altogether unworthy purpose. After all, you will always have your personality with you while you may lose some of your learning.

But to me, the primary purpose of going to college is to work—for what other purposes are the well equipped labs, good lecturers and big libraries but that students may have the best chance of following their line of thought and working on it with the best resources possible. This to me is a great challenge—that here we have a rich chance to dig deeper and deeper into interesting, stimulating discoveries.

10/25/34

Some days just grab you right up—filling all your capacity until the end, then dropping you into bed, hardly conscious of their passing. Others seize you in sequent little cupfuls of concentrated effort—until at the end of the day you look back, no particular things absolutely finished—just little heaps or squares of things scattered! One thing after another—on they go—never stopping that you may consider— that you may take a census of your changing outlooks. I wonder whether this perpetual draining and refilling of energy, strength, and resources can be ultimately strengthening. Thank God we may form our own ideals, programs, and, to some extent, our activities, at least the main line along which these activities shall lie. It is wonderful to be essentially free, to know that your self is always with you.

The family picnic

3/7/35

I can think of nothing more perilous in anticipated pleasure than a family picnic. Let all those who believe in the participation of the "little dears" in all family activities beware. I do not hurl an invective upon family picnics. They can be, and in my case, almost all, are happy, beautiful and enriching experiences. But let me call an observer's attention to the fact that the "little dears" do not always consider themselves sufficiently "little," and are rarely considered "dears" among the older members of the group, who have come out for a "vacation" to escape the over-solicitous neighbors, with their incessant, "Well now, really you ought to take the family off to the hills one of these fine days. So delightfully refreshing: the silence of the everlasting hills gives one such a feeling of comfort and peace. And the freedom from responsibility that you get as you look over vast plains from high mountain peaks in the clear, pure air is such a relief. Besides, you really ought to take a rest, my dear."

So the family decides to go, and after I have decided I can miss the first aid class, and Barbara has picked out her favorite doll, and Elinor has just lost the field glasses, and the baby has just cut his finger, and Dad has seen his last "chappie," and Mother has remembered the hundred and one necessary things that must be taken, and the beloved dog has been tearfully shut in, we are ready for the phrase as old as the serpent in the garden of Eden, "Hurry up!" We set out, laden with bags and bundles of every sort, from Barbara's dolly's toy umbrella to Dad's best camera, which necessitates turnings of the head every other step to be sure that someone has it, or that it has film in it.

At last the car is packed and the delicate adjustments of elbows and knees being made, we wave goodbye to the smiling servants that come out to help with the exodus, while Margaret wipes a tear from her eye as the forlorn yowling of the desolate dog reechoes from the deserted house.

But at the hills we pile stiffly out of the car, and mother starts the "delightfully refreshing" day with an inventory of what hasn't been squashed, and decides who is to carry what, and why, and when it is to be done.

"In the silence of the everlasting hills" we sit down near the top of the first low hillock, and after a short session of bowed heads we eat, bursting out with what we have, or haven't done, seen, or heard, and want to know why. The conversation degenerates after a while into who is to go where to rest, for sound theory and frequent experience have shown that solitary confinement is the best arrangement for a family group after a picnic lunch. Again, Mother gets her "feeling of comfort and peace" while she folds up the greasy papers, packs the picnic basket, invariably leaving out the cups, and tries to find a comfortable place for the baby to sleep. Just as he is quiet and comfortable, the renewed energy from the rest brings us flocking back with a desire to "go to the top." Since the baby needs his sleep, we scamper off, to climb with decreasing energy until we reach the top.

Dad, wakening from his nap, suddenly remembers that he has a meeting at four o'clock sharp in the afternoon. The "clear, pure mountain air" fails to conduct our parents' piercing calls for us to "come down at once," and since the baby is now wakened and howling, Dad sets off to find us.

Half an hour later we come tumbling down the hill, flushed and footsore, Barbara with a toe "that hurts right there, Mummy." Dad impatiently picks up the baskets, we gather rugs, camera, sticks, and any other collectibles we have accumulated. Mother collects the baby and his accessories, and with one last look at the "vast plains below" and the "high mountain peaks" drives her tired flock down the stony path to the car.

Once at the bottom, everyone stands on first one foot then another, making increasingly pertinent comments, as Dad can't find the car keys, and knows he gave them to Mother, who never saw them. They are ultimately found in Dad's left-hand vest pocket, which is "very strange" since he never puts them there. At last we are in the car, and everything is stored, and we are off in a cloud of dust. For the first five minutes silence soothes the tired minds. Then everyone starts saying what a grand day it's been, and how nice that this happened thus, and that happened so! Dad, appealed to, says, "Yes, it has been a jolly day." Mother smiles wearily and says, "Yes, wasn't it nice?" The baby, lulled by the car, is mercifully silent.

The servants again smilingly greet us back home, and the car put away. The dog adds his yowls of delight and wagging tail to expressions of the great day. Dad bangs the door as he leaves for his committee meeting, *amah* has received "the littlest dear" and Barbara has discovered that her dolly lost a shoe, and wants to go back and look for it. Elinor has discovered that the field glasses no one could find on the hill "were right here all the time, Mother, and we didn't see them." Mother is left to receive the congratulations of the neighbors as they exclaim, "So you did take the 'little dears' out to the hills. I'm so glad, for you certainly needed the rest."

The persimmon
[undated]

Consider this persimmon with me—how it sits solidly on the plate, shining in a bright orange glow. It looks very hospitable and cheerful —very wholesome and promising. Its cheeks bulge with maturity, the dried up leaves in the top only increase by contrast the vivid effect of the thick, juicy skin. All this persimmon has done to acquire this blooming maturity is to sit quiet and let itself grow, fed by the sunlight —automatically receiving and assimilating its food. It gives pleasure to people almost invariably, through no exertion of its own Yet we rush around from day to day, at no time giving absolute pleasure, or ever completely acquiring perfection. But we have a priceless possession which no persimmon in its most inviting stolidity ever has known, that of moving and acting in accordance with our own free will, and so directing our actions as to give pleasure to those around us.

The year at Yenching was a hinge in my life, chiefly because it propelled me into the world. I had lived a relatively sheltered, wholly circumscribed life, unaware of the struggles going on around me. Yenching not only required that I see the world in a language and culture different from mine, but that I see the world as it was. And now I was about to face the world away from home, and alone. Yenching was a stepping stone, laid in a beautiful garden. The real path was ahead.

VIII

THE LONG ROAD TO COLLEGE

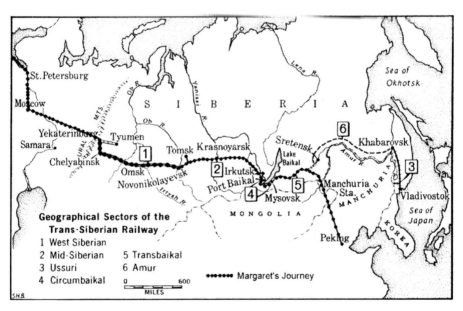

Geographical Sectors of the
Trans-Siberian Railway
1 West Siberian
2 Mid-Siberian   5 Transbaikal
3 Ussuri   6 Amur
4 Circumbaikal   ●●●●● Margaret's Journey

A t last, in 1935, the time came that most missionary children in China knew would come: I had to leave the country to go to college. From the time I started school I had known this. It was such a general expectation that it was part of being a missionary kid. I had last been in America as a six-year-old. Like the first time I went, it would be a country strange to me. Where would I buy a safety pin? We had friends on the east coast of America, and the Mission Board was in New York. But there would be no checking back for

149

parental advice or consent unless I could wait for three months for the mailed answer, by which time the relevant circumstances might have changed. Oddly, I remember no real fear or worry. I had learned how to be a foreigner, and I trusted academia. It was almost as if learning was my country.

I had applied to Wellesley College partly because it was a sister college of Yenching. Also, I thought I would be in a good position to get a scholarship, and an alumna I knew at Yenching spoke warmly of Wellesley. Mme. Chiang Kai-shek, the wife of the Generalissimo, had gone there and blazed a trail. I was interested in being a scholar. Social life was not important for me then, and I thought I would learn more and be more comfortable learning in the company of women. I had never seen the college, but beauty had become important to me at Yenching, and Wellesley was famous for its lovely campus. And it also had a lake.

At Yenching, I finished term papers, said goodbye to friends whom I almost certainly would not see again, and parted from faculty members. Some of them had known me as a little girl. In Peking, I packed my new carved Chinese chest, the standard gift for high school graduates in my family, with a caracal fur coat, also a standard gift, and the clothes I would not need until winter, and saw it crated and sent off. I was to travel with a large green baize (a rough wool cloth) suitcase and a purse.

But first it was summer. We went to Peitaiho as usual, for what would be my last summer there. I did not mind leaving Peking; Peitaiho was another matter. I loved every stone in the house, every bush around it, every breeze that blew across the porch, every glimpse of the great, fringing mountains to the north, every sharp stone on the path to the beach. The main event this summer was a play Elinor staged. There was a party after the last performance, and I was busy saying goodbye, when to the north of the house came a thump and a cry. Barbara and John had been sent upstairs to play and had been scooting balls at each other down the grooves of the corrugated tin roof of the house. Barbara, aged eight, had missed a ball and, trying to retrieve it, had gone over the edge of the roof, falling into a ditch under the eaves.

Fortunately, she had only broken a leg, but there was no infirmary or emergency service at Peitaiho. Her leg was strapped to a board and she was carried to bed. It was close to the time that I was to leave for

America, so Father and I were to take her the following day to the nearest hospital, at T'angshan, a mining city about two hours away on the railroad. That evening, with Barbara in pain and the party breaking up, I said swift goodbyes to the friends I had spent summers with, collected my summer clothes and the green suitcase, and set my face to the west, beyond the beloved mountains and the quiet beaches they overlooked.

I took a quick, early swim the next morning, kissed my sisters and brother goodbye, and boarded the train with Father and Barbara. Mother came with us to the station. She stood in the morning sunshine, waving goodbye—a tall, Scottish woman in her light summer dress, refusing the moment that had come at last, watching her first child leave for another life in another country. Barbara was a brave, plucky patient, talking cheerfully with Father on the bumpy journey, while I tried as best I could to buffer her leg against the jolting train.

T'angshan was a large, grimy mining town on the edge of a river, with a hospital run by British nursing sisters. As soon as we took Barbara into the hospital lobby, the sisters took over, walking the gurney into her room, talking with her, and settling her in bed. Then the chief nurse came out, took down some information from my father and said they would be in touch about any developments. Could the family visit, he asked. I still remember the sister's firm reply: yes, if the hospital thought it was in Barbara's interest, but anyone who planned to come should contact the hospital first, to find out. The calmness, the assurance, the confidence that one could help, and that one's help would heal, seemed like a world I would like to enter. At that moment I decided to be a British-trained nurse. Father and I left Barbara, already supplied with toys and books, and continued on a train to Peking.

Back in Peking, Father settled into his usual busy life, and I made preparations to leave. First I cabled Guy's Hospital in London to apply. Why Guy's I don't know, except that I knew it was one of the older hospitals in England, and presumably the centuries of experience would tell in the quality of training and care. I spent the next day arranging an elaborate display for the dining table—a glass lotus flower (my Chinese name, Ai Lien, meant lover of the lotus) with little presents and messages for each member of the family to be found when they returned from Peitaiho in the fall. Father was very busy, and I already missed my family.

I was to leave on the Trans-Siberian railroad with a small group from Yenching, including a young British faculty couple, Mr. and Mrs. Taylor, whose sponsors could no longer afford to keep them in China, and a young American physical education teacher returning to America after his tour of duty. Mrs. Taylor was pregnant and uneasy about the seven-day train ride, so part of my reason for going with them was to be of help. Father and I met up with the Taylors and the others in the great Peking railroad station outside the city wall, Father cheerful and competent but with just a shadow in his eyes as he helped me climb the steep steps to the carriage, the green baize suitcase firmly in my hand. I knew I would not hear from anyone in my family until I reached America.

Harbin was the exchange point from the Chinese train to the Russian Trans-Siberian train. We stayed overnight at a travelers' hotel and spent part of the next day stocking food for the seven-day trip. We were going "hard class"—bare wooden bunks, four to a compartment, to avoid the lice and other crawlies that infested upholstered cabins. We had been told not to trust the food in the dining car, so we bought wonderful foot-long Russian chocolate bars, crackers, cheese, raisins, and other staples. We knew that we could get hot water, tea, and hot roasted chickens when the train stopped at stations along the way.

We boarded the train, the engine puffing impatiently, and settled into our compartment, the Taylors in bunks on one side, an unknown Russian lady and I on the other. The compartment was stifling, the window nailed shut to prevent us from putting our heads out over bridges and construction sites.

I remember very little of the actual countryside, although Lake Baikal remains in my mind as the most sinister body of water I have ever seen. We approached it at sunset, the mountains dark around it, the train slowing as it edged the shore. I had read about the building that was going on in the area and about the working conditions of the laborers, who may have been from the notorious prison camps. The dark waters seemed to bear the burden of that knowledge.

On a journey of that length, the train became a community. Guards walked along the corridors, poking their heads into the compartments and sniffing to be sure there was no cooking going on. Kerosene stoves were not permitted, at least in hard class. For exercise, passengers rambled along the corridors, stopping to look into compartments and sometimes to visit, passing along information from car to car. Children would peer into the compartments, looking for other children to play with. The great steppes outside and the dark forests through which day after day we passed enhanced the feeling of being in a moving village. But there was danger. Sometimes it was tempting to find an open window, just to get air, even if the cinders blew into your eyes. While the train was going over a bridge one day, a passenger did put his head out, and it was shot off, the body slumping back into the compartment. After this story was passed along the corridors, parents kept their children close to their compartments for a day or two.

The tracks skirting the shore of Lake Baikal, circa 1935.

When the train stopped at stations, passengers rushed out to get hot water and look for things to eat. The stations were vivid, with Russian women in bright skirts and shawls bending over bread and chickens and pouring steaming hot water into the kettles we carried out. A short blast from the engine would send everyone rushing back to the carriages, hustling the children ahead, climbing the steep steps while guards whistled and shouted warnings. I was especially interested in these forays. Students at Yenching who were interested in the communist cause had told me that in the west of China, soldiers did not steal food, but helped the peasants produce more, which they then shared. I also knew from the newspapers that much of the rest of the world in 1935 was on the edge of starvation, yet here, in this regulated society, long wooden counters of bright fruit, vegetables, bread, and sausage stretched past the station house, and rosy-cheeked, well-nourished women were selling them to us.

Siberian station.

The Trans-Siberian at that time was still single-tracked, and occasionally we would pull onto a siding to let the train coming from Moscow go by. These stops were of indefinite length and tempted people to get out and stroll around. The guards warned us not to do this, that as soon as the approaching train cleared the track our train would start immediately with no warning, but since in that great silence it was easy to hear the approaching train, we had plenty of warning before our train started. At times like this, the physical education instructor would sprint up and down beside the train. One time he said he just couldn't stand the restrictions and he was going to run around the whole train. The guards and we tried to dissuade him, but he insisted. He was just clearing the end of the train when the Moscow train flew past, and our train started off without him. I never found out what happened, but I heard he made it back to America.

I loved the trip. I could watch for hours while the steppes and their villages, their animals and their people stretched my imagination and stirred my senses. I was profoundly moved by the great experiment Russia was making that I knew so little about, and was naive enough to believe that in these profound distances the future was incubating. The great raw cities of Irkutsk, Omsk, and Yekaterinburg loomed up from the plains and shrank again as we left them, scaffolding for a better world, I thought.

Finally we passed the Ural Mountains, with their dense forests, and descended into the Russian plain. At Moscow, I left the group. I had decided to go to America by way of the socialist countries, Russia, Finland, Sweden, and Norway, to see how those countries arranged for their citizens to eat in the depths of the world-wide depression. The hunger in China had scarred me, and I was passionate about the issue. I went immediately to the Intourist office; I had booked passage through Thomas A. Cook Travel Service and was told to be quick about reporting to Intourist. It was good advice. The state agency was expecting me and took over my schedule, showing me the approved sights, checking my housing. I remember little of Moscow except being in the fabled Red Square, with its gorgeous cathedral, and the great wall of the Kremlin.

I was impressed beyond expectation by being in an ordered society, but was unprepared to make the most of such a wonderful chance to learn. In St. Petersburg, however, coming from the less ordered museums of China, the Hermitage was one of the most transporting experiences of my life. Room after room, corridor after blazing corridor, painting after painting, the tour opened my senses to the Western canon and to its history.

I remember vividly, too, the first railway station in Finland. The official who came to check my passport emerged from a brightly colored house with flowers in front of it. He smiled and tried to speak English, laughing at his efforts and asking me to correct him. I was on my way to Sweden and could not stop, but even then I felt there was something about Finland that made sense. In Stockholm, I saw the great university, which I wandered through, again too ignorant to profit from what I was seeing. All around me were blond people, having fun, joking, so different from the stern society I thought was necessary to be sure everyone was fed.

Arriving at my hostel in Norway, I was informed that I had a message from Scotland. My grandmother's nurse wanted me to come directly to Edinburgh. My grandmother, in poor health, was now very ill. I abandoned Cook's imaginative plans for the Norwegian midnight sun, glanced wistfully down a fjord, and hurried to the Oslo dock front. As it happened, a ship was sailing for Scotland early the next morning, and I had to be at dockside to be allowed on it.

There was no hotel, just a long, low building beside the dock that looked like housing. I walked in and said I wanted a room for the night. A middle-aged woman with hair in a bun and sharp blue eyes told me that no, I didn't want a room there. I told her my story, that my grandmother was desperately ill and that I had to get to her. The woman took my money, told me to be careful, and led me down a long hall to a room at the end. As we passed along, doors opened slightly, and I heard men's voices and suddenly I realized that I was in a sailors' depot.

The woman left, wishing me a good night and my grandmother's improved health, again telling me to be careful. I closed and locked the door of my room and listened. I heard shuffling outside and more voices. I looked around to see what fortification could be arranged. The room was furnished minimally, but adequately. I pushed the washstand against the door, put the ceramic washbasin and water pitcher on it, urinated in the chamber pot and piled it on top. I heard pounding on the door. It finally gave way, and the man who entered received a shower of broken crockery and urine on his head. There was no more trouble that night, but in the morning as I was leaving, I was presented a bill for the crockery. I paid with a light heart and went down the gangplank to the little coal steamer that took me over the sea to Scotland. It seemed to me that the crew kept their distance, but the coffee was wonderful and the salmon delicious.

My grandmother's nurse met me at the rail station in Edinburgh when I arrived, her brown eyes bright and welcoming as she searched for the American girl she had never met. She was short and friendly, Scottish and competent. I was aware of being tall and anxious, American, and tired from the long trip. There was something about being in Scotland that was reassuring. This dour, rocky country, which had provided half my ancestors and a wonderful school years before, seemed instantly hospitable. Nurse reassured me about my grandmother's health; the telegram had been sent during a downturn from which she had recovered, but not in time to reach me before I changed my plans.

My grandmother, when I reached her, was sitting up in bed, lacy bed-jacket around her shoulders, her hair glistening white, her eyes blue and just this side of severe, welcoming me in the Scottish upper-class burr that I sometimes heard in my mother's voice. She was eager for news of the family, asked about my plans, and tried to bridge the five-year gap since I had seen her in China at my brother's christening.

Everything in the apartment told of her life as the wife of a famous minister: the silver trowel that had been used to start the foundation of a church in the west of Scotland named for him, the silver tray inscribed with her name from "a grateful congregation," the beautiful Scottish shawls, the gleaming tablecloth, old heavy forks and knives, and the books my grandfather had written, hard-bound, in sober colors with gilt lettering, dust-free, lined up on the shelves behind her.

My Scottish grandmother, Ellin Kelman.

I went for walks with Nurse. We went to the neighborhoods the Kelmans had lived in and went inside St. George's Free Church where Dr. Kelman had preached on Sunday mornings and given lectures

Sunday evenings on poets and authors to the young medical students who lined up on the sidewalks to hear him. At my grandmother's insistence, we shopped for a beautiful blue wool suit that for many years afterwards was the outfit I would wear for occasions. Soon it was time to move on. I had never been close to my Scottish grandmother, but I was sad to leave her, knowing I would not see her again. Nurse was firm on that point, walking me to the station as if behind a coffin.

While in China, I had heard about the "Red Dean," Dean of Canterbury Cathedral, Dr. Hewlett Johnson, and had written asking him if I could pay him a visit when I was in London. I was ardent for socialism and wondered what its support would be high in the Church of England. I had not left time to hear from him, so called him from my hostel. He answered the phone, said he would be glad to meet anyone interested in social justice, and suggested a train time convenient to him.

I rode through the beautiful English countryside in a state of excitement. Dr. Johnson was on the platform, in full regalia, gray spats and all. We settled on the last train of the day for the return to London. He took me through the cathedral and its gardens, naming the flowers along with the legends of the cathedral and some of its history. We had just started in on socialism when I realized I was going to miss my train to London. "No matter, my dear," he said, "I have an extra pair of pyjamas you may borrow."

The evening came on, and we went down to the twelfth-century kitchen, with its great brick and clay oven and hood, where he made supper. We talked about socialism and its problems, the cathedral's aristocratic old bells tolling for evensong above us. I had to leave before breakfast to make the appointment at Guy's Hospital. The Dean rose and took me to the station, cheering me on to "see what you can do about that capitalist nation of yours."

In London, at Guy's Hospital, I walked in to the reception area, a large, dark place, with a registration desk to the right. In front of me, a number of young women in blue striped uniforms with black stockings were scrubbing the eighteenth-century cobblestones that formed the floor. I approached the Sister at the desk, told her who I was, and that I was hoping my cable had been favorably received. She looked up at me briskly and said that they had been waiting for me, that they were always glad to have people from other countries come, and gave me a form to fill out. I thanked her, thrilled that I was considered acceptable, and then asked who the young women were that were working on the floor. "That's our first year class," she said cheerfully. I handed the form back to her, thanked her for her welcome, and said that I had probably better keep my original plan of going to college in America. She smiled and said that if that was my reaction I would probably not fit in at Guy's and wished me well.

I hurried to the ship for New York, and, during the voyage across a wonderfully calm Atlantic, walked the decks trying to revive my academic goals. So I was not the ministering angel I had been so eager to be; I was to be a musty scholar, mistress of some yet unknown subject, maybe teaching other musty scholars. The immediate world of a white crisp nursing uniform, with its alluring head-dress, moving among suffering human beings, healing as I went, doctors approving my skills, sank into the waves that splashed against the sides of the ship.

Our family had a wonderful friend in New York, Mrs. Kate Auchincloss, a parishioner at the Fifth Avenue Presbyterian Church. She lived on East 69th Street, in a three-story brownstone that had an elevator and a greenhouse and is the place I locate every American Victorian novel. On the day my ship docked, she was in Connecticut but had arranged for her chauffeur to meet the ship. I walked down the gangplank, careful to look my very best, glancing about for anyone who would claim me. An elegantly uniformed man came up and asked if I was Miss Hayes, and upon my eager reply welcomed me, then looked at my green baize suitcase asking somewhat hesitantly if it was mine. I claimed it, realizing how different it was from what he would be comfortable carrying, and said I had been carrying it all the way from China and would like to continue to do so.

Relieved, he agreed, and we rode in Mrs. Auchincloss's Rolls Royce to her house. There I was warmly welcomed by a maid and given a room to myself on the second floor. There was supper in an elegant dining room where the leaves from the greenhouse trees threw sunset-lit patterns on the windows. The maid told me that I should put outside my door things I needed washed and they would be ready the following day, and then she wished me goodnight. Aunt Kate called, welcoming me and asking if all was well. I felt as if I had arrived in a novel. I put my suitcase with most of its contents outside my door and fell asleep. It was gone in the morning and never came back. Nor did its contents.

When Aunt Kate arrived, full of welcome and eager for news, we had a wonderful time together. But by teatime, when my clothes had still not appeared, I was concerned about what I would wear the next day. She went to consult the maids and came back to say, cheerfully, that we would go to Bloomingdale's the next day to replace the clothes. There would be a new suitcase too. She explained that the clothing made in China had not "borne the journey well," and the maids couldn't be asked to wash them. The suitcase had also not borne the journey well and, in her courteous words, was "beyond repair." She and I went to Bloomingdale's the next day. The Mission Board provided $100 to outfit missionaries' children for school when they first arrived. I had brought the list that Wellesley required: the gym outfit of a navy wool tunic and bloomers cost $60. Aunt Kate arranged for a basic wardrobe, one of each kind of clothing, and another suitcase, acceding to my proud claim that I could take care of the rest with my $40.

The next day I left for Wellesley. Looking back over the seventy years since that extraordinary welcome, I marvel at the simplicity of its elegance, the warmth in that tall, stately stone house, the immediacy of Mrs. Auchincloss's help and its kind restraint. It framed the country for me until I could move into it and make a life of my own in it, and it left me with the memory of a friend whose cheerful and discriminating generosity opened my way like a golden gate.

IX

WELLESLEY

It was the end of one long journey and the beginning of a longer one. In Grand Central Station in New York I joined a large group of excited women boarding the "Wellesley train." I immediately became aware that I had a lot to learn at college that had nothing to do with the academic curriculum. I sat silently in the carriage while the other passengers, most of whom were returning to school, caught up with each other about what they had done during the summer. "It was wonderful! I went to Italy with my parents, and I met this Italian man...." "Mom and I were shopping in the city for weeks. The ball will be on December 16th." The ball? She was to be a New York debutante that winter. "I don't know if Rita will make it back this year. Her family's had a hard time; her father lost his job. So I don't know who my roommate will be."

As the train rode through the unfolding fire of my first New England fall, I was torn between the glory of the countryside and the equally absorbing conversation inside the railway car. I listened intently. This was to be my world for the next three years. I had been in America just two days, escorted about in a chauffeured car. Now I was on my own, equipped only with fluent Chinese.

There were others in the railway car also coming to Wellesley for the first time. They were also primarily listening, but they had been part of the culture and mastered it. They knew the references being made, they had done well, they knew the clothes to wear. I had been twice around the world, with four years of Latin, and I didn't know where to buy a safety pin. During the ride, someone turned to me and asked where I was from. I did not say Peking. Somehow I sensed that if I said I was from China, I wouldn't hear what I desperately needed to hear: what it was like where she was from. So I said "New York." After all, I was born there. She whipped back, "Oh, which borough?" Which indeed? I grasped to remember my birth certificate—I had had to show it for my passport in Peking—and answered, "Manhattan." She said, "That's nice," welcomed me to the college, and turned back to her friends. Whew! A close call.

I remember that vans met us at the Wellesley station, but they were just for luggage, of which there was plenty. With the others, I walked the two miles to a college I had never seen. As I glimpsed the college tower above the trees, I wondered how I was going to discover what the college would mean to me from the chatter I had heard on the train.

Having applied late, I was assigned to a room meant for two that had only one person in it. Ruth Osterman was already there when I arrived. She was slender, lovely, with dark hair and dark brown eyes, and welcomed me cautiously, as new roommates reasonably do. The room was on the third floor of Severance Hall, one of a group of older buildings set on a low rise near the lake, and the view out of the gabled window was of a grassy lawn and the library beyond it. I was glad the library was visible. It somehow grounded this whole fairy tale. There were books in there that I did know about, chairs and tables I knew how to use.

Ruth and I talked briefly while I unpacked. This was her second year at college. At the end of the year, I learned she was Jewish. Much later I learned of Wellesley's quota system, now abandoned. Was that why there was no roommate for Ruth until I arrived?

Tuition and board at Wellesley cost six hundred dollars in 1935, one half of my father's salary. Missionary children were sent twenty-five dollars a month from the Presbyterian Board of Foreign Missions for clothing and sundries, and there was in our family a mysterious trust fund in Hartford that mother would mention in hushed tones. Everyone in our family knew about it. My mother's father never believed his daughter would be able to handle money, and had established a trust fund for her that she could not access directly. The chief trustee was Francis Sayre, son-in-law of President Wilson and then Assistant Secretary of State, a kind and gentle man to whom we could apply in case of emergency. I had one set of clothes, the blue wool suit, and a caracal fur coat in a Chinese chest, along with assorted winter clothing made from pictures in the Sears catalog. I felt ready for Wellesley.

Since I was transferring into the sophomore class, registration was relatively easy, and I was not required to go through freshman orientation. Unwisely, it turned out. I would have found out where to buy safety pins, for one thing. I was to take Introduction to the Study of the Bible, then required of all freshman students, Introduction to Philosophy, required of all sophomores, Ancient History, and Introduction to Physics. I also discovered the Student Aid office, where students and alumnae donated clothes. As winter came on, the clothes in the chest were adequate only for a religiously circumscribed life, and, in a Wellesley setting, dowdy. Moreover, the clothes no longer fit. Missionary children coming to school in the U.S. swiftly gained weight. The food was so much richer in America, the eggs larger, the bread more serious. Student Aid became a way to transform myself into an apparent American.

Just before classes started, I got a notice that my Chinese chest had come. It had been crated, and for a long time I didn't open it. I didn't want to be the girl from China. But after the cold weather forced the caracal coat into the open, the secret was out. In a few months, letters would come with Chinese stamps, so there was no way I could hide it. I became the girl from China.

At last classes started, and I could be just a student and not this timid girl who had yet to taste her first grilled cheese sandwich and milk shake on the way to the Saturday movies in Natick, the picture of college social life in the Saturday Evening Post I had read about in Peking. But the big change was ahead.

*   *   *

My parents had not been strict about the authorship of the Bible; it was certainly required reading at home, as it was everywhere else in my childhood. However, I vaguely assumed it had a single author, or editor, and it was a jolt in Ms. Louise Pettibone Smith's level, historical-method Bible Study class to learn of the varied sources of a text bound in black leather, on the second page of which the translators wished to King James the Sixth, "grace, mercy, and peace." The old was becoming new, and I did the class assignments recognizing "J" and "P" and their styles, the reasons for Deuteronomy and Leviticus, and some of the prophets' backgrounds.

But it was Greek philosophy, specifically Heraclitus, which shattered my faith, that sturdy faith that I had carried like clothing. Our first text was a small buff-colored cloth-bound book with brown lettering, *Fragments of Greek Philosophy*. As someone historically inclined, I was intrigued by people whose thoughts were so important that a sentence or two was worth our study over two thousand years later. Heraclitus lived in the sixth century BCE and was known as an enigmatic philosopher, widely quoted by philosophers who followed him. He was vaguely known and sometimes only by reference, but he is the author of a sentence that changed my life: "You cannot step twice into the same river, for fresh waters are ever flowing in upon you." It knocked everything over. Life as liquid sequence?

Winter view of the Wellesley campus.

The Bible as I had known it was slowly unraveling in one classroom, and the feeling that somewhere there was an orderly, institutionally sanctioned cosmogony—one my parents had given their lives to and had brought us up in—was in another classroom evanescing, simply the water of the moment. The vision that all life is flux strongly influenced Plato and other philosophers to the present day. For me, there was now no room for the concept of a stable and powerful God. A verse from my favorite hymn, which hitherto steadied my doubt, now lost its power:

> Before the hills in order stood
> Or earth received her frame
> From everlasting Thou art God
> To endless years the same.

My philosophy teacher, Virginia Onderdonk, was brilliant, clear, and organized. However reluctant I was to abandon my faith, there was no way to avoid the implications of what she taught. The intellectual and spiritual structure of my life fell as completely as the fragmented pillars lying on the ground in Greece that illustrated our text.

It happened, however, over time. I went daily to morning chapel. Although the center did not hold, I needed the walls, the scaffolding, and above all the music. The Scottish psalms, especially, held me steady. In the divided psalter of my mother's childhood, and a staple on our piano rack, the psalms, converted into various metric schemes, were printed on the lower pages of the book. Tunes were separately printed on the upper pages, so that a psalm could be matched to any tune with the appropriate meter. The Twenty-third Psalm, sung to the tune "Kilmarnock," was a favorite in our house.

> The Lord's my shepherd, I'll not want,
> He makes me down to lie
> In pastures green: he leadeth me
> The quiet waters by.

And now those quiet waters were a river. However hard I tried to disbelieve hymns, to refuse their false comfort, they would not abandon me, and they are still with me, but as Bach is with me, or requiems. Before sophomore year there had been no alternative. Now there was a rational, questioning, fluid approach to everything, it seemed. A confining wall had tumbled.

I didn't approach the college chaplain, a kindly and learned man. It seemed too personal a subject for a stranger, and I had somehow known all along that the spiritual universe and its population made no sense to me, but the collapse coming from great thinkers and scholars was a blow.

Then there was physics, another mystery. It was taught by Ms. McDowell, white-haired, elegant, who stood in a sharply tiered lecture hall in front of a large blackboard and, with a few lines and arrows, opened up yet another world. She had a dry, this-is-what-this-subject-is-about delivery, which I clung to as one would a board at sea. She was also one of the professors who invited students to her home on Sunday evenings and continued to contact them years after graduation.

Introductory physics was a required course, so she could invite only a few of us into her home each year, but she recognized a drifter and drew me in. It was in her class that I became aware of how sparse my reference points in this society were. She was illustrating some principle by saying it was like the changing noise a car horn makes when it goes past you. No road I remembered was sufficiently paved so that a car could go fast enough to make that sound.

The professor of ancient history, Ms. Carr, was tall, dark-haired, and intense. She wanted us above all to think. Think about what those Roman farmers felt as they lost their lands to pay taxes to emperors. I was afire for them; I had grown up in a land where exactly the same thing had gone on since long before the Romans lost their hectares. I decided to major in history.

I wanted to talk to someone about all these changes, but the only people who would understand would be others who had the same experience, and there were no others at Wellesley that year. Much has been written about children growing up in lands other than their own, and names have been attached to them—third-culture kids, global nomads, ex-pats and the like—but I thought of myself as always having been between. Between parents, between cultures, between places. Between was not unpleasant, and there were even advantages, but it was difficult having no base where you could relax.

In America, there was no home to go to for vacation. In friends' houses, however kind, one was always still a guest. I didn't know where to go for counsel, comfort, or consent. I looked and sounded like others around me, but had no clue about how to move about autonomously in a secular society, ignorant of movies, radio programs, social norms and expectations.

I applied for jobs. Twenty-five dollars a month, my mission stipend, even in those days did not furnish a person. I got a job almost immediately selling Amana upright refrigerators to dormitory residents. We had never had refrigerators at home. I knew nothing about them, and selling full-size refrigerators to women who had no use for them in a dormitory was ridiculous. No wonder the job was available. But I plugged away, going from room to room through the three dormitories in my territory. I sold not one.

I applied for employment again, and the job I finally got I might have designed. It was my habit, when I finished studying in the library at night, to push my chair back to the table purely out of the reverence for learning my China background had made indelible. There was no virtue in it, just the Confucian way—learning is sacred and the place of learning therefore hallowed, or at least reverently maintained. A college librarian noticed me and asked if I would like a job doing just that, pushing the chairs back each night. People would leave chairs at various angles, sometimes pushing them off to a window or to the stacks. Would I come in daily when the library closed and put the chairs back where they belonged? Yes. I had a library job all three years I was at Wellesley. I moved to shelving books. And in my senior year I cataloged them.

I also signed up for crew. Thanks to my father, I knew I had the shoulders for it, but I was mainly lured by the beauty of water. Instead of the willow branches that brushed the Yenching lake, brilliant-hued trees and low undergrowth lined the edge of Lake Cabana. One rowed through their reflection, the tapestry of autumn. As the leaves began to fall, the oars, dipping into the water, would lift these fallen leaves into the sunlight, for their farewell to the year. I loved being part of a group that had to act precisely, backs leaning together, oars going in at the same time, shipped together, and placed exactly in tiers in the boat house, the water slapping freely in the dock, freed of our invasion.

The winter sport I chose was modern dance, almost the most useful course I took at college, because the first thing we learned was how to fall, a handy skill for the rest of my life. Some of my delight in modern dance was the flinging of the body into positions I hadn't seen before. It was like defying all the correct poses of the past, feeling the floor and the air almost as extensions of my body, inviting experiment and abandon. And always there was tennis, which I did not sign up for. I wanted to learn new things, and tennis was already in my blood. However, whenever a court, an opponent, and a set of white balls converged, I played pickup games, invoking memories of the sea, the skies, and the mountains that were the setting of our court in Peitaiho.

Surprisingly, I was never homesick at college. The newness of it all absorbed me. But as the first Christmas away from home approached, I began to wish my family were in America. Everyone else, it seemed, was going home, and there were invitations. But it had been arranged that I would spend Christmas with family friends of ours who had been missionaries in China. My hostess, a lovely, warm, and merry woman, was a close friend of my mother; there were four children, two near my age. I arrived with gifts and gratitude and immediately set about trying to be useful. We had been raised to think we had value for people only if we were helpful to them. So if during a meal something needed to be gotten from the kitchen, I leapt to get it. Sturdily I volunteered for every possible job, forestalling anyone who might be planning to do it. Finally, after a week it was time to go back to college. As my hostess said goodbye, she told me that I had ruined their holiday by being so eager to help. Perhaps if she had drawn me aside when it was beginning to affect the family, I could have learned more about how to be an American. As it was, I was devastated and left profoundly unsure of myself.

College was now my refuge. I returned with a fierce determination to "make it" somewhere in my new world, which for me meant doing very well academically. My roommate, when I contacted her many years later, remembered my setting back the room clock at midnight on Saturday night so that I wouldn't be studying on Sunday. I had a scholarship to work for, one that would make it possible to move next year to another dormitory where the boarding fee was reduced by jobs. The women on my floor gave me a group gift for Christmas, a woolen hat, scarf and gloves in a lovely dark green with yellow bands, which eased the sting of the vacation and went with me like a friend to classes and to the library. I listened, mesmerized, to stories of others' vacations, trips, debutante balls, with a sense of participation. I had made it through the first Christmas without my family, and now all these new and glittering scenes were laid out, like a slide show, for me to imagine and imagine myself in. I was learning what my world was to be.

I was oblivious to what was happening outside my world, the rise of Hitler, laws against Jews.

Spring vacation came, and I was to be a guest again. Francis Sayre invited me to Washington to be with him and his family, which included his daughter, Eleanor, who quickly became a friend. I met him in his quiet, wood-paneled office in what is now the Executive Office Building, then the old War, State, and Navy Building. He rose from his desk and greeted me affectionately, sunlight on the dark red draped windows behind him, Pennsylvania Avenue traffic moving below. This was the United States government! President Franklin D. Roosevelt, in his wheel chair, was next door! In Peking, the marines and the embassy were the symbols of the US government. Greeting this warm, friendly Assistant Secretary of State we called Uncle Frank, I instantly became a Democrat, and have been one ever since.

Mr. Sayre took me with his family to see a play based on the trial of Sacco and Vanzetti. In the dark theater, fresh from the hidden tribunals of China, I thought, "My country executes people too." I had heard only vaguely about their trial and executions, and I suddenly became aware of how little I knew about my country and what had gone on in the last decade. We had, of course, been acutely aware of the Great Depression. Many missionary families had to leave China in 1929 because their churches could no longer support them. Now, in the Washington spring time, I became absorbed in knowing the country, doing the appropriate thing, wearing the right clothes, taking in the sounds and smells and surfaces—American wood panels, American furnishings, American linens.

Government itself was new to me. In the chaotic twenties in China, warlords ruled. Even after Chiang Kai Shek restored order, the country was torn by the growing Communist movement along the western mountains, while Japan menaced from the north. As missionaries, in spite of my father's friendships with Chinese and American officials, we were concerned chiefly with the kingdom of God and related to the kingdoms of men only in so far as they might promote or preserve God's prospects. And, shamefully, we did not live under Chinese law.

Mother was disinterested in American politics, and Father was busy with political problems Christian students might be involved in. Franklin Roosevelt's election first stirred my interest in politics, but it wasn't until I arrived in America that I became aware that problems or programs had a political base rather than a purely social or moral one.

I finished the first year at Wellesley academically exhilarated, spiritually adrift, and registered eagerly for my junior year, already admitted to the scholarship dormitory. After a job at a summer camp washing dishes, I happily greeted my family who had come for their furlough year. Father registered for a year's study at Yale Divinity School, and Elinor entered Wellesley, while my mother and the three younger children took a house in Cambridge in order to be near Elinor and me.

Shakespeare Society cottage.

I went joyfully back to college, excited by the philosophy class taught by a legendary teacher, Dr. Procter, and by an invitation to join the Shakespeare Society, one of the social clubs at Wellesley. These were technically based on interests and were expected to offer programs during the year, but they also had cachet in the college community. That year, the Shakespeare Society claimed many of the campus leaders and was a vibrant, engaged group of people. On the steps of the chapel in bright morning sunlight I watched its president approach me with the red rose and society pin that informed me I had been elected a member. I was stunned. I had not applied. I wrote in my diary: "I can't imagine how it happened. That grand bunch of girls—and me?"

Wellesley itself was buzzing with energy. There was a new president, Mildred McAfee, later to become head of the WAVES. Brimming with new ideas and vigor, she had a brisk, friendly way about her. A story sums it up. Seeing a burdened student on a campus road, Miss McAfee stopped her car to offer a ride. The student got in, saying that this was the most honored day of her life, upon which Miss McAfee whipped back, "You've never been in a Chevy before?" At my graduation ceremony, she warned us that though we were the salt of the earth, nothing damages a dish more than too much salt.

In the scholarship dormitory I met new friends, and chose a job polishing silver and putting away linens in order to be free to see my family during weekends. The school year was in full and vigorous swing, my second New England autumn broke out its flaming colors, and I began to feel the seduction of a career in history.

But midway through October, Elinor and I went to Cambridge for a weekend visit. I found my mother sobbing in bed. Father, who had started classes at Yale Divinity School, had also come for a family weekend. With the three younger children, we stood around Mother's bed, trying to understand what was going on, but she had no answers beyond turning her head into the pillows and crying even more. Over the weekend, Father, Elinor, and I discussed what to try. Through the Mission we arranged for someone to come the next week to manage the household while we went back to school. Mother's condition did not improve, and by the end of the month it was clear she would need intensive care. I struggled with the decision to drop out of college. By early November I moved to Cambridge, and Mother went to what was then called an asylum. As my sister Barbara noted in a memoir, for her my decision delivered "mixed results."

For one thing, brought up with servants, I had never kept house or even known anything about it. The house was a big, wooden, three-story New England cake on a corner lot, painted three different colors on the outside. A coal-fired furnace growled underneath; there were an ancient gas stove, an icebox, and four bedrooms. Janet, now 13, was in junior high school, Barbara was in elementary school, and John was in kindergarten in yet another school. I hadn't a clue. By now, I knew where to buy safety pins, but I had no idea of how to keep a household together. A Mrs. Crowley came sporadically for cleaning. The furnace challenged me every morning and frequently won, plunging the house into the New England winter, requiring large supplies of Vicks VapoRub. John and Barbara had great fun playing with a mysterious chain that hung on a pulley in the dining room, until it was discovered that it governed the furnace below, which then required hours of relighting. Groceries were delivered by a grocery boy with whom I fell

22 Linnean Street, Cambridge, Christmas 1936. Left to right: Janet, Elinor, me, Kipper (the dog), Mother, Barbara, John, and Father.

briefly in love, a charming high school dropout who introduced me to secluded spots around Cambridge. We got a dog, Kippy. I learned to drive the British car we had been given, and on weekends drove down to New Haven to get my father, the dog sitting in the left front seat, prompting lively comments from other drivers and from the Massachusetts State Police. The year rolled on with its share of crises, birthdays, holidays, and finally Christmas, when my mother came home, and we were all together again. I briefly considered going back to Wellesley for the second semester, but it was clear that my mother was not well enough to take over, and I registered for a course at Radcliffe.

There were adventures. I had never had a stable relationship with a house key, and we would all too often have to devise ways to get in, the favorite one being to have Janet's boyfriends scale the front of the house, climb in through Janet's second-floor window, and let us in, to general merriment and cookies. My attitude toward keys resulted in the car being frequently unavailable at crucial times, and that led to unplanned relationships with neighbors, with, again, mixed results.

But my most difficult problem had nothing to do with the house.

> [From my diary] Why is there no love between Mother and Daddy? Our home's going to go onto the rocks. Oh God, or goodness, or whatever there is, grant that we may by love and faith knit Mother and Daddy more closely...It's all so bitter, so full of quarrels and little irritations and over it all the sense of disunity, of constant friction.

Was this why Mother was crying?

I don't remember the course I registered for at Radcliffe, but while scanning the catalog, I noticed a philosophy course being given at Harvard by Alfred North Whitehead, author of *Adventures of Ideas*, among many other books. I had read the book, and decided to ask him if I could audit the course. I went for an interview. He was a thickset man with dark eyes and a bald head, dressed like the English professor he was. He heard my request and then answered that he regretted that his position at Harvard prevented him from giving a lecture to a woman, but he added that his eyesight was very poor. If I wore a white blouse and a black tie and sat in the last tier of seats, he would not be able to distinguish between a man and a woman, and I was in.

I still have notes from Professor Whitehead's class, some of them undecipherable and others beyond comprehension. I struggled as hard with his course as I did with the furnace. I never fully succeeded with either, but Dr. Whitehead's course was the easier to understand.

Finally it was summer and time for the family to go back to China. Elinor and I waved them goodbye—suddenly, it seemed—on the train platform in Buffalo where our family had gone to see Niagara Falls. I rode the bus back to Boston and to my job as a waitress at The Snuggery in Cambridge, relief mixed with longing for them. Saying goodbye was easier to bear than knowing they were leaving the continent; the sailing date of the ship that would take them back across the Pacific remained in my mind. But the year of trying to hold together a household and a family was over, and my life was again my own.

I had chosen for my major medieval history, and I was happy. I was doubly entranced by the field. The world of peasants and animals pulling carts, of hovels and palaces, of unpaved streets and walled

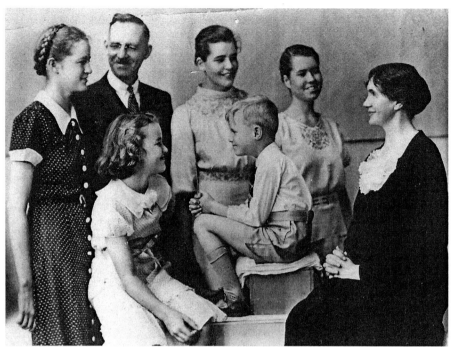

July 4, 1937, Cambridge, just before the family (except for Elinor and me) left for China. Back row, left to right: Janet, Father, Elinor, and me. Front row: Barbara, John, and Mother.

towns was familiar to me. I had grown up in a country of many dialects, and medieval Latin, with its infinite variations, beckoned me as the street language of Peking had livened my life and tongue. Also, having lost a personal God, I was fascinated by the idea of a unified religious governance on earth, the Holy Roman Empire, the City of God. In the spring of my junior year I had the option of enrolling in the honors program, which required an original piece of research, acceptable to a committee of professors from Wellesley and other nearby colleges, and providing additional credits. I enrolled in it for no other reason, however, than that I was terrified of the other option available for graduation, the formidable General Examination, which covered all the major subjects studied at Wellesley. Having missed the first year, I didn't think I knew enough to pass it. My childhood had been almost entirely free of competition. Father's job was ordained by God, and secure. We were likewise sure of everything except for our fate after death, and that wasn't decided competitively. So I chose a field that I knew something about, and burrowed happily into the thirteenth-century text of Marsilius of Padua's *De Civitate Dei*, essentially an essay on the application of Christianity to political life. I had set my course, strengthened by my election at the end of the academic year to Phi Beta Kappa. I was so excited that for the first and only time I cabled home. My mother received the cable. According to her, she relayed the message to my father, who was coming down the front stairs. "Margaret?" he said, stopping briefly. "There must be some mistake." Looking back, it is probable that he simply didn't expect women to succeed, but at the time it stung, partly because I was so eager to keep my scholarship in order to be no burden to my family. And why had she told me?

The wonderful Wellesley curriculum rolled on, and suddenly it was summer. Suddenly, too, that summer offered up a part of America I had not seen, although I knew about it from novels. I signed on as one of the maids at Randhill Inn, on Cape Cod, a complex of cottages and a hotel. Each staff member had responsibility for a given number of cottages, and since we lived on the site we were on call twenty-four hours for maid service, as well as maintenance: cleaning the rooms and bathrooms, making beds, and the like. I took it because, with Peitaiho as my image of summer, it gave access to a beach and sunrise over an eastern sea. The first night I was on duty I was called about midnight to clean up vomit in the bathroom of one of my cottages. I hadn't seen people wholly drunk before and I was sad. I didn't mind the mess—I was used to cleaning up messes. I just didn't like seeing people not in control. At college, drinking on campus was forbidden. The house mother presided at the front door, sniffing, as we came back from late dates or from the movies. Mornings at Randhill Inn, I trotted back and forth from the central kitchen to my cottages with assorted remedies for the night before. Only the rich, in 1937, could afford Randhill Inn. I was grateful for an introduction to that lifestyle as an observer. I went back to college, to my Remington Rand typewriter, sobered about my country, ready to become knowledgeable about the rowdy inns of the middle ages, and scared witless of drinking.

Senior year was a delight. My scholarship required that I read weekly to a blind Harvard student, Don, who lived in Eliot Hall, and to whom I read his college assignments and the notes for the Boston Symphony concerts we attended. He was handsome and merry, and of course I fell in love. He came to my senior prom with his seeing-eye dog, whom he could not persuade to leave him when the dancing began and whose enthusiastic tail-wagging caught many a taffeta skirt.

At the end of the year, standing at Back Bay station in Boston, waiting for the last train to Wellesley, I asked if he would marry me. He smiled and said it was a lovely offer, but he had promised his mother he would never marry a sighted person.

Our association had other advantages. Eliot Hall was not far from Widener Library at Harvard, where I found much of the material for my honors thesis. Marsilius of Padua was a physician and philosopher who in the early 14th century published a tract, *Defensor Pacis*, arguing that the people were the source of power in both church and state. This challenged the prevailing doctrine that all power, especially in the church, came from God, and moved on to claim that the secular power was over the church also. I was fascinated by this plucky rebel, and was directed to another paper in his name, *De Civitate Dei* (*City of God*). I worked for months examining the document, relating it to the time and to other works of his, and finally presented it to a joint committee of Wellesley and Harvard faculty. It was accepted and credit duly given. A few days later, a member of the committee called me and courteously informed me that it should come to my notice that Marsilius' *City of God* had recently been discovered to be a 17th-century forgery. I still got the credit, however spuriously. The chief value of taking honors, then, was actually that I had had to take an additional course to complete the required number of credits for graduation. The only one that I could arrange for was on urban architecture, and as a result to this day I am fascinated by the fenestration of any city I visit.

Finally I graduated. None of my applications for scholarships for graduate work was accepted. Although by now an excellent waitress and thus able to earn a living, I went home to China, diploma in hand. Elinor had had a difficult time at college; she failed her courses, or, as the wonderful President McAfee put it, she was too creative for Wellesley. My uncle took my parents' place at graduation; he accompanied us to the Wellesley railroad station, and we left it behind us, eager to be home in China.

X

BACK TO AN OCCUPIED CAPITAL

In June of 1939, Elinor and I stood on the Wellesley railway station platform, two great continents before us. Elinor was adrift in her life; she had left Wellesley and had no firm plans for continuing college. I had enjoyed college: the contact with good minds, the association with friends and faculty, the lectures, concerts, sports, and the whole world of privilege and work that balanced the long hours of study. I had worn a rich tapestry gown, and now it was time to go back to the cotton clothes of home in China. I had fallen in love with a blind man, who had searched for my hand on our last walk together, but who did not want to marry me. Time to change continents.

We crossed North America by train, changing at Chicago and St. Louis, before transferring to the Canadian Pacific at St. Paul and marveling through the Canadian Rockies to Vancouver. There we boarded a trans-Pacific ship, survived a ground swell off the Aleutian Islands, and were met by my father in Yokohama. As always with my father, there was suspense. He had cabled, "If not Yokohama, then Kobe." This was insufficient notice for the immigration authorities in Japan; they had to know before we reached Yokohama whether or not we were getting off there. We told them we didn't know, and showed them the cable. After considerable discussion, and relying heavily on our transient status, they agreed to let us debark if this rather casual father should appear. He did, and a sympathetic steward helped us off the ship.

We settled in to a few days of seeing, and trying to understand, what we could of the Island Kingdom. Japan was amazingly beautiful, gracious, green and exquisite. Everywhere we were treated with courtesy and thoughtfulness. Leaving, the journey across the Sea of Japan was like sailing in a silken sunset. The world seemed made of clear, quiet color, and we were part of its gleaming texture. Slowly the Japanese islands slipped behind us into the night, and the next morning we were out in the open sea again, on our way to Tsingtao, in China, where we met my father's parents, and caught up with the typhoon we had missed on the way there.

We then went north by boat to Dairen and by train to Peitaiho, the summer resort that was more home than any other place. As the land began to look familiar and the mountains began to take the profile we had remembered, and as we began to hear and to see the sort of people among whom we had grown up, I realized how much a part of China I was—an inalienable part forever. Now, in the shining morning, we were going home. Finally the train crawled around the last corner to Peitaiho Junction, and there the family was, every single one of them, waving their arms, and in danger of derailing the train. At last came the wonderful time when we all got on to the little local train that ran from the Junction to the Beach, and just sat and looked at each other and began to find where we had been the last two years, and where we were now, and how surprisingly little we had grown apart. There were daily swims, various games of tennis, long cool evenings with moonlight on the water, lights across the bay, and quiet talking on the porch. I was leaving soon for Peking and my job as assistant to the Dean of Women at Yenching University, where I had studied my first year in college. Elinor would be leaving later to finish her degree at Wayne State University in Detroit. As it turned out, it was the last summer we were together as a family.

1939 was a terrible year for floods. I was fortunate to get away from Peitaiho on the last train that came through before the appalling Hai River flood in Tientsin. The trip was a harrowing one; dead bodies of people and animals bumped against the slow-moving cars. The train was so full that those standing could not even stand erect. People with tickets could get on the train; hundreds of refugees were turned away, perhaps to drown. Used to Boston subway crowds, I marveled at the way these Chinese took the crowding—no grumbling, jokes the whole way.

Peking was hot, very hot. Soon the railway line was cut, and it was difficult to get food. But I became aware of other changes. During the last year at college I had been absorbed by my work, and noted only occasionally in my daily diary the somber news from Europe. I hadn't even paid much attention to the Japanese occupation of my home city. It was thus a shock to return to an occupied Peking. The city as I had known it in the early 1930s was proudly self-conscious—its residents were *Beijing ren* (Peking people), its public buildings the center of government of a proud nation. Now, disembarking from the train, I was greeted by small men, who ushered me into a smoke-filled office, and in heavily accented speech, asked for my passport. I was accustomed to the humorous, occasionally deferent courtesy of Chinese officials, usually slender, and in dark-blue, natty uniforms who recognized a Mandarin accent as the sign of a native, and the insolence of Japanese officials was a shock. Far worse, however, was the way they treated their Chinese employees, slapping them about, occasionally kicking them if they didn't move fast enough. Sometimes they would summon rickshaws, often for long rides, then refuse to pay, and kick the rickshawmen in the shins if they protested. Coming directly from the gracious and almost deferent hospitality in their native land, I was amazed at the changes the position of being conquerors produced.

In August I moved to the campus and to my job, which was to be in charge of dormitory administration, to be available for secretarial work for the Dean, and for anything else that she wanted. Ms. Speer was tall, erect, gray-haired, the daughter of a well-known China scholar, and beloved. Her work was concerned almost entirely with

The Two Sisters: I lived in the building on the left and worked in the Dean of Women's office on right.

either making decisions or giving advice, both of which were likely to be final. Yet after a day of that she was the best sort of company at tea or dinner. I loved her and was excited to be working for her.

The college year began to unfold. Gradually faculty members did and didn't arrive, houses were assigned, and I was to live in one of the dormitories. Suddenly students began to pour in—students and students and more students. We had accepted the entire waiting list which brought our enrollment up to the highest it had ever been—292. The maximum capacity of the dormitories was 270, so even though thirteen students lived outside and three left, all of them couldn't fit in. We turned storerooms into bedrooms, and found old pieces of furniture. I moved out to live with four young Chinese instructors, and finally we managed to squeeze in all those who had applied. I was excited. I had decided on an academic career, and the crush meant that women in "my" country were anxious to learn.

I moved to the upper part of a building across from my office, one of two buildings known as the Two Sisters. The five of us set up a household in Chinese style with a cook. We ate Chinese food, each paying 15 mex (about $1.34 U.S.) a month for it. Food, boarding, and the cook's wages came to $16 a month for each, which we paid to the cook with the understanding that he would supply us with a sufficient amount of food. Since he had to get enough from the $75 a month to feed both himself and us, there was no waste. Both sides watched carefully, and any discrepancies were immediately adjusted.

Living expenses in China were minimal. In comparison with the people around us in the village and countryside, I maintained a fabulously high standard of living, having a fairly warm house, white bread, enough clothes, and bus fare into the city every weekend. The month's other expenses rarely went above $5 U.S. and were usually well under that sum, which included amusement, travel, supplementary fruit, and even money for mistakes. One Chinese family of seven that I knew lived on eight U.S. cents a day. Only the rich could think of attending the college that I worked for.

In September I wrote my impressions in a letter to college friends.

> Life [in China] is strangely real and yet unreal. The earth is all around, and life is lived simply and openly, in all its frankness and beauty. Underfed, ragged, expressionless suffering surrounds one in the city alleys, and on the country fields, in the sterile, hard-turned earth. But deep in the soil the life of ages stirs, and the swinging loads

are carried below smiling faces. The Chinese say that when the moon is full the stars grow on the tips of the willow branches. It is true, in a way, for there is little in China through which either old or new life is not surging. I think the greatest thing that greets the Westerner here is that life is a living, not a standard of living. It seems strange to say that in this land of conventions, but everyone here knows that those conventions are convenient vessels for life, and no more. It is the most supremely sensible attitude that I have ever met. And it is all so much of a whole.

The great spaces that give power and beauty to magnificently proportioned buildings, the barren mass of the hills, where temples are set jewel-like in their dark green nests of pine, the lift of temple roofs where the wind-bells court the distant stars with their clear tinkling, the clear cold moonlight edging the warm, low-lying smoke with silver, the slow, bent figures going home on the ridges between the paddy-fields, the crisp, pungent smell of coal fires on winter mornings, the sturdy, wadded figures endlessly bending, endlessly plodding, endlessly bargaining, the patient deep eyes of women, and the gay, curious stare of little children. It is all mysterious and baffling, and challenging.... Pain and tension rule our lives...we stand in the despair of the present. A phrase which I think should be above every college gate, not so much for those who go in as for those who go out is, "Sanctify our knowledge with the power to make response."

Although the campus life seemed much as it had before, there were new tensions. Yenching was a private university, supported by American missions and other institutions. Japan had not occupied America. We Americans, who identified strongly with the Chinese, were not treated as they were, and had to stand aside while our friends and colleagues faced indignities and abuse. Chinese on public buses entering or leaving the city were routinely asked by Japanese guards to get off the bus at the city gate, to be searched in varying degrees of intensity. Once I rode on a bus into the city with friends, a professor from the university and his wife. I was the only American on the bus. Arriving at the city gate, the other passengers were asked to leave the bus, and as a gesture of solidarity I got off also. When we were all on the bus again, the professor turned to me angrily, scolding me in easily understood Chinese for acceding to the order to get off. "You did not have to get off. You are an American. They have not conquered you. You should not defer to their ridiculous request. You should have stayed on to illustrate the defiance we cannot show."

*   *   *

In 1939 Hitler had begun his conquest of Europe; the Japanese had occupied much of China; the Communist Red Army was slowly coming up the western edge of the country. The world was in turmoil, yet Yenching University remained relatively untouched by the convulsions. Shocking to me now, my daily diary reflects teas, suppers, folk-dancing, Chinese boxing (*t'ai ch'i*), concerts, lectures (on imperialism in the Caribbean, for example), trips to the mountains, music-making, and the delights of faculty and staff life in a beautiful

Visit to a temple with colleagues, circa 1939. I am third from the right.

setting. Different nations were represented on the faculty—Americans, British, Germans, Russians, Chinese; we met together for many social functions, a favorite being tea. I joined a faculty "little theater group," called *Je Nao*, meaning an excited disturbance, which accurately described our efforts to produce plays and skits. Almost daily I played tennis or went skating, or, often with others, bicycled to the hills or to Peking, or to one of the many temples or abandoned palaces near the city. Often, in the evening a group of us would huddle over a short-wave radio in someone's house, and try to hear through the crackling noise something of what was going on in the world, but it seemed very far away. As we listened, I remember only a feeling of sadness and doom about the international news. It was as if, in China, there was so much immediate disaster that one could not encompass more.

One American faculty member came late, to much critical comment. He had been visiting his grandmother in the south of China, beyond the Japanese lines, and was working his way north, delayed by the fighting. Other faculty members were teaching his English classes; there was no word about when he would arrive and considerable

Peking, 1940: Mother, Bill, John, Janet, a friend, me holding Lucky, Father, and Barbara.

anticipation about the report he would give when he did. His name was William Hollister, the son of former Methodist missionaries in Fukien province, and he was at Yenching on a two-year contract as an English teacher. One October day he finally appeared, and headed straight for the newspapers in the library, burying himself in the news from Europe before catching up with colleagues who had carried his classes. I was impressed. He had been out of touch with world news for several weeks, and his eagerness for it was conspicuous and dramatic.

At Yenching it was customary for faculty members who had been on trips of special interest to give a report to the college community, and Bill's report was eagerly awaited; he had been through battle lines, had traveled with Edgar Snow, the well-known reporter and Red Army sympathizer, and spoke Chinese well enough to have gathered possible inside information about a murky battleground. As the most recent young, single woman, I was told that I would find him interesting.

The college community gathered for the lecture, and Bill walked to the lectern. He had dark brown eyes in a long, square-jawed face, thinning hair, and a wide, gentle mouth. He carried no notes. I waited eagerly for the organized, event-crammed, analytical report I had been given to expect. It never came. Instead, in the simplest of language he told us why he had gone, described the route, explained the reason for his delay, thanked the faculty members who had taken his classes, and, to sparse applause, sat down. He answered questions in the same minimal way, and the meeting ended early. I decided this was a man who would never be a major part of my life. As young American members of a small established community, we were frequently invited together for social events, so there was no way of avoiding him, but I early signaled to my friends, and to him, my disinterest in any formal relationship with him.

Rudi was the man I loved. He was a medical student at the Peking Union Medical College I had met while skating at the Summer Palace in Peking. Part of the lake was cordoned off for skating, but there were surrounding areas where the willow branches came down to the ice, and made dark little passages along the shore. Through the branches you could see the bright lights of the marble, boat-shaped restaurant, and the lantern-lit passageways leading to it, people sitting on landings, putting on skates, other people rounding up groups to go home. Watching all this, I failed to notice a branch frozen in the ice ahead of me and skated up against it, twisting my ankle. I sat on the bank, taking the skate off, and wondered how I would be able to make the half-mile back to the gate where my bicycle was. Suddenly a skater whirled into sight, pirouetting, jumping, circling in patterns, a phantasmagoric shadow against the lights. He caught the glint of my skate blade and drew up beside me. "My name is Rudi Fleischer," he said in a pleasant, accented voice. "Have you hurt yourself? I am a medical student, and I thought I might help."

The camel-backed Moon Bridge at the Summer Palace in Peking, circa 1939.

That was the beginning. We met when we could, when he could get away. We were tentative. Rudi was part of a group we called "white Russians"—those, many of them Jewish, who had fled from Communist Russia. Though Peking was an international city, the foreign enclaves were separated by large areas of Chinese houses, low-roofed, gray-walled, private. The streets were our own, and there was little chance of meeting anyone we knew.

In early February of 1940, my father had just become acting head of the Language School, a prestigious graduate school for teaching the Chinese language. The presidency was an honor, especially for a missionary, since students came not just from the missions, but also from foreign departments of state, the armed services, and business groups. A celebratory party had been arranged at Christmas time, and my father and his family were expected. However, Rudi had a few hours off, and I asked him to come for supper, telling my father only at the last minute that I would not be going to the party.

The family would be out, I knew; Rudi and I had been somehow shy with each other, learning slowly what the other wanted to hear. He came on his bicycle, whipped by the north wind, a parcel in his hand. Parking his bicycle by the front steps, he walked in. We were wary; we had never met in a place where one of us lived. The novelty of the situation intrigued us, and we had a wonderful time. After supper we listened to the present he had brought—Beethoven's Ninth Symphony. As we sat together on the couch near the hearth fire, the music slowly drew us toward each other. Even then I was aware of an eerie feeling: we were listening to German music, brought by a Jew in the winter of 1940. Words came in the fourth movement, and I asked him what they meant, especially one phrase, *Seid umschlungen* (be embraced). He turned and said, "I'll show you what that means," and hugged me for the first time. The front door opened, letting in cold air and my family. My father's displeasure filled the room. He didn't express it, perhaps because he, too, liked Beethoven, but it was clear that he did not approve of what and whom he saw. Rudi rose, introduced himself and what he was doing in Peking, greeted everyone, wished everyone a very good New Year, and sat down. Beethoven stopped. My father said, "Well, if you are a medical student you probably need to be getting back to your work." As I watched in shame and despair, Rudi rose, took up his coat and cap in the hall, again wished us all a good New Year and went out the door. His bicycle light shone briefly and he was gone.

The next day I went to my father's study and asked why he had been so abrupt, and, I thought, rude, to my friend. He said, "Margaret, you made two mistakes. You did not come to a party important to me, and you invited a Jew into my house." That did not stop me or Rudi, but our relationship slowly diminished as his schedule became heavier, and he spent more time with his fellow refugees. He was the first man

Marble boat at the Summer Palace, Peking, circa 1940.

I longed for, and I still think of him, dark-eyed, dark-haired, funny, with a doctor's curiosity, every time I skate.

There were other men friends: a young, handsome Britisher, a journalist, an earnest young YMCA staffer. Peking and its surroundings offered seduction, all the stronger for being surrounded by poverty, dirt, dust, and stench: temples in the city and on the hills, with their quiet pines and gently clinking bells; former palace grounds, with their marbles, shrubbery, low benches and stone-edged ponds; the great city walls with their views of countryside and city, and, near the astrolabe, evocation of the sky—these were romantic destinations easily reached. In the absence of electronic entertainment or formal "seasons" of drama or music, we tended to get on our bicycles and just go.

But slowly, over the winter, the cozy, intense, multi-cultural university world brought Bill Hollister and me more and more into contact. Bill was a fine pianist, and I played well enough to join him in piano duets adapted from Mozart and Beethoven symphonies, and we played tennis at levels sufficiently alike to give pleasure to ourselves and to our partners. He was bright and thoughtful, planning to take a

Caption on the back of this picture: "1940, Erh T'iao. Margaret, Barbara, Mother, John, Father, Janet. The night before Janet left."

Ph.D. in philosophy when he went back to the States. By mid-April I had a token ring. This was followed, a month later, by a reversal. In the winter Bill and I had been elected co-producers of the little theater group, *Je Nao*. A hastily arranged skit was to be given which supplanted an abandoned plan to put on the "Merry Wives of

Windsor," and he was to arrange for the stage props for the skit. The night of the dress rehearsal the props were not there; I foresaw a lifetime of bungling and failure to provide together, and returned the ring. His two-year contract at the University was up in June and early that month he left. A hectic time followed. Details poured into the office as Ms. Speer, my boss, left for her summer holiday. The dormitories closed for the summer, faculty residences were arranged for the following academic year, staff and faculty slowly began to disappear for the summer interlude. Terrible news from France and England, Hong Kong and Indochina snapped from the radio. Finally it was August, and time to join the family at Peitaiho amid the silence of no phones and the precious sound of the sea. Our family was at breakfast one Sunday when my brother called out: "There's Bill." And there he was, on the path leading from the beach to the house. He had seen pictures of our house, had come to the Peitaiho station, and all night had simply walked the miles of the beaches until he recognized the house. My family enjoyed him; I was guarded, but it was a pleasant time. He left three days later, after a predictable quarrel and the equally predictable make-up on the moonlit ride to the train station.

At the end of August 1940, I returned to Yenching, to my work, which now included teaching an English class, and watched my city and my university struggling with the brutality of Japanese occupation. Deeply involved in the constant problems of women students from all over China during a war with an occupying force, I had left behind my life in America, isolated as it was from wars all over the globe. I was therefore startled in November to receive a letter from the University of Chicago inviting me to apply for a fellowship in medieval history. It was to start the first weekend of January, 1941, and an immediate answer was requested. With history exploding all about me, I had completely forgotten the application I had made just before graduating from Wellesley the year before. To go to graduate school then had seemed profoundly desirable, seductive, an opening to the academic career that in college I had discovered I wanted.

I struggled with the sudden option. How could I abandon my suffering homeland and the people who, as an American, I was in a unique position to help? With anguish I discussed the situation with Ms. Speer, whose disposition, as well as her job, inclined her to support any move that would enhance a career.

As war spread in Europe and news of it worsened, I began to feel

Bill, John, and Lucky, Peitaiho, summer 1940.

that the understanding of history was never more important, that the great legacies of the middle ages were stirring and had answers for our time. The languages I had with such difficulty begun to learn—medieval Latin, high and low German, Anglo-Saxon—tempted me by my incomplete command of them. Somehow I felt by going back to the study of my chosen period of history I was going toward the war, not evading it.

So on November 12th I cabled the University that I would be applying and hastily booked passage on the next possible ship. It was the *Asama Maru*, sailing November 29th from Kobe, Japan. Father, ever ecumenical, had—in spite of the general hatred of Japan in China—Japanese friends, who kindly invited me to stay with them until the boat sailed. They provided wonderful experiences, the tea ceremony, visits to famous shrines, and again I was aware of the graciousness of the Japanese society. As soon as I boarded the boat, however, the attitudes shifted. It was as if, when Japanese were in charge, they changed and treated us gruffly. It seemed that American passengers were tolerated only for their tickets. Midway to Hawaii I developed stomach pains. The ship's doctor, mentioning American physical decadence, pre-scribed exercise on the machines in the ship's gymnasium. By the time we docked in Hawaii, on December 7th, I was in severe pain, and dur-ing the ship's brief stay there sought a local clinic. I returned to the boat, but was called back, and within hours I was in an emergency room. At one o'clock the next morning my appendix was out. I knew no one on the island, but had to be discharged the next day from the hospital; it was the Christmas season, and the only facility with a bed available was the Kapiolani maternity hospital.

I was admitted to a large ward, with mothers and babies all around me. The staff, though aware of the diagnosis and the circumstances, would look on me, a single woman in a maternity ward, as somehow fallen; they insisted on calling me Mrs. Hayes. The mothers around me wondered about the lack of a child; why was I there? Christmas carols sounded on the air: "A child is born," "What child is this?" "When a mother had her baby." As the evening came on and the ward lights dimmed and the babies were taken away after the evening nursing, I felt barren and abandoned. I had never believed in the Nativity; Dr. Robinson, the wonderful mission doctor, had seen to it that missionary kids at school at Tungchow knew the facts, but now I understood why, perhaps, others did believe that beautiful story.

Four days after the operation a cable came from my family in Peking, with a hundred dollars. I was so glad to hear from them! When it came time for discharge, a kindly missionary family offered a room until the next ship for America would be leaving. The maternity hospital administrator came by my bed to tell me that I did not have to pay the sixty-one-dollar fee for the hospitalization. The surgeon's wife brought me flowers and books, and took me for rides around the island. Sustained by the kindness of those who were living by a faith I had abandoned, I finally boarded the ship that would take me to the country that housed the University of Chicago, and held my future.

XI

A WARTIME MARRIAGE

On Sunday, December 22, 1940, the passengers and crew of the Japanese ship that took me to America celebrated Christmas. A service—secular, almost anecdotal—was held in the ship's lounge. Gilded pillars ringed the room. Passengers' fur coats over the backs of chairs gave it the look of opening night at the opera. At a party in the afternoon there were packets of dates for the ladies, and toys for the children. A band jazzed up "Silent Night," but no one danced to it. The next day, as if in response to a synthetic Christmas, the sea was turbulent. The ship tossed and rocked; plates slid off tables, glasses fell onto counters, people fell out of their berths, and some of us did not risk going to bed at all.

The following day we landed in San Francisco. After inspection, red tape, and general bustle, the ship slipped into the quiet port. Strings of lights lit the piers and lined the bridges in the mist. Customs offices were closed, but I finally persuaded Railway Express to bond my trunk and send it to Chicago. That night, after a calm ferry ride across the harbor, I boarded the eastbound train. At 8:35 on Christmas Eve, I was on my American way, in a Pullman car all to myself. The next day passengers wished each other a merry Christmas and exchanged memories of more stable occasions. There was no celebration on the train. It seemed odd: a Japanese ship offered an ersatz Christmas, an American train nothing at all. A couple gave their little girl some gifts, giving the day a small sparkle.

On the 27th, Bill Hollister and his mother met me at the train

191

station in Chicago, where I was to stay in the home of a family friend, Dr. Gilkey, Dean of Religion at the University of Chicago, until I was somewhat stronger from the appendectomy. The next day I found that I had been accepted for the fellowship, a relief after the long risk I had taken, and went off to spend the rest of the Christmas vacation with the Hollisters in their home in Delaware, Ohio.

Dr. Hollister was a tall, gentle, brown-eyed, quiet man, who looked like the professor of religion that he then was at Ohio Wesleyan University. We became instant friends, bantering and affectionate. Mrs. Hollister was a short, friendly, hospitable woman, an author of children's books. She was interested in her home and in its furnishings. The family included Bill's brother, a high school teacher of automobile repair—merry, companionable, and practical—and his high school sweetheart, Eleanor Turner. The Hollisters had been Methodist missionaries in the south of China until 1929, when funds were cut by their mission board. I felt especially close to Dr. Hollister: he used to tease me about being interested in "all those saints in the middle ages; how about those at home?" We tossed scripture back and forth between us, and I felt like a daughter to him.

To my surprise I also felt immediately part of a classic American small-town family. I had never lived in a small town—the kind that had one drug store, one grocery, two garages, and a university. The days were pleasant, but scarred by the terrible news from London. We gathered around the radio to hear President Roosevelt's patrician voice, from the White House fireside to ours, reminding us of America's responsibility toward England, and I wondered whether the next Christmas would find us all together. Night after night Edward Murrow's gray, gravelly voice brought the darkening of Europe to the softly lighted living room at 179 West Winter Street, Delaware, Ohio.

Bill proposed marriage again on New Year's Eve of 1940. "Margaret, I love you a great deal. I have loved you for a long time. Will you marry me?" I was not ready to decide, and the next day he drove me to Chicago, through the wet gray air, along shining roads. I was about to study the formation of European society, even as it was being destroyed.

The History Department at the University of Chicago was at that time one of the glories of the university, especially in medieval studies. In addition, to be on the Gothic-style, gray-stoned, cloistered campus was to feel like one of the wandering scholars of the Middle Ages. I met my adviser, Mrs. Gillespie, and opened the graduate catalog in medieval history. The offerings burst forth like a Chinese New Year's fireworks celebration: Einar Jorensen on "The Culture of the Twelfth and Thirteenth Centuries," "Laboratory Course in Historical Method: Europe" with Louis Gottschalk, "The Intellectual History of Europe in the Seventeenth Century" with J.T. McNeil, "Medieval Schools" with J.L. Cate, Margaret Rickert's two courses: "Introduction to Christian Iconography of the Medieval West" and "French Gothic Architecture and Sculpture." I felt as if I had been given the gift of the Western world. The next day, dazzled, I went to five classes, but was reined in by Mrs. Gillespie, who wisely suggested that two would be appropriate for a post-appendectomy, first-year graduate student. I went to see Dr. Cate, a short, slender, bright-eyed man, whose friendliness and curiosity seemed as valuable to me as the scholarship he arranged. Returning to the Gilkeys' house, preparing to search over the weekend for a place to live, I was greeted by Mrs. Gilkey with an offer to stay with them for the academic quarter. It all seemed too good to be true. The next day I found a bank and some brown-and-white saddle shoes. In two days' time I had become an authentic American graduate student with a scholarship, a place to live, and a career. A few days later I retrieved my trunk from the Railway Express. On opening it for customs inspection, I was overjoyed to see the contents packed in China, but they were beginning to feel like imports from a foreign country.

The first class with Dr. Gottschalk was terrifying. He was a large, handsome, dark-eyed man, with dark hair turning gray, and the acknowledged foremost scholar of historiography. His required class, History 301, was held in one of the rooms in the university library, with rows of documents just behind the door. It was exciting to discuss how one knew anything in history; how even to verify a date, much less a fact; how to approach documents; what could or could not be stated with any degree of validity—all were tossed in the air, examined, challenged. I loved the class, but was constantly frightened, and took an incomplete.

I approached Dr. Joranson's class, "The Culture of the Twelfth and Thirteenth Centuries," with some confidence, having done some work in that field, but soon found myself floundering among original texts and ancient languages. I chose Heloise, lover of Peter Abelard, for my first paper; I thought a medieval woman would be good company, and

I, too, was caught in a bewildering bond with someone who loved me. We were required to do progress reports; delivering my first one, in Dr. Joranson's class, I stumbled on a wire, fell, fainted, and ended up in the infirmary.

When I got home I found that my sister Elinor was planning to visit from Detroit. I tried to study, but noted in my journal that Elinor was "full of wandering ideas. Smoke and mess, lunch in room, very difficult." I also heard that owing to the increasing anti-American attitudes from the Japanese, most of my family would be coming to America; I began to worry about what arrangements I could make for them, but then learned from the Board of Foreign Missions that my mother was taking the Language School to the Philippines for safety, and my sister and brother were going with her, while my father and his parents remained in China. I was relieved. I just wanted to be alone and get my work done; even my family was a distraction. In addition, the Gilkeys' household was an engaged one. Dr. Gilkey was a busy dean, his wife an efficient and voluble activist; I felt the burden of their hospitality, and their generous concern.

I loved the scholar's life, the great libraries, my carrel in the library with its piles of books and sliver of a window, through which, however, I could glimpse the branch of a tree and its seasonal life. I enjoyed the shared intensity of other scholars, the vigor of old languages, and the luxury and excitement of being in contact with professors distinguished in their fields, who knew a lot. I was on my own; I wanted to borrow another age and live in it.

But other far more consequential currents were swirling in my life. The terrible 1940 year-end bombing of London had shattered the city and many memories of it on this side of the Atlantic. It was not until the following March that Congress finally passed the Lend-Lease Act. On April 6th the Nazis invaded Greece and Yugoslavia; what was I doing? During the spring term I moved from the Gilkeys into "a nice room, with charming neighbors." A few days later I got a job working in the campus restaurant. A paper was due on a magnificent medieval abbot, Suger, and another paper for Dr. McNeil's course, "Christianity and the European Nations." I had chosen the subject: "Preaching 1066-1235 in England," since, with two grandfathers famous for the art, I felt I was in a position to know something about exegesis, and I was fascinated by the entangling of politics and religion, even, or especially, then.

I was in turmoil over a recent visit to see Bill in New York, and fainted in a class, "The Philosophical Works of Cicero"—a class that would normally prevent loss of consciousness, exciting as it was for the professor's delight in a political philosopher's vigor. The next day I noted in my diary: "Tooth awfully sore. Tried to have it taken out, but the $3 man away, and $5 the only other." In April I broke down, weeping, and was sent to a psychiatrist. The triple pressures of studying at the graduate level, the need to decide about marriage, and the terrible news about the bombing of my mother's country—while my own country held back—had taken their toll.

I got a job for the summer of 1941 as a waitress in a chain drug store—all complete, for $5 a week, a little blue-checked uniform with cap, and lunch. Other graduate students would drop in and look at me quizzically as I ran up and down stairs with their orders. "Slumming, Margaret?" they would ask. Slumming? I needed to eat, and decided to work where there was food. For the summer term I enrolled for only one class, "Medieval Schools," taught by my favorite professor, Dr. Cate. The war in Europe continued to intensify, and was going badly. On May 10th, London was heavily bombed. And what was my diary entry for that date? "Beautiful day, strawberries for breakfast." In June of that year the Germans began their attack on Russia; by August they had reached Leningrad.

Meanwhile, I had moved my desk to a carrel in a library closer to the religious texts, and met a gentle, quiet, bright fellow graduate student. He was good at languages and helped me with the texts, and slowly we began to do things together. We met for breakfast, for lunch after my drugstore shift, for rides on the lake, for movies, and to go to museums. His mother lived nearby, a warm, supportive little woman, and the summer and fall slipped by. America finally began to take steps: an oil embargo, the Atlantic charter. In September, 1941, I enrolled for the new semester: Professor Joransen's "The Crusades," Professor Margaret Rickert's "Romanesque Architecture and Sculpture," and a beginning course in Old English. Small news items began to appear: Jews in Europe were ordered to wear yellow stars; on September 3rd the first use of gas at Auschwitz; the murder, in late September, of over 33,000 Jews in Kiev. And what was I doing on that date? "A cloudy, fresh day.... Convocation in the morning, wonderful —seeing faces and the whole rich solemnness of it. To lunch downtown with Gene." It felt as if I was fiercely protecting Europe by studying it, while country after country succumbed to its obliteration.

Bill and Gene knew about each other. Bill had signaled that he was going to be too busy to visit or to call, and Gene was happy just to do things together that committed neither of us.

*   *   *

And then it was December 7th. Every week I had been stepping out from the Anglo-Saxon texts, from the stained glass slides of tenth and eleventh century churches, from the tangled economics of guilds, from the restless crusades, to a comfortable twentieth-century Sunday. I had a regular schedule for Sundays: laundry, letters to my family, the weekly two o'clock broadcast of the New York Philharmonic on CBS, and in the late afternoon the gathering with graduate students around a fireplace in the Commons hall at the University, where we would discuss the world, the day, and the academic week ahead before going back severally to our rented rooms.

On that December 7th I was looking forward with special interest to a Brahms concerto scheduled for the afternoon broadcast. My undergraduate days had seemed sometimes to be intervals between Boston Symphony concerts, and I was eager to hear what the Philharmonic would do, given the acknowledged dominion of the Boston string section. Laundry done, letters written, lunch over, I settled down in my room, turned on the radio, and Brahms' Second Piano Concerto filled the air. The second movement had begun when suddenly a voice broke in: "We interrupt this program to bring you a special bulletin. The Japanese have attacked Pearl Harbor, Hawaii, by air, President Roosevelt has announced. The attack also was made on all naval and military activities on the principal island of Ohau [sic]." The music continued, but I could no longer listen, and I turned the radio off. Yet it seemed as if there was now no silence; the words hung in the air, and the imagined sounds of war seemed in the room. It was as if everything had changed, the world had burst open, flinging apart the two continents that held my family. Unable to be alone and knowing where to find others, I put on my coat and hat and left the room to go to the university.

I passed people I didn't know who were out for their Sunday afternoon strolls. They didn't know, and I didn't tell them; let them have peace a little longer. When I arrived at the Commons though, I was aware of something different. Although a small group of students was at our usual fireplace, most of the men had moved to the hearth at the other end of the room, and were gathered there in a small circle, talking in low voices. We heard "war" and "tomorrow" and the names of the armed services. It was as if what was taking place in that long, low-lit, wainscoted room paralleled the enormous division taking place outside in the world, as if history was in that room. It is impossible to verify, but it is my memory that within four weeks the male graduate students in history were gone from the university, their papers and careers on hold. They had enlisted.

My own family was scattered around the world. Two sisters were in college across America, my grandparents and my father were in Japanese-occupied China, and my mother, my 15-year-old sister, and my 11-year-old brother were in the Philippine Islands.

On my way to babysit at the Cate household, I wondered what might be happening to my own family, but knew it would be a while before I found out. Entering the front door I saw the children playing in the living room, in front of the radio. I went straight to the kitchen, where Mrs. Cate was cleaning up and asked if she had heard the news. "What news?" I told her Pearl Harbor had been bombed. She flew to the bottom of the stairs and called up, "Jim, Pearl Harbor has been bombed." Dr. Cate had been in the shower and came running down the stairs, water dripping about him, walked to the radio, turned it on, and stood in front of it, oblivious to everything else. His wife ran upstairs for a large towel, draped it about him, and we all listened intently, the children close to their parents. The Cates still kept their evening engagement, while I sat with the children and tried to explain what had, or might have, happened. The next week I turned in my paper for Dr. Cate's course, but nothing about the university was ever the same after that night. America, of course, went to war the next day.

I wondered when I might hear about my family. No word came from them or from the mission board; all the usual cable connections were cut. A few weeks later I learned that most foreign nationals in the Far East were interned, either in homes or in camps, and the long silence began. For two years my family overseas did not hear from those of us in the United States, and we did not hear from them. Missionary families are accustomed to separations. We were used to separate deployment; letters, written usually on Sunday, carried love and information around the globe. But this was different. Now the silence was absolute and inimical, and we must learn to love each other without information and without contact. And, in fact, we never met again as a family.

The Christmas holidays at the end of 1941 seemed unreal, a shimmer of former times. The two days without mail seemed a mere extension of uncertainty about what was to happen. When would "Greetings from the President" arrive at 179 West Winter Street, in Delaware, Ohio, or in the boarding houses of Chicago? Soon Bill's brother was in the army. I went back to the university wondering whether I should continue my courses. Suddenly it seemed that there were no civilians.

The war demanded two decisions: the ongoing one about marrying Bill, and the new one about my responsibility to my country, and, for that matter, to my mother's country. Unable to make an immediate decision on either, I registered for the winter term: Margaret Rickert's wonderful courses in medieval Christian iconography and French Gothic architecture and sculpture, and a reading course in the period. Even as we studied from slides the stories they held, the stained glass was being taken down from cathedral windows all over Western Europe and stored for safekeeping. In April German air raids began against the cathedral cities of England.

I was unable to work well, with the uncertainty over marriage creeping into the news from Europe. Late in the month, American forces arrived in Britain. I invited Bill to Chicago for a firm decision. We had what had become our usual brief, bitter quarrel, and ended up putting the engagement ring back on my finger. The next day he bought some flowers, and I saw him off on the train. Entries for my diary for the following days are stark:

> 2/2 Sad and bewildered. What have we done again? Waited for joy to come. 2/3 Still waiting for joy to come. 2/4 No joy. 2/5 Tension mounting again. 2/6 Tension high. Sent Bill a telegram. Wrote him a letter. Called him up. Seemed so sure. 2/7 Toward end of the day reaction started. 2/8 Ghastly day. 2/9 Cried most of the day. Ghastly. I am not this person. 2/10 Set Sunday as time limit. Home every noon to try to fight this thing out. But it shouldn't be this way.

Finally no decision was made. At the end of the month I wrote:

> [I] feel as if I were living in some half way existence that will break, and either leave me nothing at all, or will leave me crippled and worse

than useless for the rest of my life, for I will still be able to hurt those I love. And yet I feel sure that this won't be settled by punching the time clock. There's more to it all than that... If I'm engaged to him, why don't I love and marry him?

The struggle to decide continued through April and May as I took the spring-quarter courses—a reading course on the Italian Renaissance, Medieval Latin, The Iconography of the Greek New Testament—and in June passed the German language examination.

But by the end of May I had begun to feel unreal, as if I were not participating in real things—"war, friendships, people." I felt I had lived "too long and too much" in thought, "and I am so able in that." I began to feel "a little insane" and to "wonder what life is, anyway." I worried about germs and went to the University psychiatrist to ask about the danger from germs on the thick, mug-like cups we used for serving coffee in the drug store. (I knew how they were washed.) She gave me a level look, and said the coffee was hot enough to take care of any danger I was worried about. I left her, unconvinced but aware that there were greater dangers in the world, and frantically wrote papers for my classes. I also tried to put some of my bewilderment in a journal.

> This is truly an incredible existence.... Is it fear of marriage, fear of Bill, or fear of self? In any case, fear is self-centeredness essentially? Otherwise why is it so consistent and so varied? Any way I turn I am afraid. Obviously because I must take responsibility. First time in life that I have had to take responsibility for direction, and this time it must be final. War is a ghastly thing, and it will take Bill where he hates going, and he needs someone else's faith in him, but I must be sure that I mean that faith, or I am not the one to give it.

Finally some friends of my grandfather Kelman somehow heard of my distress, and made plans for Bill and me to marry at their Victorian house in Cincinnati, Ohio, where Dr. Barbour was Dean of the Engineering School at the University of Cincinnati. Hitler was advancing on Stalingrad. Was it memories of Rudi that made me feel that I could not bear to have Stalingrad in the hands of the Germans?

I capitulated to the plans being made on my behalf, left the University, and with it all plans to continue working in my field. With war claiming our lives, the medieval world receded into the faded tapestries that depicted it, into the hidden slides that told its stories.

The great High German language that I loved had been conscripted into the service of murderers, its long periods used to destroy a civilization. There was no use trying to be a teacher of the culture of a crumbling world.

In the living room of the Hollisters, Delaware, Ohio, 1942: Mr. and Mrs. Hollister on the left, their daughter-in-law Eleanor on the right. Some of the caption I wrote on the back to Bill: "Taken Sunday during the Philharmonic.... My picture files are messing up the room.... The living room rarely looks like this, but I thought you wouldn't mind it. Dad often sits like this nowadays getting his muscles a little more relaxed. The files have spread into 2 cartons. They may prove helpful for our own home some day.... Some of the pictures are truly lovely, some are interesting, others we will throw away. But this is one thing at least that will make our home a little more real to us both. I don't know why I look so big here! Actually I've lost a little weight recently."

I moved to Ohio and started making my wedding dress. The date was to be June 27th, a day when Bill's brother Robert could get leave from his army post. On the 25th I moved to Cincinnati to stay with the Barbours, uncertain still. Bill and I had our medical exams and got the license. His father was to marry us. On June 26th I decided I couldn't go through with it, and packed my suitcase to leave. I had underestimated Mrs. Barbour, a woman made almost entirely of conviction. She locked me in my bedroom. I looked out over the neighboring roofs, thinking to climb out. They were on similar houses, well-spaced apart; it would be impossible to reach them. My sister arrived that evening, and made a coronet and veil. Dr. and Mrs. Hollister, Robert and his wife, Eleanor, came the next day. The service was to be at two. After lunch Dr. Hollister knocked on the locked door. I let him in. "Margaret, do you love William?" he asked. I could hear Bill playing the piano downstairs, and the preparations for cake and celebration. I wanted to say, "Apparently not," but I loved Dr. Hollister, and said, "Yes." "Then I will marry you," he said, and left, turning the lock. Later I realized I had not married to be Bill's wife, but to be Dr. Hollister's daughter-in-law.

June 27, 1942.

Bill and I were married at 2:10 in a big, empty Presbyterian church, Dr. Barbour walking with me down the aisle, my sister Elinor at the altar, Robert standing beside his brother. Eleanor's mother kindly played for the ceremony, the organ echoing grotesquely in the empty sacerdotal space. I remember the sound in the huge church: fake, staged, and devoid of pageant or joy. Back at the Barbours', around a decorated table, Bill and I cut the cake, posed for pictures, said thanks and goodbye, and left for a few days at Clifty Falls State Park. The war-time posters were already up around the highways: "Is This Trip Necessary?" I remember noting them as we drove toward the park and thinking to myself, no, it was not. Looking back on that day I think now that the only thing that prevented it from being farce was that this is what war was precipitating, all over the country.

June 1942: Margaret, Bill, and Andy (the dog) on our honeymoon at Clifty Falls State Park, Ohio.

When we returned to our rented apartment in Delaware "Greetings from the President" was on the hall table. Bill was to report to his army induction unit within the next ten days.

Finally the war claimed the pattern of our lives. When inducted into the army in July, 1942, Bill could speak Mandarin Chinese and understand both the Mandarin and Cantonese dialects. He could also type. The army, accordingly, assigned him to the typing pool at Fort Benjamin Harrison, outside Indianapolis, Indiana. At least it was in the States, and families could join the soldiers posted there.

Dr. and Mrs. Hollister's response to their sons being drafted into the war was to buy for each a car-trailer which could accompany him and his wife to any post in the United States that had the facilities. Consequently, as soon as Bill was installed in front of his typewriter on base, our dog, Andy, a fetching little terrier mix, and I piled into our 1939 Plymouth coupe, a fourteen-foot trailer hitched behind, and headed west. A trailer park near the post offered a wide field, with a few trees, some scattered benches, hook-ups for utilities, laundry lines, and a working pump. Bill joined me, we found a site between a tree and a bench, and established our first home, Andy promptly claiming the bench. He sat upright on it, ears cocked, guarding us from our neighboring trailer occupants and from Germany and Japan.

Andy and I in the coupe.

We named our trailer Nautilus; we assumed it would travel and not sink. Cozy, compact, lined with plywood, it provided wonderful acoustics for our jazz and classical record collection, all of which we brought, not knowing how long the war would last. We had always played music every evening after supper, and we continued the custom in the trailer. Soon, in the long Indiana evenings, music-hungry soldiers, sodas in hand, would come to the trailer, sit in folding chairs, and listen until night came on, when they would fold their chairs and walk slowly across the field toward their barracks, cigarette tips glowing in the dark. Sometimes there were requests—Mozart quartets, Brahms symphonies—resulting in long silences after the music was over.

I found a job in Indianapolis at the recently established WPA, cherishing my new Social Security card, and feeling, along with other working wives, that we too were part of "the war effort." The trailer park became a suburban community; laundry lines informed us of changes within each trailer. Diapers would appear, or clothes for only a single person where there had been garments for two, or the addition of another person's apparel on a line. Bill and I suppressed the tension in our marriage; the world was too chaotic, the future immediately uncertain, to accommodate resolutions of personal relationships. The trailer park was my first experience living as a housewife in America, and I enjoyed it, a combination of assignment and adventure.

Indiana, 1942: Bill's brother Robert, his wife Eleanor, Bill, Andy, and me in front of our trailer.

Bill was restless at his typewriter, and after several attempts to explore opportunities for using a language that others were frantically being assigned to learn, he applied for Officers' Candidate School, hoping the options would be better as an officer. He was posted to Jackson, Mississippi for training. There was no workable arrangement for parking the trailer there or for Bill's spending much time in it, so the little trailer and Andy were left with Dr. and Mrs. Hollister in Delaware, Ohio, and I left for Jackson by bus.

I had never been to the South in America. From the bus window I watched as the countryside seemed to shrivel; buildings were smaller, roads dustier, surroundings more haphazard. Black faces supplanted white ones at filling stations, in the back of the bus, and on street corners. The Deep South! Notices for segregated bathrooms seemed a slap in my face. How dare they divide me from other people? Weren't we all needing bathrooms for the same purpose? Having grown up as part of a minority among people of another color, I was affronted.

However, because I was afraid of doing something controversial in a new place, and as the wife of a new officer candidate, I went meekly to a referral center in the town to get a room.

Near Fort Benjamin Harrison, Indiana: Inside the Nautilus, sitting on the couch that was our bed.

Luckily, one was available in a household not far from downtown, and I set off on foot. I soon found out how different Jackson, Mississippi was from Chicago, Illinois, and even more starkly from Delaware, Ohio. Of course, soldiers were everywhere, as were African-Americans, but I had the feeling that everything was unstable, as if anything could happen at any time. That first day I felt the stares of African-Americans as they sat in doorways or passed me on the street. What was wrong? What had I done?

On the way to my lodging I crossed a bridge over a lower street in the section of town called the other side of the railroad tracks. Upon my arrival, my landlady, an elderly white woman, greeted me, asking how I had found the house. She was appalled that I had walked alone across the bridge. "Honey, never do that again. You no'therners think you can do anything you want, and get things all upset around here." It turned out that Bill was unable to be away from his training very often, so I soon made my way back to Ohio, but I have never forgotten being watched as I walked in Jackson, Mississippi.

At the end of his training, Bill was assigned to a Liberty Ship which was to leave from Long Beach, California. This was early in the war, when we often knew at least the port of departure. I decided to accompany him there, since the assumption was that he might be in the Pacific theater, although we were not sure. In our compartment on the train, the uncertainty about our marriage resurfaced and became acute. I reached the point at which I felt I could not face a lifetime with him; his affection for me in the face of my lack of feeling for him was a burden and an irritant to us both, and a disservice to him. It seemed to me it was best that we separate now, when we were facing separation anyway. Before Bakersfield, California, the last stop before Long Beach, we had a bitter discussion, and I decided to leave the marriage. I separated my things from a joint suitcase we traveled with, packed them into a suitcase of my own, and as the station appeared—empty, blazing in the hot early morning sunlight—I moved to the door of the railway car. I looked back at Bill arranging his things, checking his orders, and saw only the soldier, his new lieutenant's bars catching the light. The train stopped, and with one foot on the top step, suddenly ashamed of what I was doing, I turned back. You don't do that to a soldier in wartime, you just don't do that, I thought, and rejoined him, saying I had changed my mind. "It's up to you," he said, and continued his preparations.

Outside the Long Beach public library, 1943.

San Francisco, January 1943, just before Bill shipped out.

The troops on the train were deployed immediately. I watched as Bill disappeared on the docks. I decided, as long as he was assigned to the Pacific area, to stay on the West Coast. Long Beach was bleak, and I took the bus to San Francisco. That wonderful city was crowded, vital, full of soldiers and talk of the war. It was also full of wives and girlfriends. I soon found the best way to find a room was to join a group of wives who would rent an apartment and settle in together. Whenever a husband showed up, the rest of us would find room with friends or coworkers while he was on leave, then move back in together until the next spouse appeared. If, instead, a telegram came, we were there for support and help.

I needed a job, applied at the U.S. Employment Office, was hired on the spot, and went to work that afternoon. It was my first experience of personal counseling in America. Most applicants for jobs were women, wives and girlfriends of soldiers. They seemed to need a job less for the money than to have something to do and, for many, something to contribute to the war effort during the long and uncertain waiting. The job market was unstable. If a telegram came from the services or a telephone call from home, people would suddenly disappear to rebuild their lives, or to attend to needs at home. Life was fluid and urgent; a moment could change everything.

Writing to Bill, 1944, from Delaware, Ohio, with a map of China on the wall above me.

I hoped for a telegram; I hoped that Bill would not return. I knew that Liberty ships were unarmed, and that he was in charge of the ammunition being carried on his ship, so it was not an unlikely possibility. There seemed no answer to the problems of our relationship, no expectation that we could resolve the predicament of my discomfort with him in the face of his fondness for me. I was appalled by my wish. I was not alone; many women had married hastily when their men were drafted, and, I found out, suffered the same shameful wish, that their husbands would not come back. But that did not solve for me the feeling that again I was bad for people, this time referring the damage to the army. Bill did return in a few months, and after we'd had a week together left again, this time anticipating that he would be away for much longer, and at last in the Far East. He was gone for three years.

I returned to Ohio, moving back with the Hollisters and Andy. By 1943 the shortage of high school teachers had become severe, and I spent a semester and a summer obtaining a temporary high school teacher's' certificate—unfortunately, given the national urgency, without the opportunity of practice-teaching in a class room. The summer of 1944 I was hired to teach English and history at Sunbury High School, a consolidated rural school about fifteen miles northeast of Delaware. During one of the winter months I lived with a farm family, but most of the time I drove back and forth from Delaware, using the gas rations provided for school teachers. I had never been to public school in America, I had certainly never taught in America, but I loved learning, and I assumed everyone else did. I was given a homeroom, persuaded the school to add a course in the Chinese language, and expected a wonderful year.

By 1944 most farmers had left for the service, and the older men, with their wives, daughters-in-law, and children were maintaining the farms. The children, especially, had farm work to do before the school bus stopped at their lanes. As soon as a boy turned eighteen, he reported for the draft. Some left to report immediately. Consequently, almost every boy in the senior class was on the football squad. One young man made it a principle to do no homework. He was the mainstay of the football team and its only possible quarterback. He was also a student in my homeroom and in my English class, for which he turned in no homework for the first four weeks of school. Coming from school settings where homework was as much a part of life as breakfast, I was unsure how to respond to his attitude and warned him that I might have to fail him. He flashed a smile. "Now you wouldn't do that, would you? New teacher and all." Fellow faculty members approached me, sensing doom. Was it not possible to give him a passing grade, considering that he showed up for class? The stakes were so high, it was his last year, he might never play football again, he was already eighteen and due to be drafted. I found myself helpless before my Scottish ancestry; I did not pass him. He was thus ineligible to play the signal game of the fall; the team played without a quarterback and lost; and my high school teaching career, at least at Sunbury High School, was over. My contract was not renewed.

I had been asked by the farmers' Grange to give a talk about China on April 12, 1945. That noon the news of President Roosevelt's death was announced on the radio. The Grange program was not canceled, and with a sad heart I set out to deliver the speech. As I drove up to the Grange Hall I heard music and shouting, and wondered if I had mistaken the date. I went through the narrow little entrance hallway, turned left to the main room, and nearly fled. The farmers and their wives were dancing, shouting, slapping each other on the back. "That man" was dead. The President who had saved their farms ten years earlier, and then levied taxes and instituted rationing to support the war that their sons were fighting—"that man" was gone. There was in the room that evening no curiosity about China, and I was asked to re-schedule the speech. Gladly. I drove off into the night, again wondering about America, and eager to be home in the safety of the radio messages and the grave music that accompanied them.

In all the clamor of war, the radios in quiet living rooms brought the voices of Churchill and Roosevelt rallying us all.

Churchill: We shall fight on the beaches, we shall fight on the landing grounds, we shall fight in the fields and in the streets, we shall fight in the hills: we shall never surrender. Hostilities exist. There is no blinking at the fact that our people, our territory and our interests are in grave danger.

Roosevelt: With confidence in our armed forces—with the unbounding determination of our people—we will gain the inevitable triumph—so help us God.

And one day President Roosevelt had used his radio address to instruct us how to re-use coffee grounds a second day. Ah, something I could do myself to push things along, to help bring this horrible war to an end.

*   *   *

The experience of that war is with me still. On the one hand, the sense of national purpose, of a giant country waking to a task, of factories working all day and all night but darkened—mandatory in the blackouts—known only by their smoke at night. Grandmothers moved in with daughters to be with grandchildren while mothers went to work, often in those very factories. So-called temporary buildings appeared on the Mall in Washington to make space for the temporary workers that filled them. Posters appeared: "Uncle Sam Wants <u>You</u>," "Rosie the Riveter," "Loose Lips Sink Ships." We would receive V-mail from our men overseas with lines blacked out; cigarettes went to the army; invited out for a meal, we would take our ration cards. Nylon stockings appeared, then disappeared. We learned to roll bandages, make hospital corners on beds, respond to blood drives. We lived a double life, the one that maintained us and the one overseas, as country after country, then towns, villages, and countrysides flamed with battles in which men we knew were fighting.

And war was inescapable; it was in the air. Radios were on all day with news bulletins—Normandy, the Battle of the Bulge—and music: "When the lights go on again all over the world," "There'll be bluebirds over/ The white cliffs of Dover," "When the Fuhrer says this is the master race/ We'll say Heil, Heil, Heil right in the Fuhrer's face," "Don't sit under the apple tree with anyone else but me," "Remember Pearl Harbor when we go to meet the foe," and "This is the army, Mr. Jones." They set the rhythm of our pace as we walked to save gas. Pictures appeared in the newspapers, of bombs with messages on them: "This One's For You, Hitler." Other pictures appeared of men dead, dismembered, sodden, and of the coffins that carried them back in increasing numbers from both coasts. Did the nation unify only to kill, or for its sons to be killed? As my trip south informed me, didn't we have more urgent matters to settle in our own country before bailing out Europe? I was no isolationist; my mother was an unreconstructed Scottish woman whose loyalty to her country we learned to share. It was the horror of intentional killing that seemed to paralyze me, even as I did my best for "the war." I was not among those who cheered the atomic bomb. That awful morning I felt that the world was now in ultimate peril, that this country, my country, had unleashed the final cataclysm, and that it was a matter of time before the world and all its tenants would disappear.

Bill in China, 1945.

XII

A DEATH IN THE FAMILY

The web of war loosened on August 15, 1945, when General MacArthur announced that Japan had surrendered, although the actual signing and ceremonies were on September 2nd. Bill came back soon after, and we moved to New York, where Bill enrolled at Columbia University to complete his Ph.D in Philosophy. In China he had met a brilliant law student who was also going to Columbia University to complete his degree, and who knew other students, so that Bill was soon part of a group of bright, politically interested friends, many of whom had grown up in New York. They enjoyed the presence in their discussions of a philosopher who could and did challenge basic assumptions of life and law, but Bill and I profited even more. These New Yorkers knew where apartments could be found, and after a few disappointments, such as arriving at a sure address to find three other prospective tenants ahead of us, we found the ultimate luxury, a two-bedroom apartment on upper Amsterdam Avenue. Within a week the second bedroom had been rented to a fellow graduate student, and the living-room couch similarly reserved. New York City was full.

From the living-room windows we could see the backyards of apartment houses, with their traceries of laundry lines and flapping garments, and glimpses of civilian life returning: crowded kitchen tables, books on the window sills, and lights, lights burning late into the night. In the fall, the busyness of a reviving city was stilled for one day. On September 17, 1945, I was awed by the silence defined by the

213

sound that broke it—the shofar proclaiming the first High Holy Days of the peace. It was as if here in New York, after all the scorning, burning, and slaughter overseas, the Jews were saying, "We are still here. We are here. It is a new year."

I wanted to be ready for another job teaching and, my experience at Sunbury High having persuaded me that a student's ability to read was a good place to start, I registered for courses in the methodology of remedial reading at the City College of New York. My student-teaching for these classes further persuaded me that the ability to read was considerably influenced by whether or not the student had had breakfast, and I became interested in the lives and conditions of urban children. Between classes I would ride the subways, subsisting on the little ten-cent chocolate bars dispensed by machines on the platforms, and listen to what people were talking about.

Along with many of our friends, we were in a hurry to start a family. I had had a long series of gynecological irregularities, and we spent much of our wartime savings on trying to make a family possible. In a few months I became pregnant, but lost the baby early. A silk-hatted, gray-cravatted Fifth Avenue gynecologist, stepping gingerly among the books, suitcases, and groceries stored in the long dark corridor of our apartment, confirmed the loss; at least our baby left well-attended. The reason for the premature birth may have been the small-pox vaccinations required that year in New York City.

Bill and I met often with other graduate students for picnics, usually in the park under the George Washington Bridge, where graduate theses would be discussed and refined. As Bill developed his, I typed it, the little Olympia typewriter set on a flat rock, the Hudson River flowing by, hardly more murky than the subjects being discussed on its shore. Bill finally turned in his work, "Government and the Arts of Obedience," a title that evoked considerable good-natured teasing from our friends: "Which one of you is the government?"

Bill and I had come to terms with our marriage; there was simply too much to do, to look forward to, to waste time tearing it apart. The country had shifted from trying to destroy people and their civilizations to rebuilding and repopulating its own, and most people were focusing on doing the same in their lives. In May of 1947 Bill accepted what was apparently the only job open to a professional philosopher in that academically frenetic postwar period: professor of philosophy at Whitman College, in Walla Walla, Washington. I was skeptical of our chances of being happy there; at that time—I was told —no Picasso painting hung west of the Rockies, and we both loved New York with its museums and concerts.

We moved west in September and found a small paradise—a group of attentive, bright people, eager for new ideas and new additions to the faculty. We settled in, bought a house, and quickly became part of this group of friends. I discovered that, absent the New York Philharmonic, violin lessons were offered by the college symphony's conductor. Bill and I bought a piano and played duets after supper. Students walked to the house for discussion groups without having to negotiate a New York subway. Professors taught their courses in the fall, winter, and spring, and worked on the pea harvest in the summer to augment their salaries. I learned how to channel irrigation water into our back yard to grow potatoes, and later spent enchanted hours with our children watching the water find and claim

Walla Walla, 1948, in the backyard garden.

its path.

On the strength of my meager two courses on the subject, I became a remedial-reading consultant for the public schools of Walla Walla and nearby counties. I would load the car with teaching materials, then drive for hours through the wide, open country, with its wheat fields stretching for miles, irrigation canals catching the light beside me, to isolated one-room or two-room school houses tucked away in the low hills to the east. I loved the work, the students, the teachers. I loved our Whitman faculty friends. From time to time Bill and I played piano duets for them in the evening as they listened sociably—and critically. The cities and cathedrals of Europe were safe from bombing. Life was good.

Six years married and still unable to have a child, we applied to an adoption agency and were accepted. While we waited, I became pregnant. Donald arrived on June 5, 1949. Almost immediately my old fears of damaging people returned. The nurse, handing me the baby as I left the hospital, told me, "He will be all right if you leave him alone." If I leave him alone? Now others also thought I would be damaging to him. Terrified, I took him home in fear and wonder that such a treasure was given to me to care for and to love.

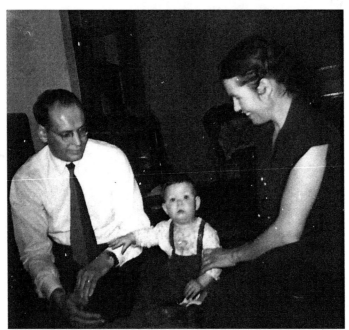

Walla Walla, 1950: Don at eight-and-a-half months.

We took the gynecologist's advice to "catch it on the run," and Paul came eleven months later, on May 25, 1950. I was ecstatic: two healthy, beautiful, responsive children, whose every move I watched and enjoyed. I was entranced by them, but still terrified that I would hurt them by providing food insufficiently sterile, or by letting them put unwashed hands to their mouths. If a fly flew through the kitchen while I was making formula, or the bottles hadn't boiled the requisite five minutes, or had subsequently cooled, I would throw out what I had made and start again. Sometimes I would prepare formula seven times over, while a hungry baby cried. The pediatrician reminded me of the thousands of Chinese infants who survived in surroundings far less promising than my kitchen in Walla Walla, but I had also seen dead Chinese babies floating in the moat of the Forbidden City in Peking, or lying in the *hutung* by our house in that city. His arguments, reasonable and concerned, failed to persuade me.

Walla Walla, November 1950: Donald and Paul consulting.

In spite of this chaotic care, the babies thrived. Donald was a bright, watchful infant, blue-eyed, cheery, though with apparent comfort silent, until he was about two, when he started to talk fluently. About that time he also began to develop some rituals that seemed strange to us: writhing his hands, bringing them up to his face, bowing his head toward them. Sometimes he would tap a rocking chair to set it moving, then peer from behind a door to watch it until it stopped. He could not hold a pencil or spoon. He would often seem not to be hearing us, as if absorbed in newspapers or books, which he could not yet read. We began to think that we needed the evaluation of a specialist, not then available in Walla Walla. Some administrative problems had evolved at the college, and Bill had been asked to merge the departments of religion and philosophy, which he refused to do. So he decided to make a change, and in June of 1950 went east to try to find a position where we could get appropriate psychiatric help for Donald and me.

Winter, 1950-51: Bill and Don outside the homesteader's cabin.

Bill found a job as an analyst with the federal government in Washington, DC, with good health benefits, and came back to teach for his last year at Whitman. We sold our house and moved to a homesteader's cabin until the academic year was up. The cabin was far out in the wheat fields; the children, now aged one and two, chased the tumbleweeds blowing across the yard and against the fence, and played hide-and-seek in the barn. I enjoyed the isolation and the far-off horizons; life among others had exposed my anxieties, and off in the country I could control their exposure, both for the children's sake and for my own.

Back in the east, in the fall of 1951, we soon consulted a child psychologist, Dr. Hanna Colm, nationally famous for her diagnostic skills. After she tested Donald, Bill and I met her in her sunny office.

She told us that Donald was autistic, that he would never be able to go to school, and that we should not allow our lives to be constrained by his difficulties. She offered to help us find an institution where he could be appropriately cared for. We could think it over and call her later, she said. We thanked her, paid, and left.

In our living room we looked at each other in silence. Finally Bill spoke. "I'm for it. We owe him as comfortable a life as he is able to handle." I told him I couldn't do it. He responded that we had sought the very best advice possible; it made no sense to turn it down. I told him I could not sign; I could not institutionalize a two-year-old. Who would tuck him into bed at night, even though he turned his head away from the goodnight kiss? We ceased the discussion and informed Dr. Colm that we would not be following her recommendation.

In the meantime Bill had started work for his then-secret agency, and we moved from our first lodgings to a beautiful ranch house in a relatively isolated development in northern Virginia, near a good child-guidance clinic in Fairfax, where we enrolled as a family. In those years most children's psychiatric difficulties were seen as caused by the unfeeling, uncaring, "refrigerator" mother, further reinforcing my conviction that I was bad for people. The polio epidemic was in full force, and my fears had evolved into what was then called a post-partum psychosis, which included a terrifying fear of the children's contracting the disease. I avoided taking them into neighborhoods where the disease had been reported. I didn't wash their faces for fear that I would let germs in. I began also to fear that I might hurt the children directly, and took all our knives to the psychiatrist I was seeing. I boiled or steamed everything until it was tender enough to eat without being cut.

About this time my sister Janet called me. Not long before, she had returned from Indonesia to New York with her husband, who was at the Rusk Institute in Manhattan for rehabilitation from the polio he had contracted overseas. "Margaret, can you care for my daughters while I get settled and find job and a house?" She and one daughter had been ill, probably with a mild form of the disease. I was scared, but of course agreed. She came down once to visit them, found that I was not keeping their faces clean, and asked my sister Barbara, ten years younger than I, and with no children, to come from her home in Philadelphia to monitor their care until Janet could take them back. When Barbara, on her arrival, told me why she was there, I was deeply humiliated; I thought I had done a courageous and loving thing by agreeing to care for Janet's daughters when I was so frightened of the disease that had been in their home so recently. A few weeks after Barbara's arrival, Janet found a house on Long Island and retrieved her daughters. I began to feel irrational, threw my wedding ring into the forest behind our house where it may be still, and began to think of suicide. We lived not far from the Potomac River.

A year later we moved further inland, and bought a house in an old neighborhood of rolling hills, tall trees, and brooks. The community was mixed; three houses from ours the boys used the owners' outside toilet; two houses away on the other side we played tennis on the neighbors' private court. Our house was set incongruously on the edge of a wide, forty-five-degree slope of grass, a heaven for pitchers in the neighborhood boys' baseball games that took place year round.

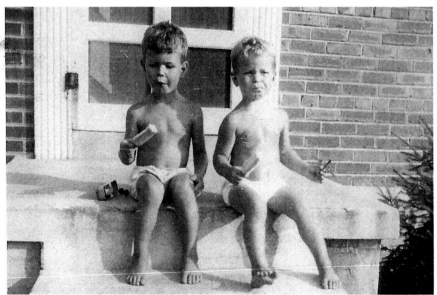

Donald and Paul, 1913 Oliver Street, West Hyattsville, Maryland, 1953.

At the child guidance clinic, Donald was progressing with a wonderful therapist, and in 1954 it seemed time to enroll him in kindergarten. At first no school, public or private, would admit him; but an old family friend of my parents, the principal of a private elementary school, heard of the situation, and offered what was at first asylum. But Donald proved to be a difficult pupil, often retreating from teachers or other students, or, alternately, screaming, and unable to participate predictably in school activities. Other parents urged that he be withdrawn and that the school in the future be more conservative in its admissions. Another private school accepted him provisionally. We invested our savings in therapy for the whole family, and Donald, with the continuing help of his brilliant and empathic therapist, slowly began to make his lonely way through the American suburban culture. At home he would sit on the sidelines of neighborhood boys' games, reading, toy pistols at his belt, twisting his fingers, occasionally leaping up to pace back and forth. A gifted teacher at school named him "the professor," and gradually in the car pool after school he would mention names of classmates. One or two came to his birthday parties; he was never invited to theirs. Bill could not bear to spend time alone with Donald, and generally arranged for Paul or me to be there also.

Paul had entered a local kindergarten and I became active in county Democratic politics. I drove in carpools taking Donald to school, but I was normally home after school. Though a famously dreadful housekeeper, I was still psychotic about food and germs, insisting that the children eat nothing my hands had touched, including the corner crusts of peanut-butter sandwiches I left for them if I was going to be out when they came home. On vacation trips Bill would take them into restaurants while I sat in the car, eating sandwiches, anxious until they came out.

The children were in kindergarten and first grade when, one day, before he started my therapy session, the psychiatrist told me that he had information for me. He had been approached by my sons' teachers, asking that the children be taken away from me. The boys had been going to school with dirty faces, he said, and the other children were making fun of them. I asked if action toward this had been taken; he assured me that he had simply been approached. I left, drove home, and found Paul eating the peanut butter sandwich I had left. As I came in he made as if to put down a corner of the sandwich. I hurried to face him: "Eat it," I said. He seemed puzzled, but did as I asked. I did not explain, and all finger food was suddenly clear of the inhibition. The next day I taught the boys how to wash their faces, and that too eventually became routine. I had read that boiling anything for twenty minutes would sterilize it, and now applied the principle to food I cooked. Most of it therefore tasted dreadful, but I could count on a hungry family.

Later, when Paul was an adult I asked him about that peanut-butter-sandwich moment, which he recalled, and about how it felt to be brought up by someone who feared she would poison him. He answered that all adults seemed to have their strange ways, and that that had been mine.

It was shortly after this that I set out from the front door of the house one afternoon, intending to jump from a bridge over the Potomac. I felt that I was hindering the boys' lives, that they would be better off with a quiet, brilliant father who would have the resources to hire better housekeeping than I was providing, and that they would be far better off freed from the anxiety with which I surrounded them.

I went to say goodbye to them outside in the yard, where they were playing, and they asked where I was going. I said, "To some bridge." They joined me, Paul beside me, Donald on the other side of him, all three of us looking straight ahead. We walked in silence about a hundred yards down the road. Then Paul touched my arm lightly. "Mom," he said, "don't."

The Hollisters, circa 1957.

I looked down at him, marveling. He was seven years old. How did he know? Then the horror of what I had done to the boys poured over me and we went to the side of the road and sat down on the verge. I apologized to them. Paul accepted it, and said he hoped I would try not to do it again, and I said they could count on that. Donald twisted his hands more tightly, bowing his head toward them, and after a minute or two we all three got up and walked in silence back home.

One day my doctor suggested I get myself a career. I asked why, and he simply said, "You're going to need one." My work in Democratic politics had taught me that it takes power to make changes, and that changes begin with people. I applied to Catholic University's graduate department of psychology and was accepted. The first week I found myself scheduled for afternoon laboratory sessions, and reluctantly left the program. Though Paul had a friend whose house he could go to, Donald was not ready to be left with anyone else. Where else to go for power for change?

I used the next year to apply to the social work school at Catholic University, which had more flexible hours. A member of the Fairfax Clinic was on the faculty and I was skeptical of being accepted, but I was, in September 1959, and was given a clinical field placement at a hospital for people needing inpatient psychiatric care. The faculty member who had been at the clinic told me at the time they just wanted to see if I could stay out of the hospital myself. The whole family came for graduation in 1961. As I came up the aisle, in cap and gown, my Master of Social Work certificate in my hand, and walked past two clapping little boys, I felt wonderful. I had acquired a set of tools of my own. If necessary, I could take care of my children. And I had a degree that permitted me to do work I believed in.

Circumstances in the family had changed. In the summer of 1961 Bill unilaterally made the decision to buy a house in a county with better schools. Because I was in a new job, I felt unable to move. We did, but the move did not hold. We found another buyer for the new house and moved back to our old neighborhood, renting this time. It was severely traumatic for us all. Donald had been prepared to move to a public school, but went back to his private one, and Paul returned to the school he had left. After a year, Bill was accepted for a Ford Foundation fellowship in economics at the University of California in Berkeley, and wanted us all to move with him. I was not ready to move, the boys themselves wanted to stay with the known, and Bill agreed to a trial separation, with a decision about our marriage to be made the following spring. The boys and I moved to be nearer my workplace, into a little carriage house, with a fireplace in one corner and loft-rooms up a narrow stair. Both the boys went to the public school nearby.

Bill came back for Christmas and urged us to join him in Berkeley immediately. I couldn't: it was too soon; it would again disrupt the boys' schooling; Kennedy had been assassinated; the world was too rickety. I needed to stay put. We agreed to meet at Easter, and in the spring the boys and I flew out to California. Bill greeted us at the airport saying that the week was clear except for one afternoon. I nearly took a return plane trip back, but decided to keep our arrangement for the trial visit. We were all together in a movie theater when he left to keep his date with a woman he had been seeing, and our marriage was over.

Don and Paul in their high school years.

I now needed to make long-term plans, and decided to live and work in a more diverse environment than Montgomery County, Maryland, then offered. We moved to the District of Columbia in the summer of 1964, to a battered apartment where Paul's friends from school spent a day with us swatting cockroaches and repainting the rooms. The next year we moved to a duplex filled with the books of its owner, a book reviewer for the Washington Post, which gave me a sense of instant stability, and would serve as our home through Paul's graduation from Wilson High School in 1968. In the meantime I joined the District of Columbia Department of Mental Health, and in 1966 started working at DC's inpatient facility near the general hospital and the jail.

Donald enrolled in a public high school, where he had always longed to be. There his classmates respected his brilliance, played with him in chess and bridge clubs, and mocked him behind his back. He exulted in winning the city-wide French language prize in a multi-cultural city, and finally graduated, triumphantly, from Wilson High in 1967, having been accepted by Oberlin College, his first choice.

From there it was all downhill for him. He had written his prospective roommate, but received no reply. Nevertheless, he left home eagerly; he had always wanted to make his own way. I once asked the boys what they wanted from me, and Donald's answer was "Less." Finally he was off, away from mother and brother and from the lifelong focus on him. At Thanksgiving, he came home disillusioned with college, but still eager to go back. He called soon after he was back in Oberlin: he had returned to an empty dormitory room. His roommate had moved out, leaving no message. Donald's voice on the phone was flat; he was reporting, but he gave me the number of the telephone that he said was "just down the hall." I never reached him on it.

In his sophomore year an erstwhile friend from high school, with whom he had often played bridge, transferred to Oberlin. Don's journal has an entry: "Someone left Jim's bridge foursome in the commons room, and Jim asked if anyone wanted to join them. I said I would, and Jim asked whether anyone else wanted to join. So I went back to my room."

He graduated, again triumphantly, from Oberlin in 1971, a history major and music buff. After we came back to D.C., Donald, a friend of his, and I went to Bethany Beach to celebrate, only to find, on returning home, that his precious hi-fi and all his equipment had been stolen. His joy in graduation seemed to leave him, and he began to be depressed. He tried to find a job in Washington, but it was 1972, and employment opportunities were moving away from young white men, especially those with a low draft number. He dutifully reported to the draft board, but, at six feet two and only a hundred and fifty pounds, was too thin. He finally found a job as a bus boy in a local restaurant. When he received his first paycheck, he handed me $10, saying, "It's nice to have it going in this direction." Through my job I found a program that offered federal employment for adults with disabilities, which he applied for, and a colleague of mine said she would try to expedite his application.

One day at the restaurant where he worked, Donald found a quarter lying on the carpet. In a panic, he reported it to his manager, saying he hadn't stolen it. The manager, seeing his distress, kindly gave him the rest of the day off, and Donald never went back, convinced he was a criminal. One night shortly afterward, as I lay in bed, he knocked on my door, and brought me a standard printed utility-bill envelope, holding it out to me in his hand. "I know the handwriting," he said. The room was dark. A chill came over me; as a psychiatric social worker I knew the symptoms of psychosis. I thanked him for it, he left, and I rolled over in bed, sobbing. All the years, the long years of advocacy for me, the brave years of guts and loneliness and forging ahead for him, seemed gone with that letter.

I urged him to return to therapy, but from then on he stayed in his room, or went on long walks, more and more agitated. At times he said he felt people were watching him. "I need new shoes, people are noticing." I urged him to return to his former therapist, with whom he had had so good a relationship, or to see someone else, but he refused. His brother came back from college and drove him to the beach cottage of friends, with whom Don had always felt comfortable. He took his favorite books there, leaving them as a thank-you gift.

By now I was working at a different mental health clinic, often late into the evening, since we were starting a new program. Finally, one evening, the call I had been fearing came. Paul was on his way to Georgetown Hospital. Don had been brought there by the fire department, after an eighty-two-foot jump from a bridge onto rocky parkland. He had suffered a broken leg and some internal injuries, and was furious that he had lived. With donations of blood, mostly from the staff of the mental health center where I worked, and six weeks of intensive care, which he resisted by pulling out his tubes, he came home in a body cast. He had to be turned every two hours to prevent bedsores; Paul left college to help care for him. The night of the Academy Awards, just before Don's cast was to come off, I threw a small party to celebrate; the neighbors and a friend of Paul's came.

After everyone left, Don found the rubbing alcohol bottle left near him and swallowed its contents, triumphantly silent as I called the ambulance.

At St. Elizabeth's Hospital he was admitted to the section for the poorer part of the city, corresponding to where we lived. His bed was in a corridor. During the first month his leg was broken again. When I suggested suing the hospital Donald refused, saying, "From what I can see, Mother, this hospital needs every cent it has got." By now, having been defeated in his attempts to die, and disillusioned with his care, he refused for four months to have his leg repaired. But an elderly attendant persuaded him that he had people who cared about him, was stuck with a life to live, and would live it better with two functioning legs.

Sensing hope and help for the first time since his graduation, Donald agreed to the operation. I had attended a recent open house at the hospital, and, shocked at the conditions for surgery—no post-operative care unit, for instance—tried to persuade him to have the operation elsewhere. But Don was adamant that the surgery be done in the hospital he was in. As his conservator, I forced myself to sign the permission for the procedure.

I went to see him on the morning of the operation. He was drowsy. "How are you?" I asked. "Mom, I have hope at last," he said. I don't remember my reply. Hearing the word "hope" from him silenced all other sounds. I sat alone in the small waiting room all day. During the day, there was a code blue (the signal for a medical emergency), and a call for blood platelets. I was told that these were not for Donald. At the end of the day there was another code blue. I rushed to the administrative nurses' office and was told that the alarm was not for my son, and to calm down. Finally the chaplain came. "Ms. Hollister, there has been a bad result. May I accompany you?" In silence we went down the hall with the surgeon to a ward room where Donald lay alone, his eyes blank, his head grossly swollen. The surgeon lifted the blanket over the bandaged leg. "A perfect mend," he said. When I got home that evening, an envelope was on the table. It contained a job offering from the federal government program, but Donald was brain dead.

A distinguished Italian neurologist, who was visiting St. Elizabeth's, was called in. I was told that Donald had a brain stem injury, that he would never recover. The surgeon urged me not to let my life be constrained by my son's condition, words I had heard 22 years before. I continued to visit him twice daily, having read that sometimes a familiar voice sufficiently heard would renew brain activity, but Don remained unconscious, gasping through the tubes. Once I was accompanied by a friend who had had a cerebral-palsied son who had recently died. "I think Don is responding," she said. And he could recognize music, as the nurses and I discovered; they sang spirituals to him at night and noticed that he relaxed. Thereafter I taped music familiar to him, which I played on visits, and Don would seem to signal choices, grossly, with a grunt. His doctors declared this impossible; the nurses disagreed and continued to sing spirituals at night. He never showed that he recognized any of us. Finally, during an early retirement option for nurses, the experienced nurses left, Donald was inadequately suctioned, and died on September 8, 1973. His father was with him at the end. He is buried in Mt. Airy Cemetery, near Cincinnati, next to his Hollister grandparents. His gravestone reads: "Donald George Hollister—1949-1973—Beloved."

Later, rehearsing the whole sequence of events and puzzled by the delay of over five hours between the time Don was picked up on the rocks and the notification of our family, I called the District of Columbia police. It seems that the police had been following him that day, that he had visited Congress, and so, they said, "There was a lot to be checked out" before his family could be notified. After all those years, how little I knew him!

Recent, and increasing, studies in autism have offered information, but no answer to the experience of loving someone diagnosed with the disease. I still question my terrible authority in denying him institutionalization that might have provided a life less lonely and painful for him. Donald's legacy is still a mystery to me. The door he went through intending to kill himself also opened to admit the ambulance that carried him to the hospital where he died. It is hard to think that with all the care and concern that surrounded him during his life with us, I failed to know him, to understand his longing for privacy, and his equal longing to be accepted as he was. What remains is the nearly unbearable experience of having loved someone honest, brilliant, and brave, and having been unable to provide for him the life he deserved.

At first it was difficult to handle, and I took refuge in blaming myself. A wise counselor, Carolyn Moynihan, reframed my dilemma with one question. Interrupting a blubbering session of self-reproach over the phone, she asked, "How arrogant can you get?" Indeed.

During the years after our sons' births, the fears of poisoning them, the disorder that came with my psychosis, and the despair that led my sons into the path of a suicidal threat did damage them. So how does one live on, in comfort, among friends, with a rewarding career, in a lovely house, taking responsibility for having hurt those you love? It was easy to feel guilty, seriously guilty, toward those whom I had hurt, and I thought it was helpful to let them know that. But that was giving them a cup with no handle, and empty to boot. Why make them carry any more of the load?

It was then that I experienced the pain, and came to realize that for me guilt had been a cover for pain, the pain that actions of mine had hurt people I loved and had been responsible for, even for their being. So with pain, what is possible? As with physical pain, amelioration seemed the way—to make things easier for them if possible, to risk staying in touch, and to enjoy each other without the carapace of guilt. It was all I knew to do.

*   *   *

Paul went to Antioch College in Ohio, then to Norway, to France, and, after college, for ten years to the streets of Columbus, Cleveland, and Cincinnati, Ohio, where he and others attempted to persuade people of the inequities of the capitalist system. Eventually the group disbanded, and Paul moved to New York to support his family—he had married twice and had three children—by working with computers.

And I had my beloved career. I was lucky in the late 1960s to find myself working in a team led by a psychiatrist who believed that the best diagnosis starts with the person's name. Such a belief fit easily with a way of working in the inner city, where we were based. In public health in Washington, D.C., both staff and patients were predominantly African-American. When our team was first assembled, we met to find out what we wanted to be called—first names, nicknames, last names, or titles? We went around the group; people wanted to be called "Jimmy," or "Ms. Briggs," or "Vin." My education in race jumped a level when the turn came for a bright, exceptionally skilled nursing assistant, mother of five children, who answered "White."

Our team leader preferred to do intake evaluations in the potential patient's home with family members present. Putting the emphasis on common family problems muted any divisions within our group. There were many crosshairs for a mixed-race team, and once an African-American advocacy group came to observe us as we discussed a case, to be sure that we were operating without bias, or at least that we were aware of what biases we had. We passed. Walking along a sidewalk anywhere still is a completely different experience for an African American than it is for me. My thirty-eight years in public health in the District of Columbia delivered every day something new, something to learn. Two years after joining the mental health staff, I was working in the inpatient psychiatric ward on the day that Dr. Martin Luther King, Jr. was killed. Streets near the building blazed. A white colleague and I stood at a window, watching the flames and smoke. He turned to me. "Two thousand years of Christianity," he said, "and now this." Just then an African-American colleague came up behind us. "Turn on your headlights going home," he said. "Then people will know you are OK."

Slowly I began to be aware. Aware of the differences, of the miserable history of slavery, of the new misery of desegregation, of the possible humiliation of someone in public housing as the white social worker, briefcase in hand, approaches her door. Aware of the passivity of a population in a city without a vote in the Congress that approves its budget, aware of the until-recently all-white Senate that must approve whether the city's citizens, voteless, go to war. Aware of the appalling condition of the city's schools while parents, believing that education is the way up and out of ghettos, tell their children to "do well in school, you hear?"

Once I asked an African-American colleague a kindness that had racial implications of which I was unaware. His acquiescence would make a painful situation easier for me. He refused. "You can't have that, Mrs. Hollister," he said. Surprised, I asked why. He leaned back in his chair. "Because I won't give it to you." Suddenly I realized the racial quality of the request, and, ashamed, fled the room. Later I began to think of the power of that response and asked another colleague why African Americans do not use that power more often—refusing the prejudice. He looked at me gently. "Have you lately checked the racial composition of the United States Senate?" he asked.

As a social worker I believed that the problems people brought with them were efforts toward solutions for them, and thus deserved full respect. Their problems were their property, and I considered it an honor that they brought them to me when their solutions weren't working for them. I usually asked, whatever the complexity of the difficulties a client presented, "What is your plan? What do you see as useful to you?" When asked what was man's chief concern, Professor Santayana of Harvard is said to have answered, "What he does next." It was an exciting moment when a person, distressed and confused, began to see what he or she could do next.

But the most exciting and productive moment of all was when a client and I could be simply human with each other. It was my experience that people of color, but perhaps especially African Americans, because they have experienced so much prejudice, often don't know what to expect from a white person. I would be approached guardedly, with innocuous greetings, often expecting to be told something. They would then back off, as if behind a scrim, to wait for what the response would tell them about whether they could trust me further. What was behind the obligatory handshake? What were they about to hear and then evaluate?

It sometimes took reminding them that as a public health worker I was their employee, and needed to hear from them what they expected from me. Sometimes, less startling, I would tell them something about myself—that, for example, I was honored to meet them, or humbled by their bringing their needs to me, or, with mothers, how difficult it is to be one, or something about my family. Once the essential humanity of both of us was established, the office air seemed jeweled, sparkling with the pleasure of being human, as we worked together on an agreed task.

Such conversation had its risks—listening to despair, raw feelings, damage to children, and an occasional scary moment—but it offered the possibility of a relationship that might be useful in itself. A teacher friend recently defined therapy as learning, which applies when both participants can listen directly to each other. Every day of my working life I have loved being a social worker.

XIII

JOYS ALONG THE WAY

Aside from the ultimate joy of family and friends, there are other ways in which I have been enchanted.

I have the pleasure of living in a house rebuilt by friends. Every corner, every step, every window frame, wall, joist, floorboard, counter-top—everything bears their judgment, work, and affection. After my husband and I divorced, our sons were with me, and we lived near their school. When they left for college, I wanted to move to the inner city in Washington to be closer to my work, and found a fine apartment with a fireplace. A house nearby became available to rent, and in the interest of being able to control an independent entrance, I moved in 1968 to the house, at the then-going rental rate of $125 a month. A couple of years later, the owner, having married a French psychoanalyst, reasonably decided to buy an apartment in Paris, offering the house I was renting for $29,000, a price my $9,000-a-year salary then could not approach. But I loved the area, it was nine blocks from my work, and the house, too, had a fireplace. I turned to the boys' grandmother, Mrs. Hollister, who had visited me there, and asked if she could help. She responded wholeheartedly. She could indeed. In fact, it would help her out, she said, since she was dividing her estate, and didn't know what to do about my surviving son's share, since he had somewhat far-left leanings. If I could buy the house with her help, Paul's share would be tied up in it, and he could profit from it when his politics had steadied down a bit. But she had conditions: an improved bathroom and kitchen.

The house before deconstruction, circa 1971.

Through a friend I met a wonderful couple, the Danielsons, who had just moved from the west. Debbie was working for the government. Dana, an engineer by training and an architect, builder, and visionary, checked over the house and decided that it was "a bunch of junk," advising me not to buy it. But it had location, nine blocks from the Capitol, and—my chief requirement—that fireplace. In addition, my furniture and I were in it, and since the divorce the boys and I had moved so often that I just wanted to stay put. So Dana agreed to work on the kitchen and the bathroom, and I bought the house. Shortly afterwards he greeted me on my return from work one Friday, and told me to sit down. I had learned to do what he said, and sat. He said he had always wanted to work on an all-wooden house, and would like to remodel this one. He estimated he would need about $22,000, and suggested we call Mrs. Hollister again, saying she could recoup the money with the refinancing of a greatly improved house.

Debbie and Dana Danielson in my kitchen, circa 2005.

I called her—again she was enthusiastic. She said she would send a check the following Monday. That weekend Dana, Debbie, a friend of theirs, and I literally dismantled the house. It came apart almost in our hands, and we piled into the back yard all we tore down. One wall had been basically tar-paper covered with cow plaster. The chimney had six large holes in it. On Monday I got a phone call. Mrs. Hollister had died on Sunday night; the check was never sent.

I at once freed Dana from any obligation—I had been raised in China, I said—and could bivouac in the back yard until I found a way, etc., etc. He refused, and for five years worked on the house, alone, with help on weekends and sometimes in the evenings from Debbie, from me, and from assorted friends. We had fun. After the house was a shell, open from soil to ceiling, we entered the front door dramatically, locking it. Debbie, a superb cook and hostess, gave parties with food served as we sat on the joists, our feet dangling to the dirt floor. After some years we needed cash, and decided to try for refinancing. I got a call at work from a bank officer at the house with Dana. "Ms. Hollister, your house needs to be in trim condition to merit application for refinancing. Your house has no stairs. Are you willing to consider stairs a trim?" We had been running up and down ladders for four years. I assured him I was willing, and at last we had some money.

After demolition, looking down from the second floor. The ladder served as stairs for about four years.

The south wall. Boards like the one hanging at an angle to the left were once part of the wall, but we removed them and used them to lay the bottom floor.

The house now, of polished old wood, cream-colored walls, and elegant open stairs, stands for me not only as a perfect place to live, but as a metaphor for the scaffoldings we build with friends to sustain and to shelter each other.

After restoration, circa 1980, looking from the front door toward the rear of the house. From the left, clockwise around the table: Polly Brown, me, Dana, Debbie, and their son Tom in the child's carrier.

South wall now with side panels of a Chinese lantern shade.

Front of the house, circa 2006.

*   *   *

There is another house, on Second Street, in Bethany Beach, Delaware, made available to me for a week in October for over forty years by a friend, Polly Brown, and her daughters. It is seven houses from the Atlantic Ocean. Through the years this cottage has welcomed all my family and most of my friends. I have come whatever the weather. Once a hurricane was predicted during my stay there. I called the owner for advice about how to secure the house. He answered calmly. "Well, Margaret," he said, "you'll find a rope coiled around one corner of the house. And down the street there's a telephone pole...."

The house, the sea, and the silence are paradise enough. The affection of the owners who offered them to me is the joy that brings the house into this chapter. Polly Brown died a few years ago. In the words of another friend of hers, Richard Gilman, "One feels her presence and her absence" at Bethany. I carry the cottage key on my keychain, so that daily the rest, the beauty, the affection of the owners, and the solace of the sea are with me all year long.

Polly Brown, seated, and her family at Bethany Beach, circa 2000. Daughters Deborah, Kate, and Suzanne are in the front row.

*   *   *

To speak two or three different languages is to have two or three totally different selves, like odd suits of clothing.

Alastair Reid, *Notes on Being a Foreigner*

Since the time I could speak, the Chinese language has been there for me, like another self, running along beside me as I grew up. I could always summon it when I needed it, step into it, as it were, whether I needed another self temporarily, or whether English was simply too exacting, too linear, too prescriptive for any particular occasion. Chinese provided a landscape—pictorial, allusive; one could walk around in it.*

---

*   Much has been written about Chinese characters, their evolution, meaning, and style: the scholarly, the "people's speech," and the modern simplified version. This brief essay is limited to my own experience with the language, without scholarly reference or resource. I am indebted to Dr. Wieger's book, *Chinese Characters*, published in 1965, for his information about early bronze characters, and to Dr. C. H. Fenn's *The Five Thousand Dictionary*, published in 1926 and edited by several others since then, including my father J. D. Hayes in 1936, assisted by Mr. Chin Hsien Tseng. It is from this dictionary that I have taken the translations and interpretations used here. The *ch'ien tze k'e*, or one thousand characters, are from a Chinese text we studied at Tungchow, and are based on the

And what have the two selves these languages, learned in infancy, taught me? Chinese is the language of myself, private, illustrated, beautiful and autonomous, fixed in images more than six thousand years old, a language I can wander in and be surprised by. English is the language I use, requiring precision, thought, and discipline, bound by rules and context, and beautiful by affection and choice. For me it is the language of behavior; Chinese is the language of being.

I did not, however, learn Chinese first from a native. When I was an infant, my mother was learning the language in order to be able to present herself as an acceptable daughter-in-law, and my father was her teacher. So not only was my first exposure to spoken Chinese from people whose primary language was English, but it was also in the context of the need to please, and even more, perhaps, woven into the forming of a relationship. Could it have taken on an intensity between these two adults living together alone for the first time—an urgency that an infant would pick up? Did relationships depend for their quality on a learned language? In our family anything spoken had to be precise. Was the legacy of those months the desperation of precision?

I was seven months old when we finally arrived in Peking. The hundred-year-old *amah* provided for me was difficult to understand, having lost many of her teeth, so my first exposure to the language from a Chinese person led me to seek others. I learned it chiefly from those who took care of us, the servants. Our household was bilingual; mother was a quick learner, and my father, born in China, spoke Chinese fluently. My parents did not use language loosely; after my mother learned Chinese, they spoke to us exclusively in English. There were thus two levels of language in our household. One was what might be called executive speech, either in English or Chinese, for running the house, working in the mission, talking to outsiders, or with other missionaries. The other was the relaxed, homely Chinese address of caretaking. If I wanted to summon the *amah*, I would call out *nai nai*, which means "grandmother," the name used for *amahs*. She would say *ai* in acknowledgement, and I might say *wah yao ni*—"I want you." She then might ask *ni yao shen ma?*—"What do you want?" And I might answer *wah chio yao ni*—"I just want you." If I had gotten hurt, she might ask, *t'ung ma?*—"Does it hurt?" And I would answer *tui la*—"Correct."

_____

most commonly used characters in the language. I have used the Wade romanization system of pronunciation, which was standard when I was in China.

So the Chinese language for me is that of intimacy, the language of an insider, the language of care. When as a child I visited America, I used to hide the fact that I knew it, because I would be asked to "say something in Chinese" and it would become an exhibit, artificial, bought. It was to me a precious, private possession that I owned. Since I learned it in Peking, my accent was perfect Mandarin, which gave me the feeling of being another kind of insider, one that I have mentioned before, a Peking person (*Beijing ren*).

Household matters were carried on in both languages, English between my parents and us, and Chinese between family members and the servants. I attended a Chinese kindergarten run by the mission, and soon learned to read and write this intimate language; it was then that I fell in love with it.

The language opened up on the pages of the little kindergarten books, and the beauty of it entered my speech. I learned *shan*, the word for mountain, *mu*, the word for tree, and speaking Chinese became a walk in the world. The written words in Chinese were much easier than English ones. They were pictures, monosyllabic, chanted as we sat on benches, small books of hand-sewn thin paper spread on low tables in front of us. Numbers: *I* (one), *erh* (two), *san* (three) [一, 二, 三]. The teacher would stand in front of the blackboard and patiently teach us the correct way to write the strokes for each character: left to right, top down, horizontal lines first.

In the Peking American School and from then on, I learned Chinese formally as a scheduled course, and it never lost its pictorial enchantment. I always felt that rather than just portraying a character, I constructed it, stroke by stroke, almost as if reproducing its evolution. Later, using a brush and ink, I felt the lure of calligraphy, writing the characters in a form that illustrated their meaning, but I didn't follow that up. I preferred ordinary, pedestrian lines to text.

Most Chinese characters are formed by symbols: radicals and phonetics. The radicals, a series of strokes usually to the left of the character, give the meaning of the character, the phonetics provide the sound and contribute to the meaning. There are a little over 200 radicals. The oldest that have come down to us can be six thousand years old, often cast into bronze bells. They are usually the symbols for things: man, cover, knife, fire, spoon, and can be characters in themselves. The word for peace, *an* [安], is formed by the symbol for a woman [女] under the symbol for a roof [宀]. (Certainly those of us who live close to others know very well that a woman under a roof anywhere does not necessarily symbolize peace, but for an ancient society that valued women chiefly in that capacity, this combination may have been the closest possible way of representing it.)

I have always delighted in knowing that little dripping downward dots and strokes to the left of a character [氵] meant that the character had a watery connotation, that those with a slender form of tree [木] probably referred in some way to wood. It is this imagination in the language that entrances me still. A favorite example of mine is that of characters with the radical for speech, *yen* [言], which consists of the symbol for mouth [口] with horizontal lines above it, signifying speech. Among the characters it appears in are words for: divine, calculate, teach, examine or admonish, remember or record, denounce, slander, inquire, promise, and it is part of 148 more. Another radical is the word for heart, *hsin* [心], which appears in no less than 375 other words, including certainty, purpose, evil, to endure, be jealous, dread, err, cherish, love, like, and delight in.

How can the English word "heart" stand up against a curved chamber, with three little heart-beat strokes over it? When I use the Chinese word *hsin*, I find myself being careful of it, aware of movement, of the genesis of the word, the long ago rendering of it, and its insertion into hundreds of words that it affects. I am also aware of the honorable etymology of English words, of "heart" and its thousand-year history in the north of Europe, but the ancient Chinese characters cast in bronze seem to have more force, more insistence, than the English words, whatever their derivation.

I have a sense of movement in the Chinese language, among and within words, that I do not find in English. An example is *yao pu yao*, meaning, "do you want?" The Chinese words are literally, "want-not-want," the "you" being understood. There is a choice, a back and forth in the question, giving a vigor to it.

Another example, *hsiang pu tao*, meaning, "I wouldn't have thought it (possible)," has a direction to it. *Hsiang* means "thought" or "thinking," *pu* is "not," and *tao* is "to come to or reach." The meaning is the same, but the phrase has a sense of destination.

One of the most useful of all Chinese phrases is *ling sui te*. It means "loose, following things," as applied to the consequences of a decision or a move. *Ling* means "loose," *sui* means "following," and *te* means "to get or attain."

K'e liao pu te is another idiomatic expression, meaning "disaster," or "it couldn't be helped." *K'e* means "able," *liao*, "to finish," *pu*, "not," and *te*, "to get or attain." It implies that something simply cannot be gained, or obtained. There is a transitive quality to it, a sense of movement.

The Chinese language leads me to think in a more relaxed way. Precision isn't that important, since there are so many ways to say things. The meaning of "almost," for example, is expressed by the phrase *ch'a pu tuo*. *Ch'a* means "mistake," *pu*, "not," *tuo*, "many." So the phrase means "not many mistakes" or "not much of a mistake."

Another example is a phrase that means the same as "no problem," *mei you kuan hsi*. *Kuan*, whose radical [門] is the word for door, means "the shutting of a door." *Hsi* means "connected to." *Mei you* means "none." So the phrase may literally be translated as "there is nothing connected to the shutting of a door."

And then there is the sheer poetry of the language. The character for sun, *jih*, is 日. The line crossing the oblong is a picture of the wisp of cloud that often comes across the sun at sunrise. And tree, *mu* [木], a vertical line with single strokes off each side and a horizontal line on top of them, makes me feel as if I am standing under its shade. The Chinese language uses four tones, mentioned before, expressed visually as the flight of an arrow, the bowl of a spoon, the dipping of a bucket into a well, and the fall of a camel's foot. Each character has one of these tones. The rhythm and fluency of these tones, essential to establish the meaning of each character, are lyrical in effect, so that at times I listen to Chinese as to music. A lovely phrase is *fang hsin*, which means "to free your heart," the English meaning of which might be "don't worry." *Fang* means "to let go, set free," and *hsin* means "heart." One has the lovely picture of a liberated heart, released from stress.

Perhaps the chief difference for me between English and Chinese is that in English the words depend on the context, or the syntax, whereas in Chinese words can take off on their own. It's possible, while indicating that someone has gone, simply to say, *tso la*, meaning "gone." The subject is understood, the verb is in charge. The character *tso* is so old that it is its own radical.

It is the authority of the character itself that makes the language so restful. The character may have a complex structure, but it has its own single sound, on which it relies for its impact, and which distinguishes it from all other characters. This sound can't be "spelled" or changed by the context of the words around it. Like an emperor, the sound of a character has authority in its own right. It cannot be modified adverbially. 慢, *man*, meaning "slow," is just that, and cannot be made into slowly or slower.

In the specific circumstances in which I learned it, Chinese was always to me secular. There were certainly Chinese words that applied to Christianity—*shang ti* [上 帝], for instance, meaning God, but literally "a ruler above." The language carried for me more the Confucian concepts, with their emphasis on correct behavior in society, rather than any mystical imperative of belief or sacrament. But I cheerfully sang hymns translated into Chinese, especially one that described children as Jesus's jewels, though it referred only to well-behaved and lovable ones.

These are idiosyncratic comments, but they illustrate just how different a language makes it possible to be. One of the glories of a language is that it carries its own culture. The challenge to me of a language non-cognate with English is that the language gives no assistance with similar words; it must be learned whole.

The Chinese solar calendar reflects a nation of farmers:

Start of Spring	Start of Summer	Start of Autumn	Start of Winter
Rain Water	Grain Fills	Still Hot	Light Snow
Excited Insects	Grain in Ear	White Dew	Heavy Snow
Vernal Equinox	Summer solstice	Autumnal Equinox	Winter Solstice
Clear and Bright	Slight Heat	Cold Dew	Little Cold
Grain Rains	Great Heat	Frost Descends	Severe Cold

Who cannot love a language that names March the month of excited insects?

*   *   *

And then there is music.

Looking back, music was everywhere in my childhood. Outside, the wide streets of Peking were themselves concerts. Vendors called out their wares: "persimmons, chestnuts, candy, tea." The whine and whirr of knife grinders, the sounds of elderly men whistling or talking to their crickets in cages, the crickets themselves and their percussive chirps, canaries above them singing, flights of birds, whistles lodged in their tails, circling in the sky. Shopkeepers chatted in the doorways of their shops while smoking pipes, the four tones of their language forming an aural fringe along the edges of the street. The soft bells of camels in their long lines bringing coal to the city, the back-beat of their hooves on the old paving stones, the rattling of carts along the gutters, the shouts of their drivers, the sound from a temple courtyard of monks chanting, the crisp *Ee, er, san, ssu* of soldiers drilling in their barracks yard. There were also sharper sounds: rickshawmen calling

An *erhu* player, Peking, 1920s.

Wai, Wai, ("make way, make way!") as they passed each other, the bells of streetcars and bicycles ringing out, sometimes urgently, the small bands following funeral or wedding processions playing over the creaking sounds that wooden poles made under the sedans. The piercing sound of the *erhu*, a Chinese two-stringed instrument played by a sidewalk musician at a street corner, would sometimes bind it all together. On the smaller streets one would hear women singing to their babies, children chanting lessons at a school, the splash of water thrown into the street, the occasional clatter of donkeys' hooves on stone paving. On Sundays, from churches all over the city would come the formal imported sounds of a foreign religion, earnest, separate.

Inside our house, one was aware of the low musical coursing of different dialects from the kitchen, and the perfect enunciation of the same language in my father's study as Mr. Chin and my father worked on the fifth edition of "The Five Thousand Dictionary." In the living room someone was usually learning to play the piano; upstairs our *amah* would be singing Chinese nursery puzzles to the youngest one of us, and every day would come the necklace of verses sung before meals and bed.

For breakfast:

> Father, we thank Thee for the night,
> And for the pleasant morning light;
> For rest and food and loving care,
> And all that makes the day so fair.
>
> Help us to do the things we should,
> To be to others kind and good;
> In all we do, in work or play,
> To grow more loving every day.

For lunch:

> Thank you for the world so sweet,
> Thank you for the food we eat.
> Thank you for the birds that sing,
> Thank you, God, for everything.

Finally, sleepily, at bedtime:

> Jesus, tender Shepherd hear us.
> Bless Thy little lambs tonight.
> Through the darkness be Thou near us,
> Keep us safe till morning light.
>
> All this day Thy hand has led us,
> And we thank Thee for Thy care:
> Thou hast clothed us, warmed, and fed us;
> Listen to my evening prayer.

Growing up, I had a lot of trouble with "the day so fair" and "the world so sweet." With beggars dying outside our gate? "Keep us safe" from what, if the world was so benign? Who had clothed and warmed and fed us? But the first two songs preceded food, and the last one ensured, usually, a night's sleep, so they simply became part of the denial of reality that I perceived as the missionary experience.

However, later on, this denial of religion was serious. In a long life, the loss of faith has major consequences. Friends belong to churches and believe. And early feelings of safety disperse. "Blessed assurance, Jesus is mine/ Oh what a foretaste of glory divine." Or, even more solidly, "Oh God, our help in ages past/ Our hope for years to come/ Be Thou our guide while life shall last/ And our eternal home" conveyed a feeling of event, of destination. For me, the words of hymns could be left alone— composed in fervor, but placid on the page—until the organ sounded and the music carried them out into my life. What was so powerful about the singing when the words themselves made no sense to me? Recent studies suggest that music engages all parts of the brain, and that some music enters the brain through one of its most primitive parts before even arriving at the auditory cortex.

Music itself became the solution to the problem of losing faith. I summoned all the earlier music of living, and found a ferry in it—a sort of skiff—into which all contradictions could be loaded. Now when faced with the greater lonelinesses that life brings, all I need to do is to find a church, enter, note the numbers of the hymns posted on the hymn-board, moor my skiff, wait for the organ to start, and feel the power of belief without the necessity of believing.

In 1966 a sixteen-year-old friend bought a new cello, and her old one stood in the living room of her family's house, beautiful and silent. I asked to borrow it, just to look at, and then one day wondered whether it had anything to say to me. A gifted teacher from the National Symphony took on a by now sixty-two-year-old beginner, and within a year a desperate orchestra invited me to join their single cellist. "You are sufficiently a musician to know when not to play," the conductor said. For ten years, until an accident to my elbow put an end to playing, my life was an enchantment inside the music, especially with a string quartet, and finally, unbelievably, in some selected movements of the Bach Suites for Unaccompanied Cello. Every day I tuned myself and my cello to 440 pitch; every day I knew where I was in the universe. Every week I could be part of a group similarly tuned (it was hoped), playing music that lifted us out of our ordinary lives and made me feel part of all who had in past years played the same notes for the same reasons with the same delight. I felt the generosity of a musical instrument that for the amateur must be played with others and yet, in practice at home, gave me the 440 pitch on the open string, tuning my life, a companion in solitude.

Playing with the McLean (Virginia) Community Orchestra.

In my eighties and for the first time, I found myself in love. It was as if a light turned on that flashed back over my life. The decades became bright, however dark the shadows that light created. Since my friend was not available, nothing would change, yet everything did. I was vulnerable at last to my own feelings. The cold isolation of the attempt to be perfect thawed, and I stepped into the liberating ordinariness of life.

And—the most consequential joy of all—two hundred and eleven years after their founding Constitution defined slaves to be three-fifths of a person, Americans elected an African American as their President.

XIV

THE CIRCLE CLOSED

En route to China: me, Paul, Rebecca, Michael, and behind the camera, Sarah.

My family and I gathered on the morning of June 20th, 2004 —bags packed, cameras and passports at the ready, a new video recorder over my grandson Michael's shoulder—and set off for China. The long-planned trip—to visit the places where I had lived as a child—had been delayed for a year because of the SARS threat. This year, suddenly, seemed to be the best time to go. My son Paul was rethinking career plans; I had retired during the year and had not yet committed myself to a new undertaking. Sarah had been invited to join a new ballet group, not yet active. Rebecca had graduated from college and taken her first teaching job, and Michael was waiting to start college. So we were off to a land that for 25 years in our family had been the stuff of stories told in homes, and of projects in classrooms, and into the long lines of security, verification, identification, and boarding that now constitute travel.

The beginning was not without drama. A suitcase with all the equipment for ten days' travel was missing at the first checkpoint, and the two-hour advance time for the security check for international flights was running out. Michael was the hero who boarded the JFK train back toward the city, found the suitcases sitting on the far side of the rented van, and rushed back in time to restore our confidence in our group's ability to handle anything.

The plane to Tokyo, a 747-400, was full, mostly with Oriental people, which gave me the old, comfortable feeling of being in a small minority. Landing in a typhoon at Narita airport in Japan, we changed planes and the order of languages. Announcements were made in Japanese, Chinese, and Korean, with English last. We were at last in the East! Delayed while the typhoon whirled off, we arrived several hours late at the Beijing airport, overjoyed at the sight of Mr. Jin, our patient and perfect guide, waiting for us at the gate. The drive to our hotel took about an hour through the sleeping city, while Mr. Jin pointed out the darkened outlines of city walls, temples, and parks, with the newer part of the city blazing around them.

The next morning we discovered what hotels in China do best—breakfast. Both Chinese and foreign dishes were offered, among them scrambled eggs, steamed vegetables, sausages, bowls of yogurt, mysterious Chinese dishes, salted cabbage and nuts, many fruits, four kinds of juices, tea, coffee, rolls, and relishes.

The first day was scheduled for sightseeing, and we set off for the Temple of Heaven, where in earlier days my family and I had often gone for picnics. On the way our driver, the laconic and skilled Mr. Wang, cell phone at his ear, provided our group of American drivers with all the excitement a day could offer. Cars and bicycles swerved directly in front of us, pedestrians strolled into moving traffic, pedicabs darted in and out, and honking horns announced drivers' intentions. Sometimes at a major intersection a policeman would be standing under a traffic umbrella, apparently acknowledging whatever was happening in the traffic rather than directing it. During our seven days in the Hobbesian Beijing traffic, we saw only seven accidents and no dented cars. Somehow these streams of vehicles and people managed to accommodate each other.

Approaching the Temple of Heaven. The man on the right is painting Chinese characters on the sidewalk in water.

The Temple of Heaven is famous, of course, for its beauty, but also because it is the temple at which the emperor worshiped, instead of being the object of worship. He went annually to pray for good harvests. The circular temple grounds are enclosed in a square, to symbolize the cooperation of earth and heaven. There is a famous round walled space where a spoken message on one side can be heard at the opposite wall. Many families, including ours, were testing it, and some were startled to hear English coming from it. In the surrounding park we followed a whirring sound, and found a diabolo performer, who, under the old cypress trees, supervised Sarah learning to twirl it.

An elaborate lunch, included in the tour package, first established the pattern of hour-long lunches, concerning which it seemed impossible to persuade the heirs of this ancient cuisine that we wanted dishes steamed instead of fried. (We came to find these lunches, always in elegant restaurants, where we were expected, a waste of time.)

We went next to Tien An Men (Heaven Peace Gate) Square, which has been called the largest public space in the world. A young soldier

Temple of Heaven.

stands, rigid, Mao's mausoleum in the background, guarding the monument to the 1988 martyrs from further demonstrators. The Great Hall of the People loomed along one side. The square was quiet, a change from the crowded streets. Impressive and oppressive, it felt like the center of government, and a little like a grave.

Across from the square is the entrance to the Forbidden City. Mao's portrait over the main gate seemed oddly appropriate in the golden-roofed splendor. History aside, this was the place of declared power. We went through the succession of gates—Meridian, Supreme Harmony, Central Harmony, Preserved Harmony, Celestial Purity—and past the Halls of Celestial and Territorial Union, Mental Cultivation (where applicants for civil service took their final examinations before the emperor), and Ancestral Worship and Joyful Longevity. Finally our guide led us to the living quarters of the Empress and of the concubines, small sets of rooms lining intimate courtyards where one could almost hear the whispered secrets. At a gate leading to the imperial garden the large beam that usually lies across an entrance had been removed to allow the young emperor Pu Yi to ride his bicycle. That had been one hundred years ago, but it seemed as if it had just been done. Finally we reached the imperial garden, with its three-hundred-year-old trees, and a hill that older members of the court had to climb yearly to prove they could.

Sarah at the Forbidden City entrance.

Inside the Forbidden City.

For me the Forbidden City was resonant. Stories that my grandfather had been hired by the Empress Dowager to teach astronomy to the court had been confirmed, and I could imagine his stocky presence and short, determined stride on those paved stones. Within a year he left the court, in protest when a Christian student was forced to bow to the altar of Confucius.

Bell Tower as it appeared on an earlier trip in 1988.

The next day we visited the Drum Tower in the neighborhood of my old house. The tower had been built over seven hundred years ago, with its neighbor the Bell Tower, to tell time for the city. As a child I had been told that the towers were there inside the north city wall to deter evil spirits—which traditionally approached from the north—from entering the city, and when I was little, the sound of the drums would make me uneasy. Perhaps the Chinese knew more than we did about real danger? I loved the sound from the bell, which was rung ceremoniously once a year in the smaller, more intimate Bell Tower. We climbed the Drum Tower's steep steps, a full eight inches deep, which I had never ascended. A costumed group sounded the drums at noon as we looked out over a city being destroyed and reconstructed. Other forces that couldn't be deterred by the drums were prevailing. The area of small *hutungs* nearby is being preserved as a tourist attraction, but the brightly decorated pedicabs that carry the tourists through them seemed alien and intrusive, and our family went to the gift shop.

Street scene near the Bell Tower, 1988.

Our next stop was the Confucian Temple. The calm I remembered was gone. There are two shops there now, one in the temple itself, where one can buy Chinese gourd flutes, rubbings from the steles in the courtyard, and writing materials like ink blocks and brushes. Sarah found members of a ballet company from Canada there. Do dancers recognize each other the world over? It was wonderful watching them walking through the old spaces, choreographing them, bringing a grace and a discipline Confucius could not have imagined, although he would almost certainly have approved.

A friend had arranged an appointment for us with Dr. Huang, the principal of the nursing school that now occupies the Tungchow buildings where two sisters and I went to school. On the way there, the driver, Mr. Wang, for whom hearing was doing, heard me mention Erh Tiao Hutung and drove us to the site of the former mission compound, now unrecognizable. He parked at the door of People's Hospital #6, a large modern building. I went in, checked at the pharmacy, and to my astonishment heard the pharmacist say that indeed this had been Douw Hospital, which was torn down in 1974. It was the mission hospital where all my siblings had been born, and where I heard my father accept congratulations on the birth of his son, his "first-born." I glanced briefly at the street that I had so often bicycled along, swerving past garbage on the unpaved surface, and climbed into the van, which went smoothly on the paved way to my school.

Erh T'iao Hutung as it appeared in 1988.

Tungchow is now included in the far reaches of Peking, and it was difficult to find from the street address. Eventually we saw a statue of a Chinese Florence Nightingale through a gate, and the van turned in. The grounds were unrecognizable, but a lane led to the completely recognizable girls' dormitory, from whose steps the matron used to monitor the return from study hall. Now we went up those steps and were directed to the principal's office, formerly the matron's apartment. The wood floors and paneling seemed the same, and gave off the familiar boarding-school smell. In the hall I glimpsed the railing of the stairs where we presented our hands for fingernail inspection before we were allowed breakfast. Dr. Huang then led us to the school building, where the entire school had been taught, from upper grades through high school. The study hall, where I looked for signals from a boyfriend, had been changed. But upstairs the class room where I had happily studied Latin for four years was exactly the same. I had not been back since 1934.

The seventy years evaporated, especially when we visited the third building of the school. This had been the younger boys' dormitory, above which was the chapel. Although the space had been divided, the floors, steps, and stair railings were the same, and I could almost hear the sound of footsteps going down after chapel, and the click as I reluctantly closed the organ cover in the silent room after playing for the service. High rises covered the tennis courts and buildings spread over the playing fields. But the sight of student nurses seated around the grounds, studying, renewed the feeling of a place where people prepared for useful lives, and it was like a second graduation to leave, with a graciously given gift of the nursing school plaque.

Back at the hotel, exhausted, we made a desperate attempt to get western food by ordering room service, resulting in a hamburger sandwich that left Michael feeling sick for the next few days—a classic Chinese condition gallantly borne.

Jonathan Kuo and Professor Chiang at the gate of Bei Ta, formerly Yenching University.

The next day we went to Yenching University, now called Bei Ta. The campus was peaceful in the morning sunlight. We met our host,

Jonathan Kuo, at the home of the former president of the university and later ambassador to China, Dr. Leighton Stuart. A graceful Chinese courtyard house, it is now the office of the president and the center of the university administration. A lifetime ago, Dr. Stuart had been a friend of my parents for many years, and along with another family, we alternated Thanksgiving dinners with him. We now filed into what had been Dr. Stuart's living room, where as a child I had romped when it was his turn for Thanksgiving. Mr. Kuo had invited Professor Chiang, Professor of Accounting and chairman of the Yenching Alumni Association, to meet with us. Armchairs were formally arranged along the sides of the room, Professor Chiang and I at one end. He spoke about the history of the university, which, founded with Rockefeller money as a private university, is now a public institution. Hesitantly, I asked Professor Chiang whether this had caused changes in curriculum or process. Professor Chiang gave the quintessential Chinese reply. "We communicate," he said, and smiled.

Our hosts then took us on a tour of places familiar to me, including the dormitory court where I had lived, and my office in one of the administrative "sister buildings," in the basement of which a present administrator and I had a short ping-pong match, which he won. Sarah and Rebecca joined me for a photograph outside my former office window—a sharp moment, as I stood with my two college-educated granddaughters and thought of the difficulties women had in obtaining an education. The campus was now quiet, an occasional group of students bicycling along the shaded paths on their way to final examinations, unlike the restlessness and turmoil of the revolutionary era, and the oppression of the Japanese occupation. We then walked down to the beautiful lake, willow trees at its edge, the water tower in the shape of a pagoda reflected on its surface. Where the sophomores used to dunk the freshmen, we skipped stones, admired the garden memorials to Edgar Snow and to Randolph Sailer, a beloved psychology professor and family friend, and then, joined by Mr. Wang, the driver, went on to an elegant Chinese luncheon. It was a morning that I hoped would give my family not only a sense of what it had been like for their grandmother, but also a glimpse of what China is offering now for people of their generation.

Ambitiously, we had scheduled the Summer Palace of the emperors for the afternoon. This had been a favorite place for our family. Essentially a pleasure garden surrounding a lake, it had been developed in the eighteenth century to provide relief for the Emperor and his court from the stifling confined heat of the Forbidden City. My family then had enjoyed it for the mile-long wooden corridor along the edge of the lake. Every few steps, on the cross beams under the roof, there were pictures of famous scenes in Chinese history, or of fairy tales. I remembered little resting places where you could look out over the lake, watch ferry boats crossing, absorb some episode of Chinese history from the paintings overhead, or just enjoy people passing by. Now a small artists' gallery halfway along provided rest, with original paintings, cold bottled water, and the inevitable display of tourist temptations. At the end of the corridor stood—on the bottom of the lake—a marble boat, built by the Empress Dowager with funds dedicated for the Chinese navy, now a popular restaurant and tourist site. We took a ferry back to the main gate, looking up at the temples and pavilions where the court would have lived, high on Longevity Hill, catching the cooling breezes from the western mountains.

Summer Palace sculpture.

This was the last day with our guide in Beijing, and on the way back to the hotel we stopped to see the ancient Beijing Observatory, which I remembered situated on the wall near the main gate of the city. It is still on the wall, but on a fragment now, just off the Ch'ang An Chieh (Long Peace Street). The gaunt bronze armillae, astrolabe, and other instruments—there since the fifteenth century—convey a sense of peace and relationship with the stars, next to the busy street. We arrived after closing time, and were prepared for disappointment, when again Mr. Jin came to the rescue and persuaded the curator of our consuming interest in an astronomical display some seven thousand miles from our home, and we entered the deserted courtyard. The curator, eager to show off the treasures, led us to a low building, where, among other exhibits, he proudly explained the workings of a

Earthquake predictor.

structure built in the fifteenth century to predict earthquakes. It operated by the flow of water within a big cauldron. The shaking of the water forced out of a complicated series of outlets served to predict the direction and severity of the expected quake. My grandfather Watson had built a telescope wherever he lived in China, until his final internment there, and it seemed impossible to leave China without

The curator shows us the astrolabe.

some tribute to his interest in the secular heavens, as well as the heaven he expected actually to reach.

Midway through the trip, it was time for evaluation. With pizzas from the Pizza Hut around the corner, we met in one of the bedrooms to discuss what changes needed to be made. The first was "no more temples." I realized then that coming to China only six years after the dynasty was overthrown, I had seen the country through the imperial scrim of that imperial city. The second change was a request for more downtime, which required spending only one day at Peitaiho, the summer resort. This meant foregoing the sight of the Great Wall going down to the sea at Shanhaikwan, which I had never seen, but the absolute necessity of a down day clearly trumped all other options. Sarah, Rebecca, and Michael all had problems with Chinese food, felt over-scheduled, uncomfortable in a language they couldn't understand, and were uneasy with being looked at. At this point I am compelled to comment. For the first time I met my grandchildren as adults making their own adjustment to an essentially alien environment. They were unfailingly responsive, courteous, caring, efficient, meeting all the requirements of packing and unpacking without complaint, helpful, funny, observant, prompt. I could go on, but I won't. With all the other values of the trip, it was worth it to be with these three extraordinary people.

Michael, Sarah, Paul, Rebecca, and me on the Great Wall, June 2004.

What remains to be said about the Great Wall of China? It absorbs the time spent on it, and the language written about it. Various warring states began building sections of it to protect themselves in the fifth century B.C.E., but the sections weren't connected together into the Great Wall until emperor Shih Huangti began his campaign to unify China in 221 B.C.E. A barrier built to prevent invaders from the north, it stretches for nearly five thousand miles from the sea. We approached it at the Mutianyu section, which was somewhat farther from the city and less crowded than the popular Badaling approach. The van took an old two-lane road, curving through farmland and orchards, by small villages, and up into the foothills of the Yen Shan mountains. Braving the gauntlet of merchants, we climbed a stony path to the cable cars. On the ride up the mountain we could see the plain in the distance and villages nestling in the foothills. Suddenly through a small opening we were on the wall. The day was bright and clear; we could see ranges of mountains beyond the wall and the plains stretching inside it. I was first struck by the beauty of it along the mountainsides, and then by the arrogance of it, as if by merely existing, it could prevent invasion. But the slanted openings for arrows, the crenelated towers, and its impressive height brought the thirteenth century to life, and it seemed, as the Chinese refer to it, like a powerful dragon. Millions had died in its construction. Mr. Jin and I watched the rest of the party walk along it—Paul actually jogged up a section. As we sat in the sunshine, Mr. Jin talked of his life, his family, his hopes for himself, his wife and his daughter, his pride in China and in what his country is trying to do. I thought of all the lives that were lost to build this wall, now a UNESCO World Heritage site that is also a grave, and it seemed to me that China is perhaps shifting a little.

When the climbers returned, we started down the merchant row again, trying to avoid the shopkeepers who sometimes stood right in front of us, preventing our going forward, prices plummeting as we passed. "Ten yuan, eight yuan, five yuan, one yuan." Slowly the van went down the winding road through the shallow valleys, past mud villages with electricity and access to the Internet, and children in bright school uniforms returning to school from lunch. Then with a brief introductory comment from Mr. Jin, we were suddenly at the door of a pearl factory and watching a video showing the production of pearls. At a small indoor pool a woman opened an oyster and gave us small seed pearls from it. We were asked to go upstairs, and found a huge salesroom filled with cases of pearls, staffed with young women in pink outfits inviting us to buy. I felt hijacked, but was taken with the knowledge that these were real pearls, and bought a pair of earrings for a friend. The schedule called for visiting the Ming tombs, with their gorgeous treasures, and even more inviting, the Spirit Way, a long avenue lined with wonderful statues of animals—camel, elephant, horse, lion—all to protect the dead emperors. Everyone was tired, and in the spirit of the evening before, we asked that we go straight back to the hotel, thus denying Mr. Jin yet another chance to take us to a tourist shop. We had been told by the tour owner that the guides were expected to usher their charges into such shops, and that there was a penalty for them if they failed. We assured Mr. Jin that his final payment would compensate him for this loss, a condition he accepted with equanimity, as if a contract had been honored, as if we were a part of a kick-back scheme, as perhaps we were.

The next day we set off for Peitaiho, the summer resort almost all foreigners went to during the months when the cities were plagued with heat, dust, and cholera. The train was a delight—clean, smooth, quiet, fast, and on time. Seats faced each other across tables, encouraging conversation with strangers, and we found ourselves inviting more people to visit America. Paul, dictionary in hand, chatted with a middle-aged couple returning from a visit with their lawyer son in the city, an only son. This sparked a conversation about China's one-child policy, a vigorous discussion in which other passengers took part.

The great China plain showed the outlines of Mao's collectives, now broken up into individually owned plots. In the whole two-and-a-half hour ride, mostly through the countryside, I saw only one tractor, few cars, and one truck. As it had always been, people were working the fields, often alone, and trudging home when the work was done. At times it looked like a Millet painting.

The train discharged us, as it always had, at Peitaiho Junction, where we used to board a little chugging steam train that carried us to the resort itself. This time we were met by the best of all guides, Jean, running along beside the train to recognize us. She quickly understood the priority—to find the house I had lived in. Again it seemed unlikely that we would. I had been told that our house, one of the larger houses in the community of small cottages, had been taken over by the military, that it was completely surrounded by a wall so that it couldn't be recognized now, and that it was in a compound to which there was access only by approved people. We drove along the crowded beaches, from Rocky Point, past Lighthouse Point, along Big Beach, until we were in our old neighborhood.

The area was so completely built up that it was impossible to recognize anything from the beaches, so we started to explore neighborhoods further inland. At entrance after entrance we were denied admission. The government moves into Peitaiho every summer, and big new houses are guarded. But Jean, the director of the local bird-watching society, had a lively interest in identification, and in us, and finally persuaded one of the gate keepers that—here it is again—these were people who had lived in a house in the community and had come seven thousand miles to see it. The van drove into an area where my 1937 sketch map showed the house to be, but it was impossible to place among the many pseudo-Italian/French/American large houses recently built in that area. I had a sense of place, however, and it felt as if the house was near. Trudging along a hot street, I recognized from the back the big stones of the foundation of our house.

Jean and I rounded the corner, and there it was. It looked tiny beside the houses recently built around it. The porch door was open. I

Our former house in Peitaiho. The sign says: Building Number 4/ Construction Space: 594.93 m2/ American Ho Yue Han: Yenching University Professor/ Completion Time: October 1932/ Superintendent: Li Yue.

waited before it while Jean ran back to bring the others, who, tired and skeptical of success, had stayed in the van. The summers we had been there seemed to flow down the steps. With Jean's encouragement I walked in. A TV was on and we called, but there was no answer. We walked through the downstairs, the big double dining rooms, the sleeping rooms on both sides, a tiny bathroom that had not been there

Playing again the old petal organ.

before, and paused before the steps that led up to the second floor. There was no reply, the TV still sounded, and we went up the stairs. There we found two women, wakening, who got up and welcomed us, encouraging our exploration of the house.

It had always been that way in the house. Since we shared it with another family, people we might not know might always be there. So it felt natural to continue exploring, the current occupants looking on with amusement. We went onto the side porches, with their views of beach and mountains, now shrouded in haze. Beside the stairs was an old pumping organ, which I sat and played as I had so often for church downstairs on the big porch. Soon more people appeared, and we took pictures on the porch steps where for so many summers the two families, the Hayes and the Meads, had posed for the annual picture together. The tennis court and its little *t'ing sze* were gone, the view of the beach obscured by a tower, and the spirea bushes supplanted by daylilies, but the people of the house, so welcoming, cheerful, and relaxed, made it seem as if we were all on vacation together, as we had always been in that house. We ended up, as usual, inviting everyone to America, but they, like us before them, did not want to leave Peitaiho.

Current renters of the Peitaiho house, summer 2004. Our guide, Jean, is on the right.

After lunch we went down to Big Beach, now full of Chinese

families, where I tried unsuccessfully to find a sight line to our house. Then we went to Eagle Rock (now called the Pigeon's Nest for the pigeon rookery nearby), crowded with young people; schools were out, and members of our group were in demand for pictures, conversation, and fun. I stood out on the sand flats with Jean and Paul while the tide started turning, looking toward Chinwangtao, invisible in the haze. As the tide came in I remembered the expeditions to the sand dunes, when we had to be sure to be back before the tide cut us off. The tide had turned for two of my sisters. Would this be the last time I would look out on this life-renewing sea?

People were hunting for brightly colored rocks at the foot of the cliff; it was a French Impressionist scene. We climbed to the top of the cliff and read, on the statue of Mao, the poem he wrote, inscribed on the pedestal.

PEITAIHO
Summer 1954

A rainstorm sweeps down on this northern land,
White breakers leap to the sky.
No fishing boats off Chinwangtao
Are seen on the boundless ocean.
Where are they gone?
Nearly two thousand years ago
Wielding his whip, the Emperor Wu of Wei
Rode eastward to Chiehshih; his poem survives.
Today the autumn wind still sighs,
But the world has changed!

Then it was time to go to the train and ride through the evening to Beijing. In the darkening fields we could see people finishing their work, and in the villages occasional lights shone from houses almost hidden by earthen walls. As we approached Beijing, conductors went along the cars, pulling the white curtains of each booth across the window. Was it to protect the privacy of the apartments whose windows were so close to the tracks in that crowded city? The conductors just smiled at our question.

Sunday we shopped. All day. The old bazaars I remembered had been partially replaced by larger stores, including a department store, and fast food shops, including Starbucks and TCBY, but some of the old crowded cluster of small shops remained, and I watched as my grandchildren searched for gifts, trying to fit pieces of an ancient culture into the lives of their friends. After a quick trip to Sian, we returned to Beijing to leave. As the plane passed over New York, the skyscrapers sharp in the morning sunlight, I found myself relieved that it had all actually happened, that Paul and his two years of work and planning had pulled it off, that the seven years of savings had been sufficient, that—whatever their experiences—all that my grandchildren had seen and heard would forever be part of their lives. As we parted, I discovered that China still feels like home, but it is even more true that my home is the country of my family.

$$* \qquad * \qquad *$$

Out of chronological order, I have saved for last our visit to my old home in Peking. On June 22nd, two days after arriving in China, we set out to find my house. It had been in an old area of Peking, near the Drum Tower, which, with its companion, the Bell Tower, formed the northernmost axis of the city. I had been variously told that my house had been torn down, that it had been converted to a shop for older people, and that preparations for the 2009 Olympics had so widened the street it was on that the house was inaccessible.

A friend had kindly asked a long-term resident of the area, Mr. Meng, to join us, and we therefore approached the neighborhood with a cautious optimism, the target of a seven-thousand mile journey. At #48 Ku Lou Hsi Ta Chieh (Drum Building West Big Street) we found an open door in the street wall and walked in, arousing a group of men in the courtyard. Mr. Jin quickly explained who we were, and the gatekeeper hospitably confirmed that a church had been there, showing us a set of original steps to the church and a couple of beams still visible on the wall of the building that had replaced it. I climbed the steps and sang what we children had sung in Sunday school programs all over America, "Jesus Loves Me" in Chinese. Thirty years after President Nixon's visit, it seemed safe, drawing applause, although one of the men clearly disapproved, and watched us closely until we left. There was then general discussion about where my old house was. I thought I had glimpsed it through the tree tops when standing on the steps, and Mr. Meng was pretty sure that there had been a foreign house down the road, so with much bowing and thank-yous, we proceeded down the street, the suspicious man abstaining and keeping watch as we left. Foreign houses were easy to spot. It was impolite in old China to build onto the standard one-story courtyard house a second story, which would allow residents to overlook a neighbor's courtyard. Foreign houses, mostly two-story, were easily distinguished by their arrogant height.

At an iron gate in the street wall a few feet away, a young soldier responded to our knocks by saying that we would not be permitted to enter, and closed the gate. The ever-resourceful Mr. Jin quickly engaged him by saying that we were former residents of the house who had come all the way around the world to see this one house, because we loved China. The guard disappeared, the gate still closed. The stakes were high, for this trip was designed to show my grandchildren where I had lived and grown. Mike, in charge of the video, put the camera up to a slit at the top of the gate and started filming. I thought, in panic, that this was our quick ticket back to the States. But the soldier returned, inviting us into the courtyard in front of a moon gate which framed the path to the houses, saying that we could look at the house from there. I was home.

I had distributed to my family a description of the house, and was pointing out various rooms, when the wife of General Li, whose residence it now was, appeared with another young man carrying bottles of cold water. This seemed a signal to depart, and I turned to my family to leave. Looking at them, I suddenly realized how foreign we all appeared—white, camera-laden, standing in the courtyard under the mulberry trees, our Chinese guide and a neighborhood resident beside us. Earlier, missionaries must have seemed similarly out of place. But it had been my home and I was reluctant to leave. Mrs. Li continued to stand there and suddenly asked me how old I was. I told her I was eighty-seven, she said she was seventy-six, and surprisingly walked toward me as if to embrace me. This she did, and saying in Chinese, "We two old women will now show the young people your old house," led the way down the familiar path.

We entered the house, the first time in sixty-four years I had been in it. Mrs. Li briefly opened the living room door, and I glimpsed a billiard table before she closed it. Gone was the furniture of prayer, of music, of fantasy, of childhood. She led us across the corridor to the room that had been my father's study. We sat around a central square table, all equally incredulous. It was only the second day of our trip and my Chinese was halting, but Mrs. Li and I were soon exchanging information about our families, while my family sat beaming and responsive in front of us. It was an extraordinary moment: my son and grandchildren in the house where I had grown up. And I was aware, amid the unfamiliar furniture and the forbidden spaces in the house around us, of something very familiar.

Ms. Li and I enter the door of my old home.

General Li, the current owner, was absent. When we lived there, the owner was also absent, since we were God's tenants. Suddenly all the old associations of the constricted religious life were there—the losses, the unfulfilled promises. My tears came, solicitously attended to by Mrs. Li, who could not have known their genesis. But the presence of my son and especially of the grandchildren closed the circle, bringing it all to the present, somehow making my life a whole.

The conversation wound down and we prepared to leave, when the young man came into the room with a platter of watermelon slices, and we started up again, as if on another, more familiar level, bantering, current. I had achieved a certain status with Mrs. Li by having been denied entrance to the house on a trip a few years before, at a time when she was away, and she became affectionate, wanting future contact with us, which was, of course, promised with delight. After chatting a while longer, we got up to go. Mrs. Li led us to the door and out to the path—a standard Chinese custom. But she came further, all along the path, through the moon gate and courtyard and out the street gate, waving as we crossed the busy street until we were out of sight, the soldier hovering anxiously to get her back inside. We had invited everyone to America, Mrs. Li, her husband, the young man, and the soldier. On a wider level the circle was closing too. America and China seemed closer to each other.

Mrs. Li and our family in my father's former study.

XV

THE ESSENTIALS

One day some thirty-five years ago, while visiting my sister Janet in Garden City, Long Island, I found my mother in Janet's basement discarding family letters. As a history major, I was horrified, and rushed to stop her. I asked her what on earth she was doing. She said she was throwing out all my grandfather's letters that contained criticism of his son, my father, which accounted for a good percentage of them. I pled with her to let me have them instead. She looked up at me. "What will you do with them?" she asked. I have used them to tell about my immediate ancestors. Raised in China, how could I complete a memoir without tribute to them?

GRANDFATHER HAYES

I have always felt an affinity for my great-grandfather, David Hayes, who died from a sniper's bullet on February 4, 1865, in the Civil War, on picket duty near Petersburg, Virginia. A college graduate, a farmer in Mercer County, Pennsylvania, and reportedly a devout, practical, upright man, fond of his four children and of his stalwart wife, Margaret Jane, he insisted on enlisting, even though a childless uncle had offered to go in his stead.

David said that the lot had fallen to him and he had no right to dodge it, or to pay for anyone else to take his place, as was commonly done then. On November 5, 1862, having finished his field work,

273

David Hayes, Company B, 100th Pa. Vols.,
the "Round Head Regiment," circa 1862.

Watson and Will,
winter 1864 or 1865.

stocked the barn, and readied the farm machinery for winter, he said goodbye to his family—Margaret Jane, Will, Watson, Sadie, and Lou —and left their little hilltop farmhouse. He rode past the hills and farms to the county seat and was mustered into the 100th Pennsylvania Volunteers, Army of the Potomac.

Ill for much of his time in the service, he survived the battle of Cold Harbor, but was killed two months before the end of the war. My grandfather Watson once commented ruefully to my father on how different their lives would have been had David lived only two months longer. Listening to him, I was torn between pride that an ancestor of mine had done what he should, and awe at the consequences of that decision.

When mustered in ("Bounty paid $25"), David's enlistment papers described him as five feet eleven inches tall, with gray eyes, light hair, and a light complexion. He did not take easily to military service. In a letter to his wife, he described his fellow soldiers as "evil companions and an evil heart neither of which I can get rid of," and added, "You can have no idea of the weirdness and depravity of the natural heart, as it is exemplified by many of the soldiers." As an educated man, he often wrote letters for his fellow soldiers to their wives, and wrote to his own wife, "But maybe you don't approve of me writing to other men's wives. I did not think of it in this light till just now, but I have told you now. If you don't like it let me know."

He longed to be at his farm and concerned himself with its details and with how his children were doing, occasionally offering Margaret Jane advice which later he would check up on: "I am glad the boys go regularly to school but did you get them the books I spoke of for New Year's presents and the beads or something else for the girls and if not why did you not?" In a letter telling her of the deaths and injuries to the sons of his neighbors, he wrote, "Oh what misery this dreadful war is bringing on families. Our sins must be very great or God would not visit us with such tremendous judgments. And from the wickedness I see around me I fear He will yet further chastise us and grind us low in the dust of humility that we may repent of our sins and turn unto Him from whom we have departed." This from a man who had gone to war with a sense of duty to his fellow man.

A letter written by David's neighbor, telling of his death and of the disposal of his body, gives so vivid a picture of the war and its conditions that I am including it in full, as written on February 17, 1865:

Mr. William Hayes, Dear Sir,

As a friend and neighbor I thought perhaps you would expect me to give all or as far as I know of the circumstances of the Death of David. Which happened on the 4th of the Present month, however he did not Die until 1 1/2 O'clock on the morning of the 5th. He lived nearly 9 hours. Perfectly unconscious of any suffering whatever, never moved or spoke, yet lived on till past the hour of Midnight. I sat up with him till 12 then called the Captain, who was with him till he Died. The Doctor was called as soon as possible, yet could do nothing and in fact I believe the Doctor came in about once an hour and I am satisfied that all was done that could be done for we could do nothing but keep him comfortable and warm. It was his first time on Picket since his return to the Company. I mention this accident for fear that you discover the wound and he may not have mentioned it in his letters. As soon as David died the Captain wanted to know of me what we should do, about sending for you, and if we had better send the Body home. I told him most assuredly we would try to send it Home that I believed the friends would be exceedingly anxious that the Body be sent home even in the Roughest Style that you would never be satisfied to have him buried here. And that I as a neighbor was willing to try without considering expenses. All haste was necessary. A box of some kind must be made and no boards or tools, but I was bound to try. So off we went to the Quartermasters, found a few rough boards, and made a Box and that night, night of the 5th I started with the Body for City Point. And the Roads the Roughest kind. And from this fact I fear the Body may have been bruised, yet I thought only of sending him home, tried to Express the Body next morning, but could not till I would take it back to the Division Hospital and there get the Body <u>Disinfected</u>. This I knew they would not do, but I would take it back make another box repack the Body, get a Certificate to this effect, from the Surgeon in Charge U.S.H. in the field. Dr. [scribbled out] certified that in his belief the Body of David Hayes of Co. B 100th Regt. Pa. could be safely transferred to the State of Penna,. for Burial,.etc.etc. Armed with this Document, I again started (at night again) for City Point. And that night succeeded in getting the Body <u>expressed</u>. And now that it is done I'm anxious to hear if it went through safe. And in what condition, etc. Please observe that at the time of David's Death we were under marching orders and this too hurried me up or perhaps by delaying one or two days have fixed him up better. I was not authorized to Draw new clothes and Put on the Body, and this accounts for him being sent in the same clothes he had on. I was informed at the office Adams Express that the Charges must be prepaid. This I was not prepared for but fortunately I could borrow and did so giving my note. I was bound this should not stop me, you, perhaps never would have known of the expenses. As for the effects of David I know but little of them, the Captain will attend to all such things.

But when I tell you that had the Body once been buried here you could never, or at least for the Present got it home, you will excuse all hast, there is an order aginst Raising any Bodies till further Orders etc. Taking all circumstances into consideration I hope you will excuse all seeming roughness or unnecessary Pain that I may have caused in Wrightin this in my own poor way. And if I failed to do so you would wish, I can only ask Pardon, for I intended to do right. And only as I thought would be right by taking the Responsibility without any word from you. And at present can only hope that the sending home the Body rough and all as it was, is approved by the friends of David, whose loss is sincerly regreted by the whole Company for he was a good soldier, an honest, upright man in all things, and a true moral man in all things.

P.S. You will Please Pay to my Wife the Sum of $19.80 at your Pleasure and consider the whole amount of expressage paid.

Francis W. Holmes

When I first read David Hayes's letters I found myself sad; I would have liked this attractive, modest ancestor to have lived a little longer. Yet, like his second son's decision to leave his home for a cause, it had been his choice. I long to have known him, and am grateful for what I have of him in the four letters I retrieved. They were found in the Hayes family barn after Margaret Jane died, and given to my mother. My second son carries his name.

Margaret Jane Hayes, circa 1880.

The farm he left was on top of a slight rise on the Mercer-Middlesex Road about two miles from Mercer, Pennsylvania. Between the house and the barn, a short lane led up to the barnyard; to the north and west, fields stretched away, edged by woods. Margaret Jane

Watson Hayes, David's widow, the daughter of a local farmer, granddaughter of the founder of Washington and Jefferson College, just south of Pittsburgh, Pennsylvania, took firm charge of a farm deeply in debt and of four children under eight years old. She began to weave and sell rugs from cotton rags, a tradition to this day in Mercer's Unity Church. The two boys went to school and assisted with farm chores; the two girls stayed at home and helped their mother with the house and farm. A memorial resolution of the Unity Church Missionary Society after her death in 1921 describes the life she lived. "Through long hours in the field and at her loom, the mortgage was lifted and in due season a commodious house replaced the log cabin of former years. There was never a day too stormy, nor the mud so deep, that she could not hitch up her horses, if the children were well, and they generally were, and take her family to church. If the children went alone they went barefoot to church before putting on their shoes and stockings."

She was, apparently, shrewd. The story is that in the spring of 1868, after William and Watson were finished with their last school year, she called them out under an apple tree in the barnyard and handed them two straws to draw—one for further education, and one for the farm. Will, the older, drew the short straw, for the farm. Watson drew the longer one, and got the education. No one knows whether Margaret arranged it that way. Will reportedly never read a book after that, although he could repair anything a farm required. Watson became an internationally known scholar and linguist (fluent in Latin, Greek, and Chinese), a minister, astronomer, and the founder and president of a theological seminary that at one time taught most of the Protestant Chinese ministers in north China.

But getting to college wasn't easy. As soon as the summer work on the farm was over, Watson went to school, walking four miles each way, barefoot whenever the weather was warm enough, to save the leather on his one pair of shoes. One winter, in the Pennsylvania cold, he had neither a suit coat nor a winter coat. When he started college, the farm work continued, and the only time he had for preparing his studies was on the long drive to Westminster. He first rode in a buggy, but felt he could not turn down others wishing to go his way, and so lost the time for study. He accordingly changed his buggy for a cold one-seated sulky incapable of carrying others.

Watson graduated from Westminster College in New Wilmington

Watson, circa 1875, age 15.

Watson, circa 1880, before going to China.

in 1879, among three girls and twelve boys, nine of whom became ministers. Before going to seminary, he taught at Frogtown School, Lackawannock Township, in Mercer County. The school was at the edge of a populous and robust coal-mining community. Boys attended school, on and off, up into their twenties. Watson taught for one year at the Academy, the school for the older boys. Although his physique was somewhat slight, he soon decided that several of the big boys needed corporal punishment. Later he heard one victim say to another boy, "Don't let the Perfesser thrash you, he hits like the devil."

After his year at Frogtown School, Watson went on to study at the Western Theological Seminary in Westminster, from which he graduated in 1882. At the seminary he found his greatest joy and his greatest sorrow, and he never recovered from his loss. He fell in love with a beautiful classmate, Sarah Black, the daughter of a neighboring farmer. In November of 1881 they were engaged to be married, and planned to go to China together as missionaries. In the early spring of 1882 Sarah died of pneumonia. Watson could barely finish his studies, but in spite of missing much work, he graduated with his class, with honors. He carried Sarah Black's picture with him all his life. My father, who was with him when he died, wrote that my grandfather asked him to burn Sarah's picture, and further requested that my father tell my grandmother that he loved her, his wife.

Watson was a practical man. He told my father that his education for the foreign-mission field had included a course in architecture: He had learned to make and to build with lath, to mix and use mortar, to lay brick, to lay a foundation, to understand the requirements of a roof —nothing more than the fundamentals, but he could build a small house by himself if he had to. In the same way and for the same purpose, he had been trained in the basics of dentistry and medicine. From having farmed, he already knew the necessities of gardening and the raising of pigs, chickens, and cows. He could use tools, and prided himself on keeping his timepieces in good running condition. Indeed, shortly after Watson's arrival in China in 1882, he had a house built, doing much of the work himself.

In those days men could not go to missions overseas without a wife. After Watson graduated from the seminary he taught at Jefferson Academy, in Canonsburg, Pennsylvania, near Wilmington. One of the neighboring farms belonged to the Young family, whose members were teachers, lawyers, and doctors practicing in the county seat.

Watson and Margaret's wedding picture, 1882.

Margaret Young, the eldest daughter, had always admired the young seminary student, whom she had known as a hardworking farmer's son. A memorial minute of the Presbyterian Board of Foreign Missions reports, without elaboration: "Her preparation for a life of missionary service was completed in the educational institutions of Pennsylvania," and in June of 1881 she was appointed by the Presbyterian Board of Foreign Missions as a missionary to China. She and Watson Hayes married on July 5, 1882, their wedding portrait willed and sober. They sailed for China on September 28, 1882, on a clipper ship, after pausing on the San Francisco docks for their funeral service. There were stories of the danger to missionaries in the province of Shantung, to which they were assigned, and they wanted to be assured of having had a Christian service.

Their mission was a formidable commitment. The ocean journey alone took six weeks. And then there was the imposing organization to which they had pledged their lives. The Board of Foreign Missions of the Presbyterian Church in the USA was at 156 Fifth Avenue, New York, and at that time was as impressive as its address. It was supported by the national Presbyterian Church, and had worldwide responsibilities and power. It could own and manage properties all over the world, assign or recall those who worked in them, and establish standards it expected to be met. In return it paid every missionary an annual salary and provided housing. Wives were considered to be missionaries in their own right. In most countries their salary made possible the hiring of a household staff which freed the missionaries to do their work, frequently resulting in a standard of living that would have been impossible to maintain at home in the United States. The funding was in part supplied by churches all across America, one of which would serve as each missionary's home church, and which expected regular reports of their missionary's work. Missionaries went to their home country every seven years for furlough, renewing contacts with their families, being available for programs and for what we would now call fund-raising activities. The first furlough was after five years, and was eagerly awaited by relatives in the home country so that they could get acquainted with any little children who might have appeared. Letters took weeks or months to arrive and to be answered. People would scan the maritime sailing lists published in the newspapers in order to send off letters as soon as possible before a ship's departure. At the time of Watson's and

Margaret's sailing, there were no planes, and of course no telephones, to connect them with the people left behind.

What propelled them to go to such distant, virtually inaccessible places, leaving home and community behind? In a memoir about his father, my father wrote that "his prime (and sole?) reason for going to the foreign field was the burden of preaching the Gospel to those who had no opportunity of hearing it. His was the pioneer spirit as well as that of a scientist, who saw the universe one, and felt that any road of real scientific inquiry would ultimately lead an honest man to God. 'The earth was the Lord's' and 'Woe is me if I preach not the Gospel.' The Bible was to him literally the word of God." Letters Watson wrote suggest that he was also especially close to his mother, a profoundly religious person and devoted member of the Missionary Society of Unity Presbyterian Church. She was not only a charter member of the Missionary Society but a life member of its Foreign Mission Board. She sent what money she could to foreign missions. Two sentences from the Resolution of the Society after her death suggest some of what may have gone into her son's life plan: "During all these years she gave liberally of her means, was fervent in prayer, diligent in service, and was fully rewarded when one of her sons dedicated his life as a Foreign Missionary. Her joy overflowed when she learned that her grandson, John Hayes, had also dedicated his life to Foreign Mission fields."

The journey from San Francisco to Shantung province in China was a long one, delayed by a typhoon and bandit activity, and it was two months later in November when Watson and Margaret finally arrived in Tenghsien, a small town in the northeast part of Shantung province, where there was already a mission college in which Watson was to teach. The day after their arrival, Watson started learning the Chinese language. Dr. Calvin Mateer, a senior missionary and founder of the mission college, held three educational principles that Watson shared: missionary education, like all education in China, should be in the Chinese language, should be thorough and efficient, and should be Christian. Watson worked hard at the language, and during the next school year taught astronomy, geology, physics and mathematics in Chinese. He taught at Tenghsien Mission College from 1883 to 1895, manufacturing with Dr. Mateer much of the science equipment needed in the school's laboratories. (Dr. Mateer was no ordinary instructor. Once, when he was a passenger on a trans-Siberian train and the locomotive broke down in the middle of Siberia, he fixed it.) I was proud that my devoutly dedicated grandfather considered it important for his students to understand their physical world in their own language, while becoming eligible for the spiritual world.

North China Theological Seminary and missionary houses, Tenghsien. Watson was the founder (1919) and first President of this "evangelical school for the sound doctrinal training of Chinese ministers and evangelists."

For each of his courses Watson had to write his own textbook before he could begin to teach—to re-study the subject, then write a textbook in Chinese. He reviewed his college geology, exploring the countryside around Tenghsien. He noted in a letter to his home church that "hitherto unnoticed facets crop up from students' questions. It is an education to discover why they find some skills easy that you found difficult to master and vice versa. There were by-products, also, of making the tools in order to teach." He told his son, my father, that he thought he had a second-rate mind, so he had to work hard to make it do first-rate work.

My grandfather thought there wouldn't be so much conflict between science and religion in general "if both sides weren't so keen on believing things that they knew weren't so, but felt they had to accept as religious or scientific faith." Eventually Watson published twenty-six scientific, mathematical, theological and exegetical books: logarithmic tables, astronomy and physics texts, a life of Christ, works on apostolic history, systematic theology, sociology, and evolution. He was joint editor of a commentary on the New Testament in Chinese, and helped in the revision of the Chinese Presbyterian Hymnal, Confession of Faith, Book of Discipline, and Catechism.

My uncle, Ernest Hayes, remembered the college museum, with all sorts of natural specimens, maps, and models of the terrestrial and celestial globes—these to enlighten the convinced believers of the

"Middle Kingdom," as China was called, around which both the earth and the sky revolved. A model train ran on a balcony that circled the museum room. The museum's hand-press printed Watson's textbooks, and later, the first newspaper in Shantung province. Grandfather believed that students, Christians, and other Chinese—not merely officialdom, with its government courier service—should know what was going on in the land, both locally in China, and in other countries of interest to China. At its height the paper had a circulation of one thousand, but had to shut down during the Boxer Rebellion (1898-1901).

My grandmother Margaret was also busy. After learning the language, she taught. Her favorite subjects were New Testament History and "Pilgrim's Progress." She also taught Bible classes for students and for the women of the local church. She saw as her main responsibility, however, the care of her husband, who had diabetes, and who frequently overworked. In the absence of hotels, her house was a famously hospitable and well-kept establishment where traveling or visiting missionaries looked forward to staying. When we visited as children, the first thing we did before greeting anyone was to take off our shoes before stepping onto her shining floors and meticulously clean carpets.

With Watson's help she set out a garden with the trees and bushes that provided the fruit her diabetic husband liked and would eat. He had an active interest in this, corresponding with the Department of Agriculture in America, sending and receiving clippings for experimental grafts to try to combine roots resistant to disease and drought with large tasty tree and bush fruits. Once he asked the Secretary of Agriculture to send the clippings by trans-Siberian mail, because the shorter mail time would likely ensure better and healthier clippings. The Secretary wrote in return that his letter would go by Siberia. The clippings came, however, by trans-Pacific mail as usual. Watson sent them back without a word in an envelope marked trans-Siberia; the Secretary thereafter sent everything by trans-Siberian mail.

Once my grandmother noticed that peaches were disappearing from their orchard. She rather suspected a group of young boys who passed by the mission compound on their way from school, but didn't know which one to suspect, and told my grandfather, who called the boys in. He told them he wanted to find out which peaches were best, and asked for their help. One boy piped up immediately, "The ones that grow closest to the wall." The peaches stopped disappearing.

**Grandmother with one of the sundials set
up by Watson, 1913.**

In the garden of his first house in China, Watson built a small observatory and installed a telescope, and after that whenever he moved to a new place, he would set up a sundial and the telescope, look at his correction tables, and calculate accurate sun time for himself and the mission station. This was a lifelong interest. Early after his arrival in China he corresponded with the United States Bureau of Standards about astronomical and climatological considerations. When he was interned by the Japanese in 1942 he kept a diary that marked the tedious days; for every day there are at least two entries—the temperature morning and evening, and the day's weather. One of my earliest memories of him is that when we visited him, or when he and my grandmother came to visit us, no one went to bed until we had sat with him on the steps and each told him the name of a star. It had to be a different one each night. Then he would supply the Greek and Latin names of the star's constellation and finally release us, awed and sleepy, to go to bed.

Within eleven months after his arrival in China he began going out on itinerations. Typically these consisted of riding out into the country, usually by bicycle, and visiting local pastors, speaking in their churches, or going to a village without a church to talk to people about Christianity. Sometimes there was already a small church group. He would then stay the night with someone, a pastor or village leader, and then go to the next village. Any time a foreigner showed up, a group of people could be counted on to gather, to wonder, to touch, to listen, and sometimes to want to join or to form a small worship group. When conditions permitted, my grandfather looked forward to spending his two-month vacation from the college itinerating on his Montgomery Ward bicycle, discoursing and getting to know the country folk. He was revered and beloved by them. When he reached retirement age his Chinese Christian community in Tenghsien built a house for him and his wife so that the Mission Board could not claim they needed that house and insist on his leaving. He never left. After his death in a Japanese internment camp in 1944, the people in the countryside covered his grave with messages written on white paper—the Chinese expression of grief.

Margaret and Watson had three children. John, my father, was born in Tenghsien in February, 1888, Agnes Irene in 1891, and Ernest in 1897. Irene, by family accounts a sunny, happy little girl and the joy of my grandfather's life, died of pneumonia in the spring of 1897 when she was six, just 15 years after the death of Grandfather's first fiancée, Sarah Black. The pictures of him after Irene's death show the same transforming sadness as those after the death of Sarah. The year Irene died, Ernest was born in June, and in the fall my father went to a boarding school in Chefoo, on the coast of Shantung Province. From then until the family left on furlough to America in 1904, Father lived at home only on holidays from school. It is a puzzle to me that my father, who would have been nine years old when Irene died, never spoke of her, although he buried his father near her grave. I have often wondered whether, during that year of 1897, when so much in the family changed after Irene's death, she left an unacknowledged legacy.

She was buried near their house, her grave marked with a simple wooden cross. Those who knew him reported that my grandfather aged suddenly after her death. I was named partially for Irene, and early in my life tried consciously to make up to my grandparents for her loss. My grandfather used to ask me to sign my letters to him

Margaretirene, but it proved too cumbersome, and when a younger sister of mine was born and even looked like Irene, the nimbus of affection moved on to her.

Grandfather, somewhat reserved and formal with his sons as they grew, was fond of children. There was always room for them on his lap, and he enjoyed letting them play with the papers on his roll-top desk, which had little cubbyholes that he sometimes stocked with surprises. He was a relatively short, solidly-built man, and into his sixties when I knew him. He had white hair early—he loved to recount that I told him once, "Grandpa, you have white hair. You're going to die very soon." His eyes were small but sharp, and their expression could change very quickly. To us children they looked amused, often affectionate, and frequently merry, but they could penetrate and sometimes immobilize you if you were pretending to know something you should know, but didn't. He had large, gentle hands, stained a little with ink, and calloused with the hard physical work of building, fashioning laboratory equipment, and bicycling. He walked briskly, setting a pace that put him just slightly ahead of anyone accompanying him, so that he always seemed to be aiming for some private goal that others might get to if they were sufficiently committed, but that he would surely reach. He had the air of one who knows his arguments will win the day; in conversations he would often break into Latin or Greek and then look out for the perplexed looks in his audience, to offer a translation with amusement but with the expectation that it would not be needed next time.

Rural mission station: Kwan Yin Tang Compound, Tengchowfu, China, circa 1890s.

For me, Grandfather came surrounded by stories and achievements. I was proud of him in one of the first stories I was told, when I was about eight years old. In 1894, Japan and Korea had declared war on China and attacked cities along the coast. By early 1895 they had reached Tengchow, a small coastal city, where my grandfather was teaching at Tengchow College. One day he noticed that shells from a Japanese fleet were screaming over the college and onto defenseless citizens nearby. He observed that the college buildings stood up just enough over the one-story Chinese houses around them to serve the Japanese as a convenient aiming point for their bombardment. Coastal towns were usually supplied with sampans along the docks. The word sampan means, literally, "three boards," lashed together to form a small craft that, with an oarsman, and sometimes a small sail, ferried goods and people along the waterfront. My grandfather, who expected from no one what he was unwilling to do himself, walked to the waterfront and persuaded a sampanman to row him out to the bombarding fleet. Shells whistling over their heads, they gained the gunboat of the commander of the operation. Grandfather climbed aboard and pointed out that they were firing toward an American flag over the college buildings and killing citizens. If they wanted to fight, he told the Japanese, the forts were in another area, as they well knew. According to the story, the pointless killing of civilians evoked no consideration at all, but firing on the American flag did, and the shelling stopped. Returning to the shore, my grandfather was praised for his success and bravery, but he answered that it was the sampanman who was the hero of the occasion, risking his life to try to save his countrymen.

This story is confirmed in an official English biography of Admiral Togo, the hero of the Russo-Japanese War. The Admiral's intent in Tengchow was to create a diversion that would attract Chinese forces away from a projected Japanese landing at Chefoo and from a planned attack on the Chinese navy at Wei-hai-wei. The Admiral didn't care where the shells used for the diversion went, but he was quoted as saying that he considered it ridiculous for one fanatic missionary to think he could tell the Japanese Navy what to do.

As a scholar, Grandfather was revered in his province, Shantung, and treated as a man of influence. The governor of the province, Yuan Shih-kai, asked him to head the government university of the province and to devise a curriculum for it. Grandfather organized a curriculum that included the western sciences. He left a year later in 1901 when an imperial decree demanded that all students bow down to Confucius. However, Yuan Shih-kai, an ambitious man who was aware of the

Empress Dowager's interest in education, referred my grandfather to her to suggest the possible revision of the imperial educational system.

There are various descriptions in the family of what the Empress Dowager asked him to do; the one I learned was that he was invited to teach astronomy at the court in the Imperial Forbidden City, as well as to devise a system for teaching Western thought and science across the entire empire. In a long document that included curricula for both village schools and regional universities, he carefully inserted in the middle a requirement for the day of rest to be the seventh day of the week, thereby effectively changing the Chinese calendar from the long-established Chinese decimal system, in which the tenth day had always been the day off. He told us that he purposely put the statement in the middle of the document because he assumed that the Empress would not read the entire text before she sealed its approval. He was pretty sure, he added, that the students supported this change. The system was enacted first in the schools, and later for the entire empire. According to my father, Grandfather considered this to be the major contribution of his life.

For many years, there hung in my closet at home an embroidered Chinese gown with the five-clawed golden dragon—exclusive to the emperor and his court—which we were told that Grandfather wore when he taught at the palace. I thought this story had to be a myth, as so many stories about my ancestors were. But, during a trip to China with a group of social workers in 1988, I found it was true. While touring the Forbidden City, looking out over the golden roofs, I wondered aloud to a colleague about which courtyard Grandfather might have taught in. That evening a tour guide telephoned my room. He had overheard my comments and wanted to let me know that Chinese high school textbooks report that my grandfather had been among American experts whom the reform Emperor Kuang Hsi consulted during the last years of the 19th century, and that he had taught at the Imperial Court.

Grandfather also started the first inland post office, at Tengchow. He told my father it had not been difficult once the local merchants saw it to be a money-saving institution. In earlier days merchants used private messengers and were reluctant to process the mail of "foreign devils." The American consul in Chefoo, a port city, handled the coastal post office; Grandfather persuaded the consul to give him the sum to hire a postal messenger for a six-month trial and to make stamps available. A friendly local Shantung merchant gave it a try, and after some resistance the service was established throughout the province.

Watson's 70th birthday celebration at his church in Tenghsien, 1930. Watson and Margaret sit against the back wall, to the right of the flower vase on the table.

During the last years of the nineteenth century the Empress Dowager, Tsu Hsi, concerned about foreign domination and occupation in China, encouraged a group of militants, who called themselves the "Fists of Righteous Harmony," to rid the country of foreign nationals and their influence. Foreigners called them Boxers because they practiced martial arts. In 1900, as these groups approached Shantung province, the district magistrate of the province received orders from Governor Yuan Shih-kai to evacuate all foreign nationals. While the other missionaries in his station left, Grandfather wanted to stay, not wanting to "run away." The magistrate called on him and asked him to leave as a personal favor, fearing for his own safety if he failed in his duty. As the magistrate looked around Grandfather's study he promised that nothing would be disturbed. Skeptical, but not wanting to put his friend in an awkward position, Grandfather left. When he returned months later, the house had been occupied and a guard was at the door, but his study, though now covered with dust, was exactly as he had left it, even the level in his bottle of ink, which he checked.

Watson in his study. He was known and respected as *Lao Shih*, "old teacher."

In 1942 my father and his parents were interned by the Japanese at Weihsien, in the same mission compound Watson and Margaret had once served in. While they were there, farmers who had known him and his work collected eggs and fresh vegetables and brought them to the wall of the compound. A Catholic priest, his robe around him, hauled the food in a basket to the top of the wall, unloaded the basket, and returned it.

If plague, torn-up railroads, or bandits did not endanger their travel, we saw the grandparents at least once a year when they came to Peking for their annual physical examinations. I loved my grandmother, whose care for her husband, mischievous ways, and long, old-fashioned dresses made her seem to me a classic person, easily approached, transparent in her likes and dislikes. Grandfather I listened to, obeyed, and was wary of, although I wasn't sure why. Later when I read his letters to my father I knew.

Of the over 300 letters I salvaged from Janet's basement, one freed me from the bitterness that we children have felt toward our father. While he was studying for the ministry in Scotland in 1915, Father had moved in relatively liberal theological circles and, accordingly, wanted to continue his divinity course at Union Theological Seminary in New York instead of at the far more conservative seminary in Princeton, which his father favored and expected to pay for. In a letter addressing my father's preference for Union, Grandfather mounted an adamant opposition. He advised instead a place where "neither professors nor students are allowed to do their own thinking." God's words and judgments were sufficient. The letter is dated January 8, 1915.

My father's caption on the back of this picture: "Father has taken another tumble…. The dean immediately <u>ordered</u> two students to accompany him whether he wished it or not…. The students walk at a respectful distance!"

You speak of 'incurring my displeasure' by going to Union; if that were all, it would not matter so much; —it is that you wound me deeply, and needlessly grieve one who has been to the expense of all your education up to the time that you left Princeton, and who has made it possible for you to be what you are, and who has ever had your deepest interests at heart… The world has suffered enough from men who feel called on to sit in judgment on God's word rather than have it sit in judgment on them.

Should you insist on Union, then Ernest [John's brother] does not go to Princeton College. Of course Union has the money to make you very comfortable, but I would rather that we should be independent; you will have more self respect and will not finish with such a heavy moral debt as I did.

I want to appeal to you by all the care and thought given to your early years, by your own feelings of gratitude for the same, by your regard for our declining years, and by all the feeling of love and consideration that you should have, and I trust do have, not to add this needless sorrow to our hearts. If your studies in the future...should after all lead you into those errors which have taken the lifeblood out of the church in Germany (for there is the origin of all these evils) then I have nothing more to say. But do not needlessly throw yourself in the way of making a religious dilettante of yourself. Be guided by the best path for you, even though it may not be the one you want.

Father went to Princeton.

The statement that helped me to understand my father better than

Watson, Father, Ernest, and Margaret, circa 1908.

anything else came at the end of this letter. Grandfather signed off with, "With much love as yet, Your papa, W. M. Hayes." "As yet"— so love was earned, not given? I was fifty when I came upon this letter, and I immediately forgave my father his inability to be a father to us.

Watson and Margaret were proud, but uneasy, about Father's winning the Rhodes scholarship for Oxford. In July 1910, Watson wrote:

> What do you propose as your majors this coming fall? Don't forget that it is not society that you go to England for, but good, honest work. I hope that you may be able to modify the opinion which the Oxford masters evidently have of Rhodes Scholars, and show them that you have a trained mind. Can not you cut it somewhat on the dancing? I fear that you will get such a reputation in that line that it will tell against you at some inauspicious time in the future.

They were reluctant to send to him congratulations from those in the mission station because they did not want him to become "proud." And my grandmother told him that a friend had said, "It's worth more than you think," meaning the Rhodes scholarship prize. She went on:

> He said these men stand high all over the world, etc., etc. This is not to make you proud. I should think on the contrary it would almost burden you with thinking of how much is expected of you from not only your friends but from ours.
>
> The highest honor you can make of it is to honor Him who made it possible for you to accomplish it and serve Him just that much better.

*　　　*　　　*

In addition to the stress of long absences, my father, busy and enthralled with life at Oxford and in Scotland—and with courting my mother—was not a reliable correspondent, which burdened his parents, who longed for visits from him, and fretted over whether or not he had received money for that and other purposes.

Concerns other than personal ones absorbed the lives of missionary families. 1911 was a plague year. Villages where the plague appeared were often burned, which sometimes cut the railroad lines and made it impossible for people to flee. The Chefoo school was shut down; students remaining there were in quarantine and missionaries tried to provide education for their own children. My grandmother wrote in January 1911:

> We will not be surprised to hear of it developing in places along the railroad...persons fleeing from the plague in the north will get out the

quickest way.... 100% of the cases die. In one place 300 daily, in another 200 and so on. Not near here and it is to be hoped a quarantine will be established in Chefoo and make it so the schools can start up. These boys are not one bit sorry not to go back to school for a while longer.... This type of plague is pneumonic and very contagious. A lot of the furs of the little animals (not rats) which carry the plague in the far north, have been exported to America. Should the trains be stopped on account of carrying the plague you might be a long time getting a letter if mail has to be taken to the coast some other way.

Missionaries ceased going into the countryside or attending meetings, and everyone lived in fear of contamination. After a few months the spread of the disease subsided, and work and communication with ones across the sea could resume.

Grandfather and Grandmother were irritated with my father because they learned from British missionaries in their station about his engagement to my mother before they learned it from him. Grandfather wrote in March of 1915:

I had a letter just the other day from Scotland saying that you had been taken prisoner by a certain engagement! I wish that you had told us yourself for then being supposed to know it I could congratulate you. I am certain you are to be congratulated at any rate. Best wishes for a noble, useful and happy life.

My grandmother, always anxious to do the right thing, was more concerned about etiquette than with circumstance, and with what was required or "proper" for her to do:

You will probably know and if it is proper to give her our warmest love.... I once read in the Ladies Home Journal that wonderful (pretty true) guide something of the duty of the son's (mother?) parents toward the intended daughter but I dare not unless you tell me or I find sure information I would rather sit quiet.

However, she had some initial doubts about father's marrying someone of another nationality:

She may be very sweet. I have no doubt of it. She may be very accomplished and have many of the graces that I have been always hinting at you should have. I wish you could find all the good qualities of a fine English or Scottish "subject" combined in a loveable U.S. subject. I would be afraid of difficult problems in the future that would arise with both of not one nationality.

But later that month she wanted more information:

> I want to love Barbara, and I feel they are a fine family and that she, because you have chosen her for your life's companion must be a fine girl. Now it is up to you to bridge this chasm the best you can and let us know all about them.

Grandmother wanted to know the color of Barbara's hair, eyes, complexion, her height, weight, disposition—"anything that would make me know her." However, when he finally sent a photograph, she said she couldn't display it.

> I have no picture of Barbara I can put out because of your posture which makes it have to lay modestly quiet. I do not like the rudeness of you standing with your hands in your pockets and eyeing her so intently. It is all right for us but don't you want me to be proud enough of her to show our friends, those who enquire kindly of her?

**Father and Mother in the back of 52 Melville Street,
Edinburgh, circa 1915.**

But she had what was then called spunk. In February of 1916 she wrote:

> I hope I get a letter from you soon. Don't fit into the way of thinking and feeling that the women's interests belong only to a few little things in the home...that all grave, important things only the men have the way to express it? ...Don't worry about my 'short letters.' Papa has a good long one ready weekly for his mother. Why should I not write my boy?

When he came of retirement age, my grandfather wanted to return to America to be with his family, but my grandmother, having noted during their last furlough how hard women in farm families worked, preferred to stay in China. There they continued to work steadily until they were interned by the Japanese in Weihsien in 1942, where my grandfather died due to insufficient insulin, on August 2, 1944. He was buried in the little Weihsien mission burial ground next to his daughter Irene, the two simple white crosses side by side. The cemetery is now covered by a soccer field, where children strive after goals—not an inappropriate place for a man like Watson Hayes to lie. Grandmother returned to the United States with my father in 1945 and died of Alzheimer's disease at the home of her son, Will, in New Wilmington, Pennsylvania, on January 21, 1947. She is buried in Unity Presbyterian Church graveyard, Mercer County, Pennsylvania.

Irene's grave in China.

Gravestone for Watson's empty grave and Margaret's grave at Unity Presbyterian Chuch in Pennsylvania.

GRANDFATHER KELMAN

Although I spent very little time with my Scottish grandfather—a few days in China, followed by a visit in Japan in 1922, and visits in New York and Scotland in 1923 and 1924—I remember him as tall, slender, mercurial, intensely attentive. He had a thin face, wide mouth, restless blue eyes, and an incandescent air, as if the space between him and others were burning with interest and incident. His interest, however, was not in very young children per se, but in students, and in those puzzled by faith.

Scotland, 1924: John Kelman holds my sister Elinor. I and my mother sit to his right.

My mother remembered him from her late teens and twenties: entering the pulpit "like a horse eager for the race," and swinging along "the staid Edinburgh streets singing softly some Highland psalm or song." To me he was a beloved grandfather who looked wonderful in a pulpit, excited in it, born for it, transported in it until he seemed almost to be part of the congregation below.

Grandfather Kelman was crucially important in our family. If my mother set the agenda, her father set a standard. He was a reference point, defining the measure of everything personal. I loved him partly because I knew—how?—that so many others loved him. Missionaries in my experience tended to be unpopular, certainly in public, and often even among themselves. To be related to someone like my grandfather Kelman—uncontroversial, admired and loved— made life in the company I grew up in somehow more stable, warmer and safer. My mother deeply admired him; the two of them had a close relationship. It was comforting for me to know that in the bitterness of her marriage she had had the experience of loving and being loved by a man.

Grandfather always seemed to me to have treasure, lots of it, that people were instantly aware of, and that he gave away almost recklessly, so that at times he could not sustain it and one felt his frailty.

He also had a reliable sense of humor. I remember two jokes my mother attributed to him. During the war, a private is trying to persuade a mule to go up the gangplank of a ship, yelling at him, shoving him, and flailing a stick at him. His superior officer comes by with advice. "Get his interest, man, talk to him." The private walks up to the mule's head. "I coom from Manchester. Where do ye coom from?" Another joke he loved to tell, according to my mother, reflected his interest in non-believers. In a small village church, a hail-and-brimstone preacher is berating the congregation, foretelling their doom and urging immediate repentance. An agitated elderly man stands up in the back row and calls out, in broad Scots, "I'm nicht a member, Reverend. I'm jist a casual attender." According to her, Grandfather could go on and on, with tales and quotes from and about Stevenson, Carlyle, Bunyan, Browning, and the Roman and Greek classics, and spending time with him was an enchantment for her.

The material that follows is from his own writings—books, fragments of diaries and speeches his sister kept, and notes and outlines of sermons my mother kept—and from the many newspaper notices, personal reminiscences, memorials, and memories of him that were sent to my grandmother after his death. As often as possible I have used his own words.

He loved waters: the burns and rivers of Scotland, with the gleaming fish he loved to catch, and the sea, which he lived near all his life, and knew from the harbor of Leith in Scotland to the shores of Australia and Ceylon. His cousin, George Barbour, wrote that "he did holidays well," and wrote of fishing trips to a favorite river, the Stinchar near Ballantrae, where his family joined others in the summer.

John Kelman fishing in Ballentrae, circa 1907.

John Kelman was born June 20, 1864, in Dundonald, Ayrshire, in the west of Scotland, where his father, also John, was minister of the Dundonald Free Church of Scotland. In 1866 his father was called to the ministry of St. John's Free Church in Leith, near Edinburgh, where young John's sister Janet was born that year. John Kelman Sr. was a gentle man, conservative theologically but open to many different points of view, including that of Mr. Dwight Moody, an ecumenical evangelist, for whom he helped to arrange visits to Scottish churches —the same man who inspired my other minister grandfather in America about the same time.

Young John went to Leith High School and to the Royal High School in Edinburgh. He was about fourteen when he wrote a school paper about the morning newspaper, giving a wonderful glimpse not just of the news-gathering of the 1870s, but also into the Kelman household and its concerns.

> To us intelligence comes in grey-printed sheets, still damp from the press, which afford us each day a very accurate chronicle of the events which on the previous day transpired all over the world. The silence of

the long dreary hours before the dawn is now-a-day broken by the clang and rattle of a thousand printing presses, ...whose wheels flash for the morning newspapers.

The thought of the morning newspaper at once recalls the image of the breakfast table with its white cloth and steaming coffee, for the newspaper is as necessary to the complete perfection of breakfast as are the eggs and the hot toast. One of the remarkable facts of our mental constitution—a fact which has been unaccountably overlooked by psychologists—is a certain craving for "something more." Which renders all our meals unsatisfactory if they be not accompanied or supplemented by some additional element, to be ranked rather among the luxuries than among the necessities of life. A breakfast without its newspaper, a dinner without its pipe or its cup of coffee is no more complete than is a rose without its fragrance or a holly tree without its berries. Looked at in this light, moreover, the morning newspaper has its advantages over all other luxuries, for few "moral statisticians" venture to object to it on Sanitary or Conscientious principles. Some, indeed, exist under moral or physical conditions which prohibit coffee and tobacco; but no one, so far as we know, has been so unfortunate to find his morning newspaper an insupportable burden either to his stomach or his conscience!

The peculiar characteristic and chief glory of the newspaper is its all-embracing range of subject. It gives to its readers, in a very literal sense, 'a largess universal like the sun.' ...It cannot be doubted that Politics ought to occupy a foremost place in a newspaper. If we were presented merely with a record of the individual life of mankind, and no record given us of the doings of nations, and more especially of the doings of our own nation, we would have just grounds for complaint. We are citizens of the world; we are not merely Rate-payers of a parish.

What infinite satisfaction does our amateur politician find in these precious moments at the beginning of the day, when he can with impunity scorch a member of the opposition with his indignation and express freely his approval of the sentiments of his favorite Leader! The morning newspaper allows each of us to be, for the time, 'absolute ruler' for in politics at least we may be pretty certain of gaining approval for our sentiments from 'the other side of the house,' or if we are so unfortunate as to have no sweet face smiling to us at our breakfast table, we have at least a delightful sense of freedom from opposition, and may easily persuade ourselves that our dog or cat is at least as much a Liberal as he is a Conservative!

...The same newspaper which criticizes so daintily some concert or recital, narrates also in all its terrible details the story of a murder, for our newspaper is not a representative of respectable life only—it has its grim tales of poverty and crime to tell....

What a human interest is awakened, too, as we glance over the list of Births, Marriages and Deaths! We may recollect that each name we read there is the name of "Somebody's darling," and that, outside of our own small world of action and thought and feeling, there are thousands of other such small worlds in which birth and marriage and death are just as important as they are in our own.

Finally, the last two paragraphs seem to illustrate and to foretell the compassionate life of these two ministers, father and son.

> The humanity of many is perhaps the lesson which is taught by the newspaper. The great wave of horror which rolls over the land with the large-typed messages of disaster affects the millionaire in his gold and lace no less than the artisan in his moleskin. The special items of news have each their own burden of joy or sorrow, for everyone does not read them with such apathy as we do. The news of the capsizing of a fishing boat—"two lives lost"—may make little impression upon ordinary readers, but to one home it brings wailing and despair. The over sharp and heartless criticism of some literary effort may be read with amusement by most of us, but to the author it brings disappointment and depression. We may care little about the state of the money market, but thousands of men find its records the signs of prosperity or the forebodings of ruin.
>
> In this way, we may read a moral of the most poetic nature from our newspapers as we consider that they determine, as they fly over the earth, the flutterings of so many human hearts. How little they are, those hearts! How easily moved! And withal how engrossed with their own flutterings! How strange their indifference to the great light or the great darkness beyond, from which they are separated by so thin a veil!

John's teacher's comments about the paper were "transpired (first paragraph) does not mean happened," and concerning the paper itself, "A good essay: expression clear and lively and pointing very fair." But oh, to have had breakfast with the Kelmans in Leith! Small wonder that some thirty years later students from all over Edinburgh would flock to Dr. and Mrs. John Kelman's house at 57 Melville Street in Edinburgh to talk, at times, all night.

At fifteen John went to the University of Edinburgh, to its great, stern stone courtyard, the Old Quadrangle, and to its equally stern course of study. The first two years were spent on Latin and Greek, with one class in mathematics; the third year offered Mathematics, Logic and Physics or Natural Philosophy; in the fourth year, English and Moral Philosophy. For his English class he had Dr. David Masson, who introduced him to poetry—especially Dante and Browning— although he also enjoyed reading Meredith and Carlyle, and especially

Robert Louis Stevenson. Writings from these and other poets and authors appear through all his books and sermons, giving his ideas a sort of literary hospitality, an invitation to think of things in many different ways. He later wrote of his entry into "that other-world of beauty which is always either before us or behind."

John Kelman in Australia, 1885-8.

In 1884, after taking his M.A., he entered New College in Edinburgh to train for the Free Church Ministry, but after a year he suffered what was in those times termed a nervous breakdown. I could find no information about what actually happened, but there were three more breakdowns during his life, the last one an apparent stroke. In 1885 the treatment was a change of scene, to leave the country entirely, and he chose Australia. He kept a journal of his three years there, which he summarized in a speech whose date I cannot determine, but from which it is a pleasure to quote:

For the best part of three years I lived inland in Australia. Sometimes tutoring and bookkeeping on a station, sometimes out after the cattle from morning to night in the paddocks, alone with horse and dog, arrayed in slouch-hat and loose shirt, and trousers and leggings and boots. Spending the evening hours month after month in yarning around the log-fire with old stockmen and diggers and those Arabs of Australia known as sundowners, whose house is just under their hat, and whose property, wrapped in its blue blanket, travels with them on their backs. Sometimes myself wandering among the diggers' tents, or the wayside inns of the Blue Mountains, or lighting a fire and making tea and building a bothy [hut] of green branches and lying down to sleep in the open air of the Illamarra forests. And always writing down what I heard and saw....

Nature was personal to him. He speaks of the southern rivers in Australia:

The half-dozen really noble rivers grow discouraged, one would say, before they have traversed anything like 1/3 of Australia. One after another they unite their waters, and bending southwards as if ashamed, abandon their efforts to cross the great stony and sandy deserts of the interior, and make for the nearest ocean...The rivers wander solitary until they grow weary of silence and spread themselves out in marshes or bend to seek each other. Then there were the stands of dead forests, where the bark of the trees were banded to preserve the earth's value for sheep, and on "sunset rides," when I slacked my rein and turned to gaze upon the numberless network of black arms, thrown up against the blood-red West, like the skeletons of the past dark centuries waving their arms in despair at their ending or like the demons of the early days when convicts and blacks tore each other in that forest.

As I've noted, Grandfather loved waters. Returning from Australia on the cruise ship *Oroya*, he spent many hours in a canvas chair on deck, watching the waves and the sky, especially the sunsets:

[I] watched a very beautiful sunset in a burning copper-colored sky that seemed hot and glowing, as if its depths were changed to metal—a fine censer, though, for the fiery ball it held, wafting, one might easily fancy, the warm breeze as incense in the temple of Jehovah. Then the sea glowed in its long pathway of dancing gold! And then when all was over, the great evening-star came out and hung exquisite over the end of its own little silver pathway.

There was a burial at sea:

[We learned] that poor Merryweather had died.... A great hush was on the passengers. It very soon passed, for no one knew him well, but there was no game played in our Saloon all day. At 2 o'clock the ship's bell sounded, slower than ever now and solemner. This time it was to his funeral. On the main deck a crowd gathered with bared heads. The captain read the burial service and suddenly, from beneath the white bordered ensign, they raised and shot out that ghastly something which we had spoken to but yesterday. There was only a splash, short and sudden, and all was over. I turned back, filled with my own thoughts to my seat at the stern of the ship. There was little said, but our books had lost their interest, and though few tears or none had been shed, there were many solemn faces that watched far out behind. That great silent sea had become weirdly interesting, as we looked, and knew that there, hidden in the secret places, over which so many ripples were dancing, hung that shrouded man, with the heavy shot at his feet. The whole mystery of life and death were there.

John Kelman on the left with his touring club in the Lake Country, circa 1890.

Back in Scotland, he returned to the New College, and in 1890 was licensed to assist one of Scotland's great preachers, George Adam

Smith, at Queen's Cross Free Church, in Aberdeen, where he was ordained as minister. I found a charming picture of the life of the distinguished minister and his young assistant in a diary entry for June 4, 1890:

> Called on poor Debrell, the dying boy. His mother busy making the uppers of cloth shoes, for which, including machine sewing, lining, pasting in of cardboard, and some hand sewing, and find your own thread and needles, she gets 10 shillings per dozen! Tried to point him to so brave a man, who in dying still loved and had room for others. Then took car to Queen's Cross and went into 91. Found g.a.s. [George Adam Smith] and his wife sitting in the garden on chairs side by side. G.A.S. was writing his book at a table with books, pen, and paper etc. She was reading Matthew Arnold Essays. Got a hearty welcome, lay down on a rug on the grass and had afternoon tea, while he read aloud what he had written. Just going to visit when I mentioned the 23rd Psalm as subject for tonight. He had preached on it in April! Horror! Rushed home. Gave orders that no one was to be admitted even if they were my wife [he was not yet married] and family. Wrote at high pressure an address on 2 Pet. 3:3-9.... Home along the lovely road, with its mingled glory of green and copper beach warm in the evening sunlight.... So my work is slowly progressing, but my head is clear, intellect alive, jaw peaceful, heart glad.

The following year he was called to Peterculter Free Church, a small country church in Aberdeenshire. The congregation of that

John Kelman's first church, Contlaw Hill, circa 1892.

church had started by assembling under a sycamore tree, but soon after built a church on a site called Contlaw Hill, where Dr. Kelman began his preaching.

They also built a manse with walls of stone twelve inches thick, and beautiful views of far-off hills and meadows with sheep and low stone walls. The stable of the manse was an old fourteenth-century building—the original plaster still there when I visited in the fall of 2007.

In 1892, the year after his arrival, Grandfather married Ellin Runcorn Bell, the daughter of William Hamilton Bell of Edinburgh.

The Kelman manse, Peterculter, Scotland.

She descended from a large and famous clan, the Bells, who provided us with vivid ancestors. Joseph Bell, a physician at the Royal College of Physicians and Surgeons in Edinburgh, had a student, A. Conan Doyle, who used his teacher (with Dr. Bell's permission) as the model for Sherlock Holmes. Dr. Bell, known for his diagnostic skills, could tell from which part of the country a patient had come by the soil on the patient's boots, and what he had done for a living by the texture of his skin. Another ancestor, my grandmother's uncle William Bell, had inherited and developed much of southeastern Edinburgh and gambled it all away. Given our many virtuous and sober relatives, we rejoiced in his nick-name: "Wicked Willie." And then there was another branch, known as the Border Bells, who in 1404 built a stone tower on the English border, from which they poured boiling oil and assorted maidens on anyone who attacked their domain. A year after my grandparents' marriage, my mother, Barbara Monteath Kelman, was born in the manse.

The Kelmans at the Contlaw manse, Peterculter, 1893: John stands at the center, Ellin sits in the carriage to his left with her sister-in-law Janet Kelman. Mother is being held by the nanny on the right.

Soon after Grandfather came to Peterculter, the congregation voted to build a church closer to the village, and the young minister led

Peterculter Church.

his working-class congregation in raising money and then in building the church—"in journeyings often, in weariness and painfulness." When the foundation stone was laid in April 1894 by Ellin, who was beloved by the congregation, John spoke of the occasion not as "a great public display, but a quiet home gathering at their own fireside, and that as they had begun the building of the church together, that day, so might they stand together in love and friendship in the years to come."

Ellin, my mother, and John Kelman at Peterculter, 1894.

In 1895 the church opened, and on Sunday, February 17th, the minister's father preached the morning service, the son in the afternoon. That year Mother's sister, Margaret, called Daisy, was born, a beautiful little girl, blue-eyed and golden-haired.

In 1897 John accepted a call to the New North Church in Edinburgh. In contrast to the quiet, beautiful countryside of the river Dee, with its soft hills and fields of sheep and low stone fences, the New North was in a crowded, run-down part of Edinburgh near the University and the Royal Infirmary. Many members of the church had recently moved to the suburbs, leaving the area to students who could afford the low rentals. John Kelman made it his mission to speak to them, and within two years the church was full, overflowing with students who came from all over the city. Two services on Sunday were crowded; his Sunday evening classes and discussions soon attracted so many that it was necessary to hold them in the Operetta House, a tawdry theater nearby the church, where a predecessor, Dr. Henry Drummond, had led similar meetings. Frequently after the Operetta House meetings, students would follow Grandfather home to supper and to talks throughout the night. His ability to speak to their concerns and to share the interests of university students prompted the university to ask him to be the university chaplain, a post he declined because he thought it would interrupt the informal contacts he so enjoyed with the students.

Mother, Daisy, and Ellin, circa 1899.

In any event, he was at last in his beloved Edinburgh, and the move there ushered in the most productive period of his life. Between 1897 and 1907, the year of his father's death, he wrote ten books, developed and preached four hundred and sixty original sermons, lectured in America in 1902 for the Y.M.C.A., made two trips to the

Holy Land—which he later reported in two more books—gave lectures on the major writers of his day, and in 1907 moved to the most prestigious pulpit in Scotland, St. George's Free Church in Edinburgh. These are mere statistics, records only. His gift to the Scottish church and to Scotland was, as a friend put it, to be John Kelman. Every year he called on every parishioner. When he was called to account for this expenditure of energy he replied that if he could not visit he could not preach.

The family moved into one of the great gray gloomy granite houses of the city, which Ellin Kelman transformed into an open, welcoming place; vivid blue and green peacocks formed the design for the wallpaper that led up the front stairs. Shortly after the family moved, however, it became clear that Daisy's mind would not develop further, and she would be helpless. Once, George Barbour was with the family in the evening when the parents went in to say goodnight. He later recalled John's adapting the first verse of a children's hymn to sing to her, and how he bent over the cot, singing very softly:

> Day by day the little Daisy
> Looks up from her slender stalk,
> Never murmurs, never wishes
> She could run about and talk.

Daisy died of pneumonia in 1907, when she was twelve. Mrs. Kelman then had a serious breakdown from which she never recovered, and my mother became the unofficial hostess of the household. Dr. Kelman continued his strenuous work, and in 1914, when war was declared, was eager to join the British troops, and began training to be a chaplain to the Expeditionary Force.

His health again broke, and a trip to Australia was again prescribed. He was bitterly disappointed. In *Salted With Fire* (1915), his book of sermons delivered during one of the worst years of war, he wrote:

> I felt as if my chance were gone and myself flung aside useless in the
> dust of weakness and humiliation. It was bitter beyond words to be out
> of it all, when you and your sons were going, to be left behind at the
> very moment when I was ready to go.

He was a vigorous patriot. This collection of sermons, written between February and July of that terrible year, was, he wrote in a

1914 in Army chaplain uniform.   **Recuperating in Australia, 1914.**

preface, intended to convey to his readers "some appreciation of their sacrifice, some understanding of their sorrow, and some heartening for their journey." The titles of the sermons march through the book like an index of war: "Humiliation," "Salted with Fire," "Austerity," "Courage," "Death," "The Mystery of Pain," "The Answering of Prayer," "Faith," "Thrift and Other Ways of Service in Time of War," "Untimely Virtues," "The Unification of Life." In the title chapter, he counsels the value of salt, with its attendant meaning of wit. Perhaps it takes a Scotsman to suggest that "few Christians have ever frankly faced the duty of joy." He goes on:

> I think the teaching of the Bible is that the one inhuman thing, the one thing that is not permitted under any circumstances, is dullness. Dullness is a crime against the sunrise: it is a betrayal of the evening star. Life will always be difficult, it will often have to be painful, it will sometimes inevitably become dangerous, but there is no necessity in heaven or earth why life should ever be dull.

He quotes people coming up on the deck of a ship, seeing "the same old sea." And he responds, "Yet it was never the same, for one day it was an innumerable multitude of broken sapphires, and another day a vast opalescent expanse." "The modern man of science who writes down a fact in black and white is not more but less accurate than the medieval monk who wrote it in gold and scarlet, sea-green and turquoise."

He notes how the war has wakened the nation:

> Duty is no longer a slavish round, but a daily vocation and a high trust. Its voice is the call of God's bugles blowing over the ramparts of Heaven, and tells you that the time has come to march, and that He trusts you with His uniform.

And death? He quotes, without attribution:‡

> This our hope for all that's mortal,
> And we too shall burst the bond.
> Death keeps watch beside the portal,
> But 'tis life that dwells beyond.

Thrift: he advises not only savings and war bonds but early marriages, and even that "the practice of voluntary childlessness in marriage...always a selfish and contemptible thing (except under certain conditions); now it has become a crime against the state"—this two weeks after the slaughter of the Royal Scots at Ypres.

The winter of 1916-17 he spent at the front, speaking in YMCA huts and hospitals with the title given him by the Assistant Chaplain General of "liaison officer for the Kingdom of God." On the strength of Dr. Kelman's appeal to students, the British government sent him to America in the spring of 1917 to lecture on war aims as the United States was debating entry into the war. The Foreign Office was especially interested in his visiting the Midwest, with its large centers of German immigrants. This visit resulted in a book, *War and Preaching* (1919), a summary of some of his experiences and what he had found most useful in preaching at the front. America joined in March of 1917, and the burden of the book was that preaching in time of war was much as it should be in times of peace—trying to help people to reach, in their own way and in their own circumstances, a spiritual life.

In 1918 he was invited to the pulpit of New York Avenue Presbyterian Church, but declined, not wanting to leave service in

---

‡ This is the 7th stanza of the poem "Hope for the Hopeless" by John Sterling (1806-1844), originally published in 1838 by the *Westminster Review* as "Abelard to Heloise." The second line is there rendered "And we two..." The poem is simply ascribed to "a valued contributor."

Scotland in time of war, and accepting the advice of friends and colleagues, who knew what a "heavy charge" it would be. That year he was awarded the Order of Officer of the British Empire for his services at the front. The next year, the New York invitation was repeated, and he accepted because he wished to draw England and America together "in common service for the peace and welfare of humanity." He lectured frequently around the country, wrote and worked to establish the League of Nations, and was bitterly disappointed when the U.S. Senate refused to ratify the proposal. In a sermon preached on March 28th, 1920, the day after the Senate vote, Dr. Kelman could not withhold his grief. His text was "Open to me the gates of righteousness." To his rich, conservative congregation he said:

> The hearts of many of us are sore today and bleeding. Forgive me if I offend you by trespassing beyond my bounds. I am not an American. I am but a stranger among you, a British man who loves you well. But I was here three years ago at the time when my nation and its allies were falling in tens of thousands at the storming of the gates of international righteousness. I saw those gates swing open for you also when you entered the war. How you and your sons sprang forward into them! With what a shout, with what devotion, reckless of consequences, you sprang into the breach that day!
>
> Oh, my brothers, I am not here to criticize your politics. Doubtless there are difficulties and complexities which I do not understand. But listen to the cry of the world borne to you today across every ocean— the torn, bleeding, hungering, ruined world. It cries for righteousness, for international righteousness, and the end of war. It was that you sprang to, and it was for that you gave your sons. Surely every man in this continent who remembered that day turned pale when he heard the shutting of that gate but yesterday. It was the gate before which, storming it, so many of your sons have died. I am no politician, but I only sense the world weary to death, longing for new life, standing today aghast before that closed door of yours. Yes, and I see this great nation standing there, longing to enter in and yet unable now. I only hear the cry from the heart and conscience of America: Open unto me the gates of righteousness.
>
> That cry rises this day to the ears of God. It is a nation's demand for her share in the redemption of the world; it is her deep heart's prayer. Surely every man who has passed through the fires of sacrifice and who would follow in the steps of Christ will vow today that by the grace of the living God that gate of righteousness shall be opened yet.

The burdens of Fifth Avenue Presbyterian Church, whose chapel had been built on his watch, whose members he had formed into a

John and Ellin Kelman in front of the Garden City Hotel, Long Island, 1921.

congregation, proved too great, and in 1924 his health failed again. The years he had been at Fifth Avenue were years of great turmoil in the church, a struggle between the loosening of strict orthodoxy and the maintaining of it. Finally, in a speech he gave at a farewell dinner given in his honor by leading members of the church, he spoke of his vision of the good minister.

> I plead with you to find a man whose religious experience is genuine and deep, and whose expression of it is absolutely true. Do not seek to pigeonhole him, or to make him pigeonhole himself.

In 1924 he accepted the invitation of Frognal Presbyterian Church in London but after another breakdown of health, resigned in 1925 and moved back to Edinburgh, where he died in his home on May 3rd, 1929. His gravestone reads simply:

John Kelman
1864 – 1929

*　　　　*　　　　*

**Ellin and John Kelman, Blantyre, Scotland, July 1925. John's flute playing is
being accompanied by the dog**

I have changed since writing about my grandfather. One of his
sermons, which he gave several times during and after the war, was
based on a text from Ezekiel (I.2): "Son of Man, stand upon thy feet,
and I will speak to thee." He knew that men who had "trench feet"
could not stand upon their feet. He nevertheless urged them, and
everyone, to "stand as those who realize they have an inheritance in
them." The idea of standing is complex—one can stand legally,
physically, socially, in support—but I had never thought of "standing"
as a condition for an exchange, or even for a relationship. Being itself
had always seemed to me somewhat accidental—something that
happened as a result of being born; now it seemed like an inheritance,
and a joyful one. There is much more in the sermon, but I now feel as
if my grandfather, by my deciding to know him, has spoken to me.

There is a corollary to this: it is as an adult that I now have learned
about him, as if we have met face to face, each standing, with things to
say to each other.

I have also become aware of the value of letting "work speak for
itself without the prejudice of a name." Grandfather expanded this in a
sermon called "The Unknown Christ." The first secret of true
knowledge, he says, is to take men and things as they are, without a
theory, or even a name, and to let them reveal themselves. "There is
less need either for names or theories than for an open and loving eye

in the search for truth. Everything...is best explored while it remains uncatalogued." To someone raised in the Manichean world of the Protestant Church as I knew it, this was more than fresh air, it was breathing itself.

John Kelman appeared to remember everything he had ever read, and he treated it all as relevant, so that the world seemed to him of a piece: heaven and earth, death and life, love and honor. This for him was not the absence of classification, but joy in, even a love of, the world and its people. Matters secular and religious all were on the same level, so that all thought had interest and relevance. He wrote books about authors and their works—*Among Famous Books* (1912), *Prophets of Yesterday* (1912)—with as much attention to the works' literary quality and content as to their religious affiliation or lack of belief. To be in his company, then, was to enjoy a level field, open to whatever source of information or experience. He had a light touch and enjoyed that of others. He once cited G. K. Chesterton's essay on "The Twelve Men." The subject of the essay was the British jury, and its thesis was that when our civilization "wants a library to be cataloged, or a solar system discovered, or any trifle of that kind, it uses up its specialists. But when it wishes anything done which is really serious, it collects twelve of the ordinary men standing round. The same thing was done, if I remember right, by the Founder of Christianity."

Finally, I found comfort and company in his interest in non-believers. I realized that he considered non-believers to be his true audience, and he spent much time and thought on the subject of faith, its provenance and authority. In a sermon on the text "He hath founded it [His kingdom] upon the seas, and established it upon the floods," Grandfather acknowledged frankly that we do not have firm foundations for faith, and that "the point of wisdom...is to attend not to the foundations, but to the one little platform of immediate present experience which floats upon their surface." Somehow my own small platform feels more stable on the floods after reading and writing about this man.

MOTHER

Opposite my mother's picture in the 1910 yearbook of St. George's School for Girls in Edinburgh is the caption "Barbara, tall and anxious maid." And that is how, in 2006, I still think of her. In my memories she stands erect, her head up, ready for the next disaster.

She always seemed to me a single woman; my husband Bill, who was fond of her, once described her as a virgin with five children. She loved the English Victorian poets, but from all of them the line she quoted most was from Matthew Arnold: "But the deepest still is single."

Barbara Monteath Kelman was born in Peterculter, Aberdeenshire, on March 4, 1893, in the manse of her father, the pastor of Contlaw Free Church. In 2007, I went to Scotland in search of her, since I felt she had never really left that country. With a friend I climbed the steep stairs of the manse, passing the "pastor's bathroom"—on a landing, so that parishioners would not have to access the family quarters— and entered the gabled rooms in one of which my mother had been born. We decided that it was probably one that looked westward, past the stable, to the hill on which the church stood bleakly against the soft evening skies of the north. Stone fences divided the fields stretched across the valley of the river Dee: sheep grazed slowly, the long line of the hills, barely blue—hills rounded with age, lying quietly at the edge of the country. I thought of the stanza in a hymn: "Before the hills in order stood/ Or earth received her frame/ From everlasting Thou art God/ To endless years the same."

Barbara was, by many accounts, a spirited little girl. There are stories. Once, at Christmas-time, given a little whip, she said: "Here's a whip to whip Joey with."—her beloved wire-haired terrier —"Where's Joey?" Once the family, on summer holiday, composed a rhyming alphabet. Most of it was jointly produced, but, still very small, she contributed the last four lines:

> W is the Wanderer, far on the roam.
> X is the 'Xcellent tone of his Home.
> Y are the Youths whom he bids to buck up.
> Z are the Zauzages on which they sup.

Mother with sister Daisy, circa 1898, Edinburgh.

After Mother's sister Daisy died and her mother had a breakdown, Mother (then fourteen) became her father's hostess, accompanying him to public ceremonies and on a vacation trip to Italy. Once, when I was visiting her in her retirement home in New York, she told me that her father had told her she was the one person who made living worthwhile for him, and that she was relieved when, as she was entering college, her parents fell in love with each other again. Driving back to Washington that evening, I wondered what it would feel like to be the child of two people who openly loved each other. Safe?

Melville Street, where Barbara's family lived during her years at St. George's School, was a wide, severe thoroughfare, churches at either end of it, and with rows of tall, thick–walled stone houses facing each other across the street, as if in judgment of what might pass in the space between. My mother was proud of her mother's choice of the

Mother with her mother, Ballantrae, Scotland.

Mother at about 15.

brilliant peacock design on the wallpaper that lined the staircase, but her memories of the inside of the house were of gloom—with her mother and a family nurse in constant attendance on Daisy and her father off on his pastoral calls. St. George's, a progressive, private school across the street, offered a classical education, sports, and friendships, and became the focus of her life. Barbara adored her father, as did almost everyone in his orbit; she considered herself primarily his daughter all her life long, and her daughters and son were, to her, primarily his grandchildren.

This had consequences. Although she had some women friends in China, especially young single British women homesick for countries and accents, she preferred the company and conversation of men. All four of her daughters married, and, for three of us—Elinor, Barbara, and me—if our mother was aware of any difference of opinion between one of us and a husband, she landed squarely on the side of the husband. (Janet being a doctor, however, balanced the scales.) My grandfather Kelman had considered his daughter unfit to handle money, and he set up a trust for her which she could access only through Francis Sayre, a former Assistant Secretary of State, and a friend of his. She accepted this as a perfectly understandable arrangement, and Mr. Sayre's graciousness and affection for her probably made it even preferable to handling her money herself.

She loved Oxford, which she attended between 1911 and 1913, and always regretted leaving before she had a degree. In Peking she had difficulty accepting the compassionate invitation of the chapter of the American Association of University Women to become a member —she didn't want to seem a fraud.

Oxford, 1914. Mother on a
date with Father.

Mother on her wedding day,
July 6, 1916.

On occasion she sometimes brought down from a bookshelf Dorothy Sayers's *Gaudy Night*, and claimed that it was her room that Ms. Sayers referred to as having "been occupied in her day by a woman she particularly disliked, who had married a missionary and gone to China."

Most of what I learned about Mother's life was during visits I made to her retirement home in Manhattan, and later to her nursing home in Long Island. During her last ten years, I would drive from Washington to New York, and later to Syosset, on the second Sunday of every month, and we would have lunch. She would have a nap, and then she would set out tea—tea-cloth, cups, milk, and cookies or shortbread—at four o'clock, which she had done every day of her adult life on which it was possible. I would ask for her memories, but for months the answer would be, "Why do you want to know about me?" as if she were not worth knowing.

One day she asked me why I came so reliably. "Because I love you, Mother," I said. She looked straight at me. "What's to love?" she asked. It was like being slashed with a knife; I was her eldest daughter and, given the bitterness of her marriage, often her counselor in matters concerning the younger children, or in trying to help her to negotiate her alien worlds, China and America. After a couple of years of these visits, she started to answer the questions. How did she meet my father? They met in Oxford at a tea given by their tutor. How did she feel about taking American citizenship? She did not want to: she had had to swear to defend the United States against all enemies, domestic and foreign, including her own country. How did she feel meeting my father's country relatives? She was ashamed of herself, dressed "all wrong" in her elegant clothes among all these cotton-skirted, apron-clad farm wives. How did she feel about going to China? Initially she had felt the excitement of learning the language, of the challenge of evangelism, of experiencing her husband's world, and helping in his work. But, "truthfully, Margaret, I never liked China."

My mother was first and foremost a Scotswoman. One of her favorite jokes was about an American traveler to Scotland who was asked where he came from. "From God's own country!" he answered. The reply was, "Och, man, ye've lost yer accent!" Another favorite joke of hers featured a highland band. Upon their arrival at the train station to travel to a concert, one of the drummers complained that he had lost his ticket. The band leader said to him, "Man, ye canna have lost yer ticket!" "Can I not?" the player replied. "Ah've lost the big bass drum." Mother would laugh first, looking around her, to be sure everyone got it (they usually did), and I would think of her as a teenager, entertaining us all.

Mother's gaiety was soon dimmed. After Elinor was born, in March of 1919, my mother had a nervous breakdown and would have nothing to do with the baby. Her anxious parents came to China, bringing Lena, her own childhood nurse, who stepped in to help yet again, as she had when I was born. My sister Barbara put it succinctly in her memoir: "Mother had found out that Dad was not the personification of her father, that missionary work was not all preaching to the heathen, that she did not like children, and that she did not like China and the Chinese."

But she was a Presbyterian, and she had a conscience. When, in

Mother at mission meeting, Peking, May 14, 1938

college, I first read Wordsworth's poem, "Ode to Duty," I recognized my mother: "Stern daughter of the voice of God./ Oh Duty." She was indeed stern, and she was in charge. There's a letter to her from our precious Aunt Janet, Dr. Kelman's sister, written to my mother in 1952, evidently responding to some distress that mother had reported. In it Aunt Janet tried to comfort her, recounting that Mrs. Kelman had forbidden anyone to coddle or to pet my mother, even when she was an infant and certainly later, lest the child be spoiled. It was a relief to me to find that letter; to be deprived of tenderness in the service of principle seemed somewhat less damaging than being marred by an uncaring person.

My father's comfort with China—his own native country—baffled and isolated her. She could not get used to the indirectness of the language. Chinese characters in general have an irrational element that allows a vagueness in their meaning, and in China one does not expect a direct answer. Mother did, and since my father, returned to his childhood language, adopted its indirect manner in English as well, the two of them grew further and further apart. Their marriage became a bondage and it was difficult to be with the two of them together; we would wait for the cruel twist as they talked to each other. As war, internment, and my father's last assignments separated them, they seemed happier. They wrote each other long and loving letters. In America Mother enjoyed her independent association with the National Presbyterian Church, which had supported them as missionaries, and she traveled across the country, speaking and writing, settling in Washington, DC, visiting her children.

Father and Mother in later years.

In China she had fulfilled her life as a missionary wife, teaching English in The School of Gentleness, the mission girls' school, helping with the *gung-ch'ang*, a mission workshop that employed women to make beautiful cross-stitched linens to sell to the tourists who thronged from the great ocean-liners. These buyers would be Mother's own "class" of women; she would stand behind a sale counter in the Peking Hotel lobby, proud of her decision to be on her side of the counter. She was on the board of each one of the schools her children attended, she was a loyal and accomplished hostess to the many travelers and guests who came to see my father, and she was uncomfortable with it all, except in the summers, when, as in her childhood, she could be free with friends, games, and the sea.

Finally, in the summer of 1974, in the Presbyterian Nursing Home in Syosset, she was so miserable that she considered her life no longer worth living. However, that life had always belonged to God, and, accordingly, dutiful to the end, she made a bargain with Him. She told us, her children, that if she did not receive from Him any sign that He had anything further for her to do for Him, she would stop eating until she died. The five of us consulted with each other. In our lives with her she had always had her way, but we knew it would be difficult for her to carry out such a plan in a nursing home. It was decided that I, the eldest and a social worker, should approach the doctor in charge and request that her wishes be respected. We were skeptical of success because he was Catholic. I made the appointment and drove up from Washington, rehearsing the request and an approach to its likely denial. In his office he rose from behind his desk and, assuming a complaint, invited me to sit and asked what problem I was bringing. I thought fast—I did not want him to think that we expected any problem. So I abandoned all the carefully rehearsed preliminaries and said simply that her children wanted their mother's wish to starve herself to death to be respected. He sat back in his chair and answered: "The Pope has said that he does not wish members of the Catholic Church to be heroic, and I will not be. As long as no active measures are taken, your mother may die as she wishes." We shook hands, almost as conspirators.

I continued the monthly visits and conversations with her into the fall. In our last conversation, she told me with eyes shining that one evening several days earlier she had seen things far away that she had never seen before. Eagerly I leaned forward. "What were they, Mother?" She looked at me with some of her old severity. "Don't rush me, Margaret," she said. She died four days later, before I could see her again.

Mother at the Presbyterian Nursing Home in Syosset, Long Island, circa 1972.

Her memorial service was held at Madison Avenue Presbyterian Church, on November 15th. She is buried in the graveyard of Unity Presbyterian Church, Mercer County, next to the empty grave of her husband. I still wonder about those "things far away" that she saw before she died—that she might have told me if I hadn't rushed her. I still miss her, if only for her opposition.

One of my mother's favorite verses became one of mine:

> Lord, be it unforgot,
> That through these many years,
> By Thy great grace, my lot
> Was better than my fears.

My mother brought to us rills of Scottish place names, coursing down our memories like burns running through heather: Pitlochry, Inverarie, Dumfries, Cromarty, Gleneagles, Airdrie, Clachaig, Aviemore, Ballantrae, Benachie, Traquair—Inverarie for its summers,

Clachaig for its peat bogs, Benachie for its mountain.

On the beach at Ballantrae, circa 1905.

She also brought us "Songs of the North," a collection of songs "gathered together from the Highlands and Lowlands of Scotland" and dedicated "by Gracious Permission to her Majesty The Queen." At times she would play the piano in the living room and we would gather around her and sing, but she herself would be far away, on the boat to Skye or on Culloden Muir or, more happily, Doun the Burn, Davie Lad. When she decided it was time to stop, she would turn on the piano stool and slowly look at us as we stood there, waiting for the next instruction. Then she would suddenly turn back to the piano, close the songbook, and stand and say, "Off with you, we've work to do." I remember thinking as I walked away that my mother carried Scotland like a locket on a chain around her neck, the picture of a loved one inside.

And she would lie restless in her American grave if I failed to write at some point that she loved to lie in the heather.

FATHER

There were ultimately seven of us in our family: Mother and Father, four daughters (Margaret, Elinor, Janet, and Barbara) and (at last) a son, John. A family friend, after a visit to us in Peking, remarked that the Hayes family provided the best dramatic school in the Far East. We did indeed have a certified playwright: The sister next to me, Elinor, won a Kay Kaiser fellowship in drama at the University of South Carolina in Charleston for two one-act plays she wrote. They were written in one night; I know, because I typed them. She also staged plays and skits for the public in Peking and at Peitaiho, as well as the "plays" we put on at home. In one of her plays she introduced my

Father at about two years of age, circa 1890.

father with the stage direction "Enter Daddy, like a Chinese roof." The corners of Chinese roofs tilted up, it was said, in order to send any evil spirits that might have slid down them back to where they came from. It is exactly how my father entered a room, rushing into it with an expectant enthusiasm, as if everything was going to be fine now that he was there. Father was always the leading man in any script our family produced—tall and handsome, with a boyish cowlick of hair over his forehead and bright blue eyes that twinkled when he laughed or was excited, which was often. He was a conscious dresser; somehow he always looked not only appropriate but dashing.

John David Hayes was born in Tengchow, Shantung Province, China, on February 23, 1888—the eldest child of Margaret and Watson Hayes. When he was nine, his sister Irene died, his brother Ernest was born, and he was sent to a boarding school in Chefoo.

Irene and John, 1896.   **Ernest and John, 1898.**

Chefoo School, founded in 1880 by the China Inland Missionary Society to educate children of missionary families, welcomed also children from the diplomatic and business sectors. The management of the school followed the model of the British public schools; some students, called prefects, selected by the faculty, monitored student life; teachers, called masters, taught.

In the days of warlords, bandits, and plague, the trips to and from Chefoo School were often dangerous, and my grandfather would

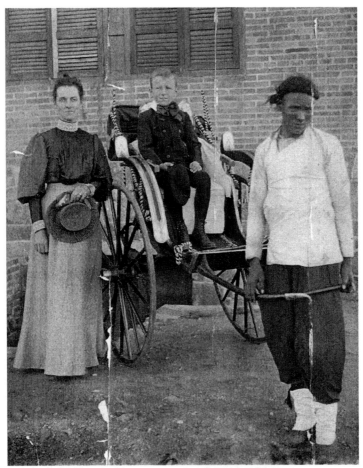

Ernest on his way to school, 1901, Shantung.

accompany my father on the day-and-a-half-long trip to and from the school. The travel was taken seriously. Grandfather, as a widely respected scholar, had civil service status in the province, and once had to attend an important provincial meeting instead of being able to escort his son from school. A naval gunboat was sent to take young John up the river from Chefoo; he was then carried by litter to his father, preceded by couriers who called out, "Make way for the son of the great official." By all accounts he was a spirited boy, handsome and resilient.

He tended toward mischief. During his last year at Chefoo he was head prefect, which he enjoyed. He especially loved to tell us about one exploit during that year. Chefoo School admitted both boys and girls, separately housed and taught. Both groups, however, attended

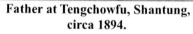

Father at Tengchowfu, Shantung,
circa 1894.

Father, circa 1900, at about the
age of 12.

weekly services in the same church. The girls would walk, two by two, along one path to the church, the boys, two by two, along a different one. The two queues had one intersection in common, through which the prefects had to be careful to be sure girls and boys passed separately. My father considered it one of his major achievements that for the last church service of his last school year, by equally careful scheduling, both columns arrived at the intersection at the same time, resulting in a confusion he had accurately predicted would be a joyful one. Father claimed no memory of any repercussions, but significantly, perhaps, he told us very little else about his time at Chefoo, except that he "respected the British educational system."

Dr. and Mrs. Hayes had delayed their first furlough until they could take Father to America and leave him there for the rest of his education, and in the spring of 1904 they went directly to the farms in Pennsylvania. Father was destined for Wooster College, then a small, religiously oriented school in Ohio, where, to the intense anxiety and equally intense disapproval of his parents, he did very well in basketball and football and led an active social life. After two years he transferred to Princeton, from which he graduated in 1910. In April of that year his father wrote, "I am glad that you did so well last Semester. I did not expect you, with all those other affairs on hand, to make first." After John graduated he taught at a boys' military academy in Peekskill, New York, while studying for the Rhodes examination, which he took in the fall of 1910.

Princeton graduation, 1910.

At Oxford, 1911.

There is a story, easy to believe because it would be so characteristic of my father if it is true. Although a graduate of Princeton, and living in the east, my father calculated that his chances of being chosen as a Rhodes scholar would be greater in Ohio, where there would be less competition. The night before the examination was to be given, a massive snowfall shut down train service in the east and Father was marooned at Princeton Junction. According to the story, which I heard from him, he noticed a locomotive idling on the tracks at the station and asked the stationmaster if it could be used, citing damage to a lifetime career if he could not reach Ohio the next morning. The stationmaster contacted an engineer, who somewhat sleepily agreed to try, if my father would shovel the coal for the steam engine. The next day Father took the examination in Ohio and passed. The probability of this unlikely tale rests chiefly on its being just the sort of escapade my father would be the subject of.

His parents received the news of his acceptance in December. His father wrote him, "Your taking the Rhodes' has struck the folks all of a heap.... As I rather anticipated, you made the hit of your life out here by taking the Rhodes scholarship," and then went on to hope that his son would improve his "small talents" and be worthy of the honor. Watson followed up with proposals for courses Father should take, the best colleges to go to in Oxford, and warnings about being interested in girls, especially English ones.

In 1911 Father entered Merton College in Oxford, living in the Old Quad, which had housed scholars since 1300. He took eagerly to the British life style. In this his mother encouraged him: "I am rough and so is papa, but we don't want you to be." She did not, however, approve of "the British use of wine."

> Wine, wine, drink, moderating drinking and smoking is so strong in all society in England. You would need to put down both feet from the start.
>
> I wrote you recently about how I felt about dancing. You said you would go to that dance but not dance. I did not think you could resist it if you did not stay away from it in the first place. You have not the strength of a kitten to resist temptation when it comes to a strong fight between desire for fun and what is straight.... I have no faith in a minister who dances. He thinks more of the dance and whirl than of his Savior.... I wonder what will become of you this year when you have more money at your disposal?

Father chose rowing for his sport, becoming captain of the Merton College crew. On the wall of the front hall of our house in Peking hung his section of the winning shell, with his rowing seat, stained with the tar that kept him in it. He also belonged to other clubs at the University, the debating society, groups available especially to Rhodes scholars, and the Leander rowing club. On international sporting occasions in Peking, he would wear the lavender Leander cap and scarf with the cream-colored jacket and its crest. His sporting achievements mattered to me. Every summer he and I tended to win the mixed-doubles tennis tournaments staged at Peitaiho. That he not only excelled but led others in sports made it easier for me, as a sportswoman myself, to accept him. What mattered even more to me was that he had been president of the Merton College Debating Society. It meant that at some time he had listened closely to someone else and had responded specifically to what that person said, while my experience was that such a thing was unlikely.

Father (fourth rower from left) at the Henley Regatta, 1914.

At Oxford he chose philosophy as his field, and once he had recovered from the shock that the texts were in the original Greek, he enjoyed the education, the intellectual vigor, and the opportunities to see Europe that the long university vacations offered. He met my mother, Barbara, at Oxford, where she was at Somerville, a women's college, and the two—flaunting rules that required a chaperone for single women students in the company of a man—explored on bicycles the old city which both of them loved. He took a B.A. with honors in 1914, and, with the outbreak of the Great War, promptly applied to be an ambulance driver with the YMCA. Permission was denied, however, because he was an American, and he returned to Scotland to become an assistant in Barbara's father's church in Edinburgh. He began studying for the ministry at New College Theological Seminary there, living in college settlement housing, bicycling through the night each week to maintain his permit as an American to remain in the country. In 1915 he asked Dr. Kelman for permission to marry Barbara. It was granted on condition that he not take her to China. On July 6th, 1916, John and Barbara were married by her father in St. George's United Free Church in Edinburgh. They left in August for New York across the submarine-infested Atlantic to prepare for missionary service in China. As his mother said, my father had a way with fences.

Father and Mother after their wedding, July 6, 1916, standing in the back garden of 52 Melville Street, Edinburgh.

In September 1916, he entered Mateer theological seminary in Princeton, after capitulating to his father's preference. Father later commented to a group on his intention to go to China as a missionary:

China was a vast mass of humanity in the midst of material resources not yet realized. 'You may smile now' but history tells us that Westward the course of Empire takes its way, and some day in China someone or in someway leadership will unite that vast manpower with the material resources and again China will have an awakening—a dragon with world power potential. I intend to use my life in sowing the seed of the love of God, so in some small way I may see the harvest of good for the world, and those people and not of evil.

A fine athlete, he moved swiftly, with long strides; it was hard to keep up with him. He had charm, vitality, and an easy way with a problem, so that he tended to be a leader in, or the chairman of, any group he belonged to, and he belonged to many. My mother's informal biography of him listed the many different positions he held in

Father looking dashing, holding a cigar in the back row, Thanksgiving, circa 1920. I'm in the center at the front wearing the pointed cap. Mother is to my right, holding my hand and looking down at me.

addition to being chairman of the mission station and carrying out his evangelical and preaching commitments: Adviser to the Student Christian Movement, Interpreter at the Organizational Assembly of the Church of Christ in China, member of the faculty and later president of the College of Chinese Studies in Peking, Language Examiner for the American Embassy in Peking, editor of a Chinese-English dictionary, flood and famine relief worker in various provinces, member of the China Council, director of Yenching University and the Peking American School, and member of the faculty of the Chinese government police college. He was often the chairman of the American community in Peking, and of the British-American society. His chief delight, however, was in work with students, for whom he

Father holding a characteristic birthday gift from one of his classes: a scroll with all the students' names written on it in fine characters.

organized groups to interest them in Christianity; these evolved into a major organization, the Peking Christian Student Union.

I remember him as a restless man, seeming to charge the air around him. Even when he sat down, which was rare, the air was never still in a room he was in. He himself seemed always to be in motion, or about to be. He also spoke very fast, in a clipped, pressured way, as if

Father with other members of the Presbyterian Mission, Peking, 1930s. Father is in the center at the back; Mother is to his left, one step lower.

what was inside him had to get out. He had a slight British accent and would use British expressions, such as "chappie" and "that sort of thing," which gave his speech a chopped up quality. I never thought of him as a religious man, although when, every morning at breakfast, he read, movingly, the prayer for missionaries that each day listed one by name somewhere around the world, I thought of him as a member of a committed group. He seemed too real to belong to an invisible God.

He also expected to get his way. For a family expedition he would caution us all to be on time, then arrive thirty minutes late, asking, "Everybody ready, folks?" He needed always to be in touch with people; upon entering a room he typically looked to find where the telephone might be, and one felt dismissed. He was always in a rush, and frequently late, but few held it against him because it was so good when he arrived. One close friend of our family wrote in his birthday calendar:

> Whish! here you come!
> Whish! there you go!
> A delightful and stimulating person to know.
> By cycle or bus, ocean liner or cart,
> You travel your way
> Into everyone's heart.

And a young son of a missionary neighbor wrote: "My childhood in Peking would have lacked something without John Hayes...the personification of cheerfulness, deadly opponent of the rut, a friend to all, and kind to me."

In Shanghai, where from time to time he went for meetings, he stayed with other missionary families. It was always a great occasion when he came home, and we would crowd around him. I learned to steel myself for what often came next. He would sink into an armchair and pull out pictures of the children in the family he had stayed with. "Isn't she pretty?" he would say as he showed us pictures of a daughter of that family. I felt this more than my sisters did, who were pretty and admired.

But my father had a vitality and delight in life and in doing things that we experienced as warmth. He could make the dullest and most routine activities worthy just by being part of them.

And everyone for him was either already a friend or about to become one. For his fiftieth birthday my mother sent out to friends and relatives five hundred slips of paper for a desk calendar, asking that each person enter on the date of his or her birthday a message for my father. All responded. Mother filled the calendar and wrapped up the extras and duplicates. My contribution read, "'What a father's smile is thine.' in loving appreciation of your great and priceless gift—the 'courage of gaiety.'" Elinor wrote, "You have opened a door for me that no man can close." Barbara enclosed a poem: "In life's journey/ with its joys and fears/ A ripple of laughter/ Is worth an ocean of tears." John thanked him for memories of rides in a special car. My mother's entry for April 5th was, "The Lord shall perfect that which is between me and thee." I was in college in America for this birthday, but one of my sisters wrote me that for the first time she saw my father look happy with something my mother had done.

Brought up in China, Father had an immediate sense of occasion, what it could bear, and what could be achieved. He recognized in the Chinese convention of "saving face" a mandate for relationships in China. That no one be humiliated was more than necessary, it was of the essence in personal or institutional exchanges. Father used this sense unerringly. He once advised a new young missionary perplexed by Chinese customs to treat all Chinese officials as Boy Scouts. Confronted with a road block, Father would salute smartly, and drive straight through.

His experience in Europe gave him an assurance in the many diplomatic tangles of an international capital. One incident I have always thought of as so typical of him that for me it defined him. He was to meet with a Chinese official in charge of a project outside the city wall in which a French embassy official was interested. The arrangement was to meet at 6 a.m. when the city gate opened. The Chinese official and my father were there a few minutes early. At six o'clock the city gate opened, but the French official had not arrived. The two waited, the Chinese official growing more and more restless. Finally the Frenchman arrived, and the Chinese official, perhaps by way of reprimand, asked my father what time it was. Father glanced swiftly at his watch. "Six o'clock," he said. It was the perfect answer, falling neatly between the three cultures, its falsity canceled by the necessity of it.

Father was often on call in Peking to help in intricate situations. I once asked him what was the secret of his diplomacy. "Leave everyone smiling, Margaret," he said. I was wary of this; sometimes it seemed to me that whatever smile I might produce was in tribute to him and to his skill rather than being part of a real solution.

He had very little sense of time, which sometimes led to others feeling disposable. Once he and I were to meet at 12 noon at the YWCA cafe under the south wall near the railway station to have lunch before I had to catch the 1:30 train for school. The café was a small, quiet room with bare tables, a serving area in a corner, and a telephone. I sat down, knowing the phone would ring. It did, at about 12:25. The waiter told me that my father had called to say that he was "hung up" with someone, but would be there shortly. He never came, and a little after one I picked up my suitcase and walked to the station. I never mentioned it to him, because I knew it simply wasn't a transactional issue with my father; he might not even have remembered the occasion, which would have intensified my hurt. It was more important to keep him in my orbit, and to let it go.

Father could be strict, rigid, and blind to others' needs, especially, perhaps, within his family. He disapproved of our wearing lipstick or of anything adventurous in clothing. On one famous occasion his feelings exploded in public. My mother had arranged for dance lessons to help my sister Elinor—at fourteen, six feet tall—move more gracefully. The annual recital was given on the roof of the Peking Hotel, the showcase site for the foreign community. It was a large, flat space, which looked out over the gray tiled courtyard houses below. My father, uncharacteristically, attended. Our family applauded when Elinor appeared, in wispy costume, leaping across the stage, but our delight was short-lived. Father rushed from his seat, grabbed Elinor by her arm, and pulled her off the stage, saying that he would not allow a member of his family to be seen in such attire. Numbly we filed out of the audience and down the stairs. No one said a word, and the performance continued. Even the fiery Russian dance mistress dared not object. No one said a word at home, either; somehow it wasn't an option.

On another occasion, however, when his family might have embarrassed him, he handled it with elegance. I was sixteen, at last old enough to attend the annual Washington's Birthday Ball, held at the same Peking Hotel and attended by most of the American community, by members of foreign legations, and by officers of the armed forces in elegant formal dress or regimentals. In rose taffeta I went with my parents in their glory, my father in tuxedo and mother in a shimmering gown with long crystal beads—the same clothes they had worn, year after year, bending over us in our beds to kiss us goodnight on that festive evening, those crystal beads glistening in the dim room. Father, as the chairman of the American community, was the host of the ball. Waiters passed trays of hors d'oeuvres and drinks; there was dancing—dancing! I was having a wonderful time. However, I felt that I should let my father know that the grapefruit juice in the drinks seemed to have turned, and somewhat blurrily informed him of the fact. He took one look, and said, loudly enough to be heard, that he was sorry I wasn't feeling well, and gallantly escorted me to the door, hailed a rickshaw, and sent me home, out of his and my harm's way. Liquor had been no part of my world before.

Father and Kanga at the Language School,
College of Chinese Studies, Peking, 1936.

Dad lived with an impossible imperative, "Be ye perfect, even as your Father in heaven is perfect," and apparently believed it to be possible. In the face of my mother's anxiety and chill, he was, however spuriously, the "warm" one, and when young we willingly did his bidding just to have the life-giving warmth of his approval. Being his daughter was like growing up with fire in a cold climate; it was necessary, but it needed tending, and if one got too close it would be damaging.

Yet other people all over China loved him and sought his company. Once a friend of my sister Elinor said, "It must be wonderful to have a father like yours," and Elinor replied, "Yes, wouldn't it be." For the most part, Chinese, startled by his immediate understanding of their speech and culture, admired and trusted him. Students especially sought him out, invited him to their meetings, and trusted his leadership. I would at times creep down the stairs and listen to conversations in our living room, with Teilhard de Chardin, the great mystic, Dr. Grabau, a member of the team that discovered the Peking Man, Hu Shih, a famous Chinese scholar and philosopher. I did not understand what was said, but I knew and revered who they were, and I knew the reason they were there was my father.

As a missionary and chairman of the mission, he was in the front rank of employees of God. I knew his allegiance was first to God, then to the Chinese, and that our family was subsumed in those priorities. There simply was no alternative to the twisted, necessary loyalty to this complex, powerful, disastrously charming man.

After the Japanese occupation of Peking my father carried his evangelical spirit into controversial territory by his open association in Peking with Japanese nationals. In the summer of 1940 my sister Barbara accompanied him to Japan for a mysterious trip labeled a vacation, where he met with powerful Japanese Christian contacts in an effort to forestall the probable war with the United States. I was then a student in America and knew very little about this part of his life. What follows is derived from records of conversations people have had with Japanese visitors, and from my sister Barbara's recollections.

Since 1935 Father had been acting president of the College of Chinese Studies, where most missionaries in north China received their Chinese language training, and where he was the language examiner for the American Embassy from 1925 to 1940. Early in 1941, with Chinese hostility toward foreigners increasing, he decided to transfer the College to the Philippine Islands, which then seemed safe, in the charge of my mother, who moved there with Barbara and John.

Our cook K'e Chang, in the center foreground, helps with the 1941
evacuation. Ch'ien Men railroad station is in the rear to the right.

After Pearl Harbor, while living under surveillance at the mission
in Peking, he served as the spokesman for mission groups in property
dealings.

Evacuation passport picture for Barbara, John, and Mother,
March 1941—on their way to the Philippines, and eventually the
Japanese internment camp at Baguio.

March 18, 1942, Peking: Father (on the far side of the table, third from right, with face resting on his hand) meeting with a Japanese general (standing) about handing over church property. Father notes on the back that there is still courtesy shown here compared with later dealings with the Japanese: the general is standing and the secretary to his left is taking notes.

Then the first of two long silences about my father began. On February 26, 1943, all foreigners in North China were rounded up by the Japanese authorities and assigned to the Civilian Assembly Internment Camp in Weihsien, Shantung Province. Until August of 1945 my sisters in America and I heard nothing of him. The man who had never been there had disappeared; I thought of him as simply submerged in the general world tumult. His parents were also interned there; we learned later, and from my grandfather's diary, that he took daily care of them until my grandfather's death in 1944. He was also in charge of the ovens at the camp, and also assumed responsibility for the children from Chefoo school who, unable to be with their parents, had been moved to the camp. One wrote a poem.

> Tall, lean and overall'd, we see you yet,
> Stained with abundant coal-dust, streaked with sweat;
> Busy, yet always ready to do more,
> Manifold tasks in Camp you gaily bore;
> Often wearing (from Chefoo) a cap long kept,
> And scarved with Leander's pink, when cold winds swept.
> Smiling we see you always happy in heart,
> And so to others able to impart

Like cheerfulness; loyal, to stop the grumble;
Steady, to strengthen those whom life made stumble,
You knitted us in one, imparted life,
Encouraged, trained, averted rising strife.
With you so hopeful for us, in each test
We could not give, or be, less than our best.

After the camp was liberated in 1945, Father wrote a report of his experience there concerned almost completely with the organization and management such a forced gathering required. When he returned

American bomber dropping supplies to Weihsien camp after liberation.

Some of the liberated captives at Weihsien, 1945. Father is near the center in the back. His mother is seated in the front.

Caption on the back of this picture from Weihsien: "U.S. flag dug out of hiding and displayed quick by Mrs. Jenness when American planes appeared. Fall 1945."

to America he joined his home church, the National Presbyterian Church in Washington, DC as assistant pastor. He considered administering communion to President Eisenhower one of the profound experiences of his ministry.

Longing to return to Peking, he found that because of his friendships with Japanese visitors he was not welcome there, and in 1947 was assigned as a representative of the Presbyterian Church to the Church of Christ in China in Kweiyang, capital of Kweichow Province, in southwest China. My mother was unable to tolerate the climate and moved to Hong Kong to work for the Church of Christ there. In November of 1949 my father went to visit her. On November 8th, the Communists took over the Chinese government, and on his way back to Kweiyang, he watched the takeover of a village.

> The Commies did come in and I saw them coming in.... I saw the red sedan chair starting off to meet them. I was surprised to find that

Washington, DC, circa 1946.

there was a tremendous milling crowd going towards the north of the town. I stood there nonchalantly and a man in the crowd called out and said, 'How about joining the crowd and welcoming the liberators to town?' I joined myself with the crowd and went out to see them coming in. Well I happened to arrive out there just as the Commies came into town. And I was surprised to see the remarkable spirit of the army that came in. The first detachment had their guns on their backs, their hands were swinging free and they were singing the liberator's song, singing it with real zest too. And I caught my breath because I realized that the red sedan chair was still wandering over the hills south of town and here they were coming out of the north. They didn't trust this town one bit. And yet these men were coming in like that. Making out that they believed that they would receive a real welcome and there proposed to give the very best they knew how.

But the next detachment wasn't like that. They had their guns across their chest and locked like real good American tommy guns and they had their fingers on the trigger, and looking from left to right. Then following them came the regular marching order, the guns over their shoulders. And I had seen symbolically expressed what I was to see again, the regular Communist procedure where they come in with their very happy, friendly promises, land to the people, control of the factory for the workmen and the redress of all grievances against the landlord class and a new feeling that was that every man was to be respected and his attitude to the government was to be considered and any suggestions he had to make were to be taken seriously. All that open approach, really remarkable. And then came the cruel stroke.

After reaching Kweiyang, my father, ever ecumenical and curious, applied to teach English in two Chinese universities there, the National Teachers' College and Kweichow University—in order, he said, to learn more about this political system which had engulfed the country that he loved.

Kweiyang, circa 1949.

In March of 1951 the second utter silence fell. The following information is from an interview he gave to U.S. News and World Report, in the March 13, 1953 issue. He had sought the position in the Government school "as I thought that would be the best vantage point from which to study Communism. I felt that in China, with a knowledge of both Russia and America, one might find some key to the solution of the growing tangle between our two nations. I also felt that this would be possible only through a Christian solution." Reading this, I was stunned. For a third time my family members felt they could solve an international crisis all by themselves! It did not last long. In August of 1951 John was placed under surveillance in his house, and then, in October of 1951, was arrested and "thrown into jail."

After two weeks in jail, lying on the floor in the pajamas in which he had been arrested, he was called before a Communist court and charged with "being a spy, with having a transmitting set as well as a

Kweiyang, 1949. My mother's caption: "Dad's deck tennis court, with our boy
Chang Ming and the dear dog, who has just produced 4 puppies. The hills
beyond, which we saw from my room in the old house—lovely in the morning
light—are very typical of Kweiyang. The one on the left, wooded, is the one we
climbed together just before I left. Note the timbered gable on the left—regular
Kweiyang architecture."

radio, with organizing all of the spy activity in the Southwest, with
being a sub rosa consular official, with training spies in the past, with
having engaged in spy activity over the 15-odd provinces in China
through which [he] had traveled, with having organized the 'third
party' movement inside the Nationalist Government..., and with
having used [his] position on the faculties of two Government schools
to set up a spy system to continue after [he] had left—all pointing to a
secret relationship with the FBI." After Father came back he told us
that President Eisenhower and J. Edgar Hoover being listed on the
church stationery as trustees of his sponsoring church, the National
Presbyterian Church in Washington, didn't help.

His first trial was for 40 consecutive days at odd hours, and from
three to nine hours each day; the second was spread over a period of
35 days.

He listed the final accusations against him: "First, the attempt to
break up the Chinese-Russian friendship; second, the use of [his]
position as a professor to foster American-Chinese friendship,

including student parties at my home, etc.; third, the use of my students and other contacts to oppose Government policies—(a) the liquidation of landlords and (b) the necessity of 'falling over to one side' [i.e., becoming subservient]." These he signed on September 6, 1952, when he was released.

Before that, under intense and irregular questioning, he confessed that he had known of, and counseled the disposal of, a fellow prisoner's transmitting radio, thus endangering his colleague, although taking full responsibility for the possession and transaction of the instrument. He had been told that if he confessed he would be released immediately, and his fellow prisoner would be killed; finally, he confessed. To the end of his life he maintained that only his mind broke; his spirit, he claimed, remained whole. Meeting this frail and confused man in New York after he was released, I am relieved he could find some comfort in that design; I think he never recovered from the betrayal.

He was asked by his Communist interrogators for one more document, a confession of the sins of his life's work as an American missionary. He wrote one, which I found among his papers after his

Father before prison, circa 1948-50.

Father after prison, as he appeared in the March 1953 issue of *US News & World Report*.

death. It was skillfully constructed, beginning with a summary of Christian beliefs, which he hoped would thus be kept in Communist files as part of an official document. He then listed the sins his mission was responsible for since his arrival in the autumn of 1917:

Missionaries had had a superiority complex, committed "extrality" (importing the American way of life in customs, clothing, etc.), established educational institutions which did not "reach the masses," committed resources to particular churches in a form that ignored the needs of the poor, failed to make the relief of the people the main aim in medical work, arranged scholarships to America for advanced study instead of focusing on their own society's needs, and brought an American way of life inappropriately to their areas of service. All these were neatly, even fastidiously, tailored to Communist political tenets.

Soon after this was submitted, my father was expelled from China, the land to which he had given his heart and his life. He and his three fellow prisoners were told to gather their possessions, and were put on a train for Canton, where they were again imprisoned for a week, before passing over a bridge to Hong Kong, where the British flag flew briskly. My father told me that one of the first people he met in Hong Kong was the very man he had imperiled, who had been freed after implicating my father, and who was surprised to see him alive. The American consular official in Hong Kong who briefed my father after his release, however, knew nothing of the matter. In November 1955 Vincent Price played my father in "The Brainwashing of John Hayes" on the TV Reader's Digest series.

After a restless six months in America, my father arranged to be sent to the nation with the largest number of Chinese outside of China, and was assigned to help build a Christian university in Salatiga,

Father in Indonesia, 1955-57.

Indonesia. On March 2, 1957, on the way to preach a sermon in Chinese, despite being an excellent driver, he swerved his Land Rover to avoid hitting a young Indonesian boy who had fallen in the road ahead of him. The car landed in a ditch, rolling over on my father. He died two days later, on March 4, 1957.

A funeral service was held March 6th in Salatiga, which the Communist chairman of the Town Council attended, and at which he requested permission to speak. My father was buried in Indonesia. His gravestone at Unity Church, near Mercer, Pennsylvania, carries his Chinese surname, *Ho*, meaning "bright, fiery, awe-inspiring." His gravestone in the Christian cemetery in Salatiga reads:

John David Hayes 1888-1957
Died in the Service of God
Remembered with love by many students and friends
in China and Indonesia
The Joy of the Lord is your Strength

Who was he? As I worked to construct this account of him, I found that the computer keyboard was covered with flames whenever I sat down to write.

Father's empty grave at Unity Presbyterian Church, Mercer County, Pennsylvania.